The Medieval English Stage

A fifteenth-century Corpus Christi procession. From National Széchényi Library, Budapest, MS Cod. Lat. 424, fol. 69ᵛ, reproduced with the generous cooperation of Mrs./Dr. E. V. Windisch, head of the manuscript division, by permission of the National Széchényi Library. This illustration, associated in the manuscript with the *Introit* for Whitmonday, was evidently copied from a northern French or Flemish original, where it was associated properly with Corpus Christi: see Elisabeth Soltész, "Zur Herkunft des Corvin-Graduals und zur Ikonographie seiner Miniaturen," *Magyar Könyvszemle* (1968): 334–42. In the left foreground are three minstrels, followed by a bishop carrying the Host (the Corpus Christi). Four acolytes bear the canopy which protects the bishop and Host. Following the Host is a procession of citizens bearing torches and staves. In the right background is a viewing stand, a raised platform covered with cloths and boughs and occupied by noble men and women (see fig. 3 for detail).

The Medieval English Stage

CORPUS CHRISTI PAGEANTS AND PLAYS

Alan H. Nelson

THE UNIVERSITY OF CHICAGO PRESS

CHICAGO AND LONDON

ALAN H. NELSON is associate professor of English at the
University of California, Berkeley. He has edited *Medieval
English Drama* with Jerome Taylor.
[1974]

THE UNIVERSITY OF CHICAGO PRESS, CHICAGO 60637
THE UNIVERSITY OF CHICAGO PRESS, LTD., LONDON
© 1974 by The University of Chicago
All rights reserved. Published 1974
Printed in the United States of America
International Standard Book Number: 0-226-57173-4
Library of Congress Catalog Card Number: 73-85247

For Judith

Contents

Illustrations

Acknowledgments

I owe this book to the kind assistance of many persons and institutions. Medieval drama and the Corpus Christi plays first caught my interest while I was studying for my doctorate at the University of California, Berkeley, on a Danforth Graduate Fellowship. A graduate student exchange program between Berkeley and Stanford enabled me to enroll in Professor V. A. Kolve's memorable Medieval Drama seminar at Stanford University. Though I engage in friendly battle with Professor Kolve in these pages, I acknowledge with pleasure that his inspirational teaching and enduring friendship have sustained me through a decade of work on the drama. The Department of English at the University of Chicago encouraged my work and provided funds which allowed me to deliver early drafts of several chapters to various conferences and seminars. It was at Chicago that I first met Professor David M. Bevington, who has been a fast friend and a source of needed encouragement and wise advice. The Department of English at the University of California, Berkeley, has supported the final shaping of this project and the preparation of the manuscript. I am particularly grateful to the University of California for a year's rest from teaching under the Humanities Research Fellowship Program. This fellowship gave me the time I needed to assemble and to revise my manuscript. The American Council of Learned Societies provided me with a Grant in Aid for a summer's work at first hand with the original documents which I cite in this study. It was this opportunity in particular which, I feel, has turned this study from a merely speculative venture into a solidly grounded historical investigation. Professors Jonas A. Barish and Norman Rabkin of the Berkeley English Department have read parts of my manuscript and have offered suggestions for improvement. I have also consulted on many points with Professor John Elliott of the Department of English, University of California, Santa Barbara.

My debt to various museums, libraries, and archives is acknowledged in the prefatory note on transcriptions, and in the notes to the respective chapters. I wish to thank here the individuals who have been of personal assistance to me: Mrs. Rita Green of the York City Archives, for frequent assistance while I worked at the archives, for maintaining a lively correspondence with me since my departure, and for consulting various wills in the York Borthwick Institute; Mrs. Mary Thallon of the same archives; Mr. B. P. Johnson, Archivist of the York Company of Merchant Adventurers; Mr. D. A. Wood, Assistant Town Clerk, and Mr. Harry Hogg, former Town Clerk of Beverley; Mr. C. P. C. Johnson of the Lincolnshire Archives Office, for sparing me hours of time searching for civic and diocesan documents; Mr. F. I. Dunn, Assistant Archivist of the Norfolk and Norwich Record Office, for telling me of his recent discovery of an early transcript of the Grocers' records and play; Mrs. E. K. Berry, City Archivist, and Miss A. M. Kennett, Assistant Archivist of the Chester Record Office, for helping me track down the family of John Whitmore, and their property in Bridgestreet, Le Blackhall; Mr. H. R. J. Swinnerton and Mr. A. E. Edwards, Stewards respectively of the Chester Companies of Painters and Coopers; Mr. J. Keith Bishop, City Archivist, Newcastle-upon-Tyne; and Colonel R. H. Carr-Ellison, Steward, and Mr. J. S. Stephenson, Clerk of the Newcastle Company of Merchant Adventurers.

Other persons have provided me with advice, assistance, and transcriptions in regard to the documents of particular cities: Professors A. C. Cawley, Martin Stevens, Alexandra F. Johnston, and Margaret Dorrell on York; Professor Stanley J. Kahrl on Lincoln and Louth; and Professor David Galloway on Norwich. Captain R. D. Risser, USN, ret., of the Morrison Planetarium, San Francisco, helped me with the astronomical details in chapter 1.

Miss Susan Grossman and Mr. Andrew Blasky, graduate students of the Berkeley English Department, assisted in securing books and in checking my manuscript for early errors of transcription. Bev Heinrich typed the final manuscript.

Finally, I wish to express my gratitude to my wife, Judith, for her loving patience during the years I have spent on this project, and for her shared interest in the medieval arts.

NOTE ON TRANSCRIPTIONS

Most transcriptions from original documents in this book are my own. Local archivists from Hereford, Bury St. Edmunds, Canterbury, and York Minster have kindly verified transcriptions for me, and in several instances have offered improved readings. Stanley J. Kahrl provided me with transcriptions of several documents from Louth, and Mrs. Rita Green suggested improvements in several transcriptions from the records of York. I have relied on Anna J. Mill's *Medieval Plays in Scotland* for the citations from Scottish documents in the final chapter. I acknowledge assistance in transcribing documents and permission to transcribe and publish documents from individual towns in the notes to the respective chapters. Documents in the British Museum have been transcribed and published by courtesy of the Trustees of the British Museum. Transcriptions and translations of Crown-copyright records in the Public Record Office, London, appear by permission of the Controller of H.M. Stationery Office.

I have employed the following rules whether transcribing from manuscripts or from printed books:

1. Abbreviations are, in general, silently expanded.
   Exceptions:
   a) "&" is transcribed as "and" in English but as "&" in Latin.
   b) The abbreviations "Xpi," "xⁱ," etc., meaning "Christi" or "Cristi," are left unexpanded.
   c) All abbreviations for the title "mister" or "master" are written as "mr" and are not followed by a period.
2. " þ " and "y" for thorn are transcribed as "th."
3. Original distinctions between "u" and "v" are retained.

4. "ff" at the beginning or end of a word is not doubled.

5. Expenses expressed in pounds sterling, shillings, and pence and occurring in an itemized list are always preceded by a comma and followed by a comma, semicolon, or period. The "s" for shillings and the "d" for pence are printed on the line, while the "li" for pounds sterling is given above the line as a superior figure: "for his paynes, iij[li] iijs iiijd."

6. The longer expense accounts are generally transcribed with each item beginning a new line, so that originally solid paragraphs of itemized expenses appear as lists.

7. Distinct clauses in civic orders are generally separated by semi-colons even when no punctuation occurs in the original. Otherwise punctuation is supplied only on rare occasions where it is necessary for sense.

8. Slashes (/) or other marks of punctuation are replaced by commas or by semicolons, or are disregarded when not significant.

9. Words written in above the line are brought down to the line and enclosed in parentheses. Words which have been deleted in the manuscript are retained where they are significant, but are enclosed in half brackets: ⌐play.¬

Note concerning the character ȝ: This letter, which cannot be modernized, represents several different sounds. In initial positions it often represents y or g; in medial positions it often represents the modern gh; and in final positions it often represents s or z.

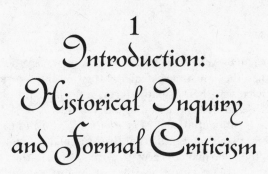

1
Introduction:
Historical Inquiry
and Formal Criticism

In fifteenth-century England many populous cities and towns celebrated the festival of Corpus Christi with spectacular pageants and lengthy
dramatic plays. Corpus Christi was a relatively new feast, held on the
Thursday after Trinity Sunday, some sixty days after Easter. The
pageants and plays mounted on this day often portrayed episodes of
biblical history from Creation to the Last Judgment.

Most students of medieval drama, including E. K. Chambers and
Hardin Craig, have held that the dramatic cycles developed from the
earlier Latin plays originally performed in the church. O. B. Hardison
believes the cycles issued from the convergence of two parent streams:
they are "a fusion of the techniques of representation derived from
vernacular tradition with the ritual form characteristic of Latin religious drama." Rosemary Woolf wishes to trace the cycles back to a
tradition of vernacular cycles which had already established its independence from the liturgy by the twelfth century. V. A. Kolve argues
that the vernacular Corpus Christi cycles constituted an entirely new
genre quite unrelated to earlier drama and that the source of the genre
has to be sought outside the traditional context of the liturgy.[1]

Scholars searching for antecedents or for missing links between
liturgical drama and the English Corpus Christi plays have uncovered
no shred of evidence to show that the cycles of York, Wakefield,
Chester, or Coventry, even in their earliest stages, were ever in the
hands of anyone but the guilds. Nor can anyone, including Kolve,
explain convincingly why the guilds should have decided to initiate
plays on their own.

If the vernacular cycles were not merely taken over by the guilds from the clergy, then they must have achieved their essential form under the guilds. But what was their essential form, and where did the guilds get the knowledge and determination to develop it?

V. A. Kolve's influential book, *The Play Called Corpus Christi,* is one of several recent studies arguing that the form and content of the cycle plays reflect the doctrinal concerns of Corpus Christi, the festival from which they sprang.[2] Because Kolve offers the most energetic defense of the proposition, his argument will receive our closest attention.

Kolve states his conclusion boldly: "It was Corpus Christi feast that caused [the Corpus Christi plays] to be written, and influenced their subject and form, but when fully grown they were free of their birthday."[3] Four propositions are packed into this sentence. Kolve insists that the feast itself gave direct rise to the commissioning of plays; that the subject matter of the plays (the history of the world centering on the Passion) and their form (their particular beginning, middle, and end) were determined as a direct response to the doctrine of Corpus Christi; but that this crucial relationship between plays and festival obtained only during the formative years: once they achieved their perfection, the plays could be transferred to almost any other occasion.

Many an occasional play has subsequently won independence from the occasion which brought it to light. But for Kolve the Corpus Christi play is not simply another *Twelfth Night.* Rather, it was conceived as the most complete possible expression of the deepest significance of the Corpus Christi festival. Kolve's problem is to demonstrate this proposition in the face of our knowledge that many plays of the same type were performed on occasions other than Corpus Christi.

Kolve does not name the agents responsible for implementing the new dramatic form. But he suggests that those who selected the subject matter for plays on Corpus Christi had a clear choice between spectacular miracles of the Host, as in the *Croxton Play of the Sacrament,* and the history of the world, as in the extant cycle plays.[4] O. B. Hardison, in a review of this argument, calls Kolve's first choice a "red herring," since in England no plays of the Host are known to have been associated with Corpus Christi.[5] The Croxton play in fact is announced for a Monday,[6] so here the connection is excluded. But clearly Kolve makes the suggestion because the most obvious topic of a Corpus Christi play would be the sacrament of Corpus Christi, that is to say, the Eucharist. Acknowledging this possibility only to reject it,

Kolve insists: "To English ears 'the plaie called Corpus Christi' meant a play of the history of world, from Creation to Judgment":

> This was a very different way of "celebrating" this maximum gift of God: instead of concentrating on the Sacrament's temporal power to work miracles, to convince and convert, it looked instead on its eternal power to alter the destiny of the human race. The Eucharist serves to recall both the Last Supper and the flesh and blood of Christ offered on the cross—events about which it is possible to rejoice only when they are related to man's fall, Christ's Resurrection, and the Last Judgment. Except for this sacrifice and gift, even the good would have been damned, guilty of Adam's sin. To play the whole story, then, is in the deepest sense to *celebrate* the Corpus Christi sacrament, to explain its necessity and power, and to show how that power will be made manifest at the end of the world.[7]

These statements will not, I think, stand close scrutiny. In the first place, the sacred history of the world provides the ultimate context of significance for *every* historical event, liturgical rite, or doctrinal statement. It is not uniquely an explanation of Corpus Christi. Further, we may wish to conceive of the cycle plays as an elaboration of the Passion; but is it really possible to understand them as essentially an elaboration of the Eucharist? Hardison notes that the Last Supper is not even included in Kolve's protocycle of plays common to all the cycles.[8] It is true that the Last Supper does occur in all the extant cycles: Kolve subsumes it under the category of the Passion. But the Institution of the Eucharist is quite absent from the Wakefield and possibly from the York cycle. Nor does it rise to great prominence in the Chester cycle.[9] The N-Town cycle, which makes most of the Eucharist, is announced for "sunday next,"[10] and thus was not, and may never have been, intended for the Corpus Christi occasion.

Hardison presses an alternative explanation into the breach: Corpus Christi signifies not only the Eucharist and the Passion but also "the body of all true Christians, past, present, and future, united by faith in Christ":

> If this concept is relevant—and it is fairly common in medieval Corpus Christi sermons— one can understand how a series of dramas tracing the history of the *plebs sancta* from Creation to Doomsday could be considered an appropriate—even inevitable—way of expressing the meaning of the Corpus Christi.[11]

This is an ingenious argument, modestly tendered. But surely the Corpus Christi festival was promoted to celebrate the Eucharist proper, rather than any metaphorical elaboration such as the mystical church. Even granting Hardison his point, we may wonder at a vision of the church which neglects its entire history and all its saints from Pentecost to Doomsday. We would do well to return to Kolve's assertion that the Eucharist properly recalls *both* the Last Supper *and* the Passion. This is firm ground, but it does not answer to the interests of the Corpus Christi cycles, which concentrate on the Passion almost to the exclusion of the Eucharist, the essential sacrament of Corpus Christi.

During the early fifteenth century, John Lydgate, the monk of Bury who spent a lifetime writing occasional poems, composed "an ordenaunce of a precessyoun of the feste of corpus cristi made in london."[12] This poem, which bears some formal resemblance to the episodic style of the cycle plays, names a series of twenty-six biblical and post-biblical figures who were to be shown in pageants. The list begins with Adam, Melchizedek, Abraham, Isaac, Jacob, Moses, Aaron, and David. Then follow prophets, evangelists, Paul, the doctors of the church, Peter Comester, Peter Lombard, and Thomas Aquinas.

No figure of Christ occurs among the pageants. The explanation for this is that the poem, stanza by stanza, points out the significance—frequently typological— of each figure. The signification regarding Christ is to be imagined, not seen:

> First, that this feste may more beo magnefyed,
> Seothe and considerthe in youre ymaginatyf
> For Adams synne howe Cryst was crucefyed
> Vppon a crosse . . .

Thus, various moments in the life of Christ are remembered, but indirectly, through figural association. Moreover, Lydgate's poem is radically eucharistic. (It also includes major figures from the history of the church.) "Sherthursday" is mentioned repeatedly, along with the wine and the wafer, the chalice and the paten. The stanza on Abraham is representative of this concentrated interest:

> Chosen of God this patryarch Abraham,
> Example pleyne of hospitalytee,
> Recorde I take, whan that the aungel came
> To his housholde, wheeche were in noumbre three,
> In figure oonly of the Trynyte,
> Set to hem brede with ful gladde chere,
> Of gret counforte, a token who list see,
> The sacrament that stondethe on the awter.

Here is a poem patently designed to suit the Corpus Christi occasion. But in its basic interest and choice of subject matter, it is quite unlike any of the surviving Corpus Christi plays.

Kolve claims that the Corpus Christi festival determined not only the basic subject matter of the plays but also their form. He discovers the entire connection between subject and form in a single concept—joy. The official explanation for the foundation of the Corpus Christi festival, promulgated by Urban IV in 1264, included the observation that Holy Thursday and the institution of the Eucharist at the Last Supper were a preparation for the events of Good Friday and thus were governed by a mood of impending sorrow.[13] Another holiday, entirely outside the Easter season, was therefore set aside for a more joyful celebration of the Eucharist. In Kolve's view, as the idea of the Eucharist dictated the plays of the Passion, so the idea of joy dictated the plays of Creation, Resurrection, and Doomsday. This is because the Passion is an event "about which it is possible to rejoice only when [it is] related to man's fall, Christ's Resurrection, and the Last Judgment."[14]

It is true that the Passion is properly regarded—at least in retrospect—as a cause for rejoicing, and that it can only be regarded this way when related to the wider context of man's fall and salvation. But Kolve's argument involves the unstated assumption that a Passion *play* can beget a joyful understanding if and only if it is accompanied by the Fall of Man and the Last Judgment presented in *dramatic* form. Certainly, however, joy and understanding are complete with the Resurrection of Christ, particularly as it implies the possibility of individual salvation. There is grave danger, moreover, in treating the Last Judgment as the occasion for climactic joy: Doomsday carries too many threats of damnation to be regarded with an unequivocally buoyant mind.

Kolve turns his argument on form, particularly in regard to plays of the Fall and Last Judgment, into an a priori substantiation of his empirical observations concerning the "protocycle." The Corpus Christi play is elevated to a genre. Nonconforming cases are forced into compliance or are dismissed as unintelligent. Thus he insists, against all evidence, that the Coventry cycle must have had Old Testament plays. And of the Norwich pageant list, which omits the Passion and Doomsday, he writes: "if we must limit ourselves to this list, we had best recognize it as the record of a civic authority that never rose to the Corpus Christi occasion with the sustained intelligence characteristic of the six or seven other English towns whose records survive in greater detail."[15]

While Kolve invokes the concept of joy to unite the Passion with the

Fall and Last Judgment, he resorts to other principles in explaining the presence or absence of other episodes: the two chief principles are typology, and the Seven Ages of the World. Kolve can demonstrate no connection between these concepts and Corpus Christi. Indeed, he concedes that "the authors of the great Corpus Christi cycles did not themselves select the incidents to be dramatized. . . . Other men before them had determined a hierarchy of significant event in Scripture, and their choice decisively influenced all art forms for several centuries."[16] In conceding this point, Kolve, to my mind, concedes all. The Corpus Christi cycles bear no distinctive relationship to the doctrines celebrated on Corpus Christi: they simply constitute one of many art forms whose structure was determined by an anciently established "hierarchy of significant event in Scripture." The cycles are not eucharistic plays or Passion plays set in a context encouraging joy. Rather, they are plays of sacred history, or *Heilsgeschichte.* Their form is determined by historical more than typological principles. Who among figures from the Old Testament are of greater significance to sacred history than Adam, Abel, Noah, Abraham, and Moses? The Seven Age scheme itself, which was originally a reflection of the political history of the Hebrew people, was subsequently adjusted to reflect the values of Christian sacred history. Thus the Corpus Christi cycles and the revised Seven Ages were both organized by priorities which were already centuries old.

Kolve recognizes that the protocyclic events bear no unique relationship to Corpus Christi: "I do not argue that cycles could only have been born in response to the Corpus Christi occasion—the Cividale records make such a view untenable—but rather that in England the decision to honor the Corpus Christi feast with religious plays determined in its turn the choice of dramatic subject and form."[17] The play at Cividale (northern Italy), which in 1304 was much like the English protocycle in choice of episodes, was given at Whitsun (Pentecost). The similar Florentine *Rappresentazioni* of 1454 were given on St. John's day (Midsummer). The Le Puy procession of 1469, which included "very beautiful stories, both of the Old and the New Testaments," was mounted on 10 July. The London sacred history plays of 1384, 1390, 1391, and 1409 were given on summer holidays. The Cornish cycle was given on some unknown occasion, possibly Corpus Christi, possibly another festival.[18] And the N-Town cycle was given on a Sunday. In fact, the sacred history of the world is appropriate to any occasion except perhaps the narrowly defined high festivals of Christmas and Easter.

Kolve also implies that the abstract decision to mount plays was made prior to the choice of subject matter. Somehow the feast itself dictated this decision: "It was Corpus Christi feast that caused them to be written." An explanation of this is tendered, but not pursued: "The date set aside for the feast can vary from May 23 to June 24. It is weather for an outdoor festival, and someone somewhere (later, many persons in many places, perhaps in emulation), had the idea to stage a play on that day. The history of this decision cannot be written, for no records exist."[19]

Kolve would not seriously claim, I think, that the combination of good weather and appropriate theme constituted a *sufficient* cause of the Corpus Christi play. And it may be that no single cause or combination of discoverable causes will ever constitute a sufficient explanation. Nevertheless, it is troubling to witness this retreat behind "fourteenth-century silence"[20] when it comes to a consideration of why plays were proposed in the first place. The good weather is all we have for an explanation.

In the course of his argument Kolve reveals his belief that a formal analysis, indeed, a *history* of a literary form, can be undertaken in the absence of full documentary evidence: "Lacunae in the records will prevent us from ever writing a proper history of the early growth of these cycles. Using a different kind of evidence, I wish to discuss instead the genesis of an art form."[21] At the end of the ensuing discussion Kolve concludes:

These facts are perhaps ultimately more important than those records which were never made or have not survived, that might have documented the history of the Corpus Christi plays between 1318 and 1376. Somehow the cycles took form, and the form they took was determined by the facts we have been examining. They are the facts behind the facts.[22]

Perhaps. Yet it seems dangerous to discuss formal causes in the complete absence of efficient causes. If historical records are indeed silent, then we must perforce resort to conjecture. But even so, we cannot entirely disregard history, and Kolve does not do so. His analysis of formal cause rests on several unproved historical assumptions: that the cycles arose from a specific moment of deliberation; that this deliberation arose from a prior abstract decison to mount a dramatic play; and that the point of the deliberation was to choose a subject matter as appropriate as possible to the Corpus Christi occasion. None of these assumptions, as Kolve repeatedly concedes, can be documented. We must insist, I think, that his subsequent formal literary analysis of the cycle plays stands or falls with these assumptions; or else bears no relationship to them.

Kolve is by no means the only recent critic for whom formal analysis of early vernacular drama has taken precedence over an inquiry into historical fact. Jerome Taylor, for example, argues like Kolve for a close relationship between the cycle plays and Corpus Christi festival. Taylor writes: "In considering the relevance of the Feast of Corpus Christi to the cyclic drama, I wish to prescind from the question of *how* the Feast and its procession came to attract drama as such. The fact is that they did." The "reasons that drama became an established part of the Corpus Christi celebration" are characterized and in effect dismissed as merely "external."[23]

O. B. Hardison, who takes great pains to ground his analysis of liturgical drama on documentary evidence, concludes a brief incursion into the vernacular drama with the statement:

> The preceding notes (and they are no more than that) are intended to suggest that the forms and techniques used in the earliest drama of the Middle Ages are important not only to later medieval drama but to Renaissance drama as well. The task of relating them to the data of history and criticism remains for the future.[24]

And Harry Berger, Jr., writes in a recent article subtitled "A Prologue to Shakespeare":

> There is a Short Course in the History of Drama which may be found in a very large number of handbooks and textbooks. This course propels the drama from the church to the church porch to the city streets and innyards, and finally drops it into the theater. In brief, it transports the drama from the first to the second world, and from the Godmade to the manmade Globe. Since this itinerary very nicely fits some of the patterns I have been sketching out, it is something of a disappointment to me that there is no corresponding itinerary in the real world. Studies by Hardison, V. A. Kolve, Glynne Wickham, and others, have rendered this short course obsolete. They have demonstrated the futility of presuming to trace the career of the drama as if it were a person taking a walk. I am nevertheless reluctant to give up the idea of transition from the first to the second world, and therefore I would like to see if there is a more viable approach to the history of drama, another frame of reference which may perhaps allow us to save appearances which I find attractive. I have neither the time

nor the competence to undertake such an approach in detail, but I should like to offer a rough and summary sketch which may suggest the lines such an approach might take.[25]

As with Kolve, the historical assumptions in Berger's argument are more or less necessary to his formal account of the rise and integrity of a dramatic genre; but any argument for their necessity, in the absence of specific documentation, must be circular.

Records of early Corpus Christi pageants do exist, however, and in the following study I will argue from documentary evidence—much of it previously unknown—that the fifteenth-century English dramatic cycles developed out of fourteenth-century festival processions. A corollary of this argument is that the doctrinal relationship of the Corpus Christi dramatic play to the feast of Corpus Christi is almost entirely incidental.

Hardin Craig throughout his lifetime was a determined opponent of the proposed theory of genesis: "The dramatic figures of the Corpus Christi procession," he wrote, "could have come only from the plays. The plays could not have come from the figures in the procession, because the plays were in existence long before the procession was instituted."[26] This argument, however, assumes a direct continuity between liturgical plays and the Corpus Christi cycles, and is based on an outmoded theory concerning the date of the Chester cycle. We know that Corpus Christi was celebrated throughout England by 1318, and that processions were generally instituted by the middle of the century.[27] But the cycle plays, as F. M. Salter has attempted to show in the case of Chester, cannot be dated earlier than the last part of the fourteenth century.[28]

Craig does not rely entirely, however, on his argument for dating. He backs his position with an a priori assertion:

Also a series of *pageants tableaux* on so extensive a scale, so orderly, and so highly developed dramatically as a Corpus Christi play, could hardly have come into existence at all until after the community involved had been educated by considerable famil- iarity with the plays. We should never have arrived at the uniform, definite result we have—Corpus Christi cycles with their general similarities, their local differences, and their constant dependence upon their liturgical predecessors—if a beginning had been made from any possible set of ideally constructed *pageants tableaux*. In other words, the particular set of subjects treated in the Corpus Christi plays are there, not because they were chosen to suit the idea of Corpus Christi, or because they were dramatically attrac-

tive in themselves, but because they were the liturgical themes and
events handed down for centuries and thus ready to be combined
into cycles on the occasion of the establishment of the feast of
Corpus Christi (with its procession) in the early fourteenth century.[29]

It is true that "liturgical themes and events" had been handed down for
centuries, but not in liturgical plays only. Craig himself writes, in
another place: "The pattern to be followed in the construction of a
Corpus Christi play was everywhere available—in the church service, in
the Scriptures, in many learned works, and in various narratives in the
vernacular."[30] To this we may add sculpture, painting, and manuscript
illumination. It would have been just as easy to construct a series of
pageants tableaux from this pictorial tradition as to make plays—
easier, in fact, since the immediate composition of dialogue would have
been unnecessary.

If a series of *pageants tableaux* lies behind the dramatic cycles, then
the selection of episodes was made before any dramatic considerations
could have been deemed relevant. *Pageants tableaux* bear a closer
relationship to pictorial art than to drama. If we seek the source of the
generic integrity of the episodic cycles, we perhaps should look to
pictorial traditions rather than to liturgical plays, liturgical texts, or
theological doctrines.[31]

This is merely one way in which a consideration of historical facts
may force a reconsideration of critical (formal) theory. Another has to
do with the plays' "address," that is, with the nature of their audience
and its effect upon the formal rhetoric of the drama. Kolve goes a long
way in loosening up the traditional view that the cycle plays were aimed
primarily at the unlettered. He calls the cycle plays "the most truly
popular drama England has ever known" and insists that "their
audience included clergy, aristocracy, burgesses, and peasants, all
together."[32] We will discover, however, that in many cities Corpus
Christi dramatic plays were presented to a select audience of civic and
ecclesiastical authorities. Presumably Kolve mentions peasants because
he believes that "The Corpus Christi drama took place in broad
daylight, in the streets and open places of the town."[33] This in turn is
part of the most sacrosanct of all theories concerning the cycle plays,
the idea that they were presented processionally through the towns at
stations along the way, and that the audiences numbered in the
thousands.

In the following chapters I will first offer evidence of a theoretical
and a priori nature against the generally accepted notions concerning

the staging of Corpus Christi plays. Then I will analyze, city by city, beginning with York, all available records that might establish how, where, and for whom the Corpus Christi plays were performed. I will assume that each city may have conducted its own affairs in its own way, and I will therefore avoid argument by analogy. For the same reasons, I will make reference to events on the Continent only rarely. Exceptions to the rule against analogy will occur only in cases where the influence of one town on another can be clearly demonstrated. The form of this study is a direct consequence of its methods and assumptions. The chapters on individual cities are more or less separate essays. The two chapters on York should be read together. The rest are best read in order but may be read in any sequence without much loss of coherence.

My primary aim is to discover how, when, where, and for whom the Corpus Christi plays were performed. My secondary aim is to discover something about their origins. We know that the feast of Corpus Christi was promulgated in 1264 and confirmed at the Council of Vienne in 1311. By 1318 the feast was observed throughout England. Evidently Corpus Christi was celebrated with a procession from the beginning. This was only natural, since processions were common to festivals of any kind. Moreover, Corpus Christi naturally required a procession for the exhibition of the Eucharist. A council of Paris addressed itself to the nature of this procession in 1323: "As to the solemn procession made on the Thursday's feast, when the Holy Sacrament is carried, seeing that it appears to have been introduced in these our times, by a sort of inspiration, we prescribe nothing at present and leave all concerning it to the devotion of the clergy and the people."[34] In England, as elsewhere, clergy and laymen combined into guilds in order to exercise their responsibility toward the procession, and the procession itself became a major *civic* event.[35] The mayor, aldermen, and members of the craft guilds, instead of merely witnessing the procession, joined it. This had certainly been accomplished in important cities of England by the middle of the fourteenth century.

Three-dimensional images were carried in English processions as early as the thirteenth century: witness the London Fishmongers' piscatory show of 1298, in which fabricated fish and an image of St. Magnus were displayed.[36] And as we shall see, images or pageants were shown in Corpus Christi processions as early as 1376. It is almost certain that these were all that existed of the "Corpus Christi play" in the late fourteenth century.

Once pageant figures were introduced into the Corpus Christi procession, a high-level decision was clearly called for. If every one of the guilds were to present a pageant, some authority might be exercised over the choice of subject matter. It is remotely possible that the civic and ecclesiastical authorities decided to make pageants all take themes appropriate to Corpus Christi, sending clerks scurrying off to do the kind of research that Theo Stemmler has undertaken in recent years.[37] I suspect that if the question had been put this way, however, the procession would have constituted a direct meditation upon the Eucharist in the manner of John Lydgate's poem.

Instead I imagine that the authorites (the city council rather than the church) said to themselves, "Let us consider: we have forty-eight (or twenty-six or thirty-two) guilds, each clamoring to put on a pageant. We must have order! The pageants must have a consistent theme, and a clear, sequential, familiar iconography. The subject matter must be divisible into so and so many parts." This supposition, I think, will fully account for the subject matter, selection of episode, and episodic nature of the Corpus Christi plays. Among pictorial narrative cycles, the history of the world had few close rivals. As for the inclusiveness of the English pageant cycles (from Creation to the Last Judgment), this was a simple consequence of the relatively large number of guilds in various English cities. In general, pageant assignments were made according to the pre-established order of processional marches, the first guilds receiving the Creation pageants, the last receiving Doomsday. In a march, it must be noted, the guilds last in priority often led the way, while the most distinguished brought up the rear. Exceptions may have been made in cases where a guild might claim an affinity for a particular pageant. Special circumstances in the organization of guilds may account for local variations of subject matter in cities like Coventry and Norwich.

The subsequent elaboration of processional pageants into dramatic cycles was at once simpler and more difficult than is usually imagined. It was simple because many important decisions—guild responsibility, selection and assignment of episode, creation of appropriate costumes for the actors—were already settled. It was difficult because dialogue (to a total of 10,000 lines and more) had to be supplied; and also because a dramatic production is quite incompatible with a moving procession. No doubt the *pageants tableaux* sometimes included brief actions and speeches. But lengthy dramatic plays can only have been given at or after the conclusion of the procession, perhaps on special stages constructed for the purpose.

Spectacular pageants were introduced into processions of various kinds by the fourteenth century. We cannot escape the question why such pageants frequently achieved their fullest and most conspicuous development in the Corpus Christi procession rather than some other occasion. Though Corpus Christi was initially an ecclesiastical festivity, the primary force behind the guild pageants was probably (granted that the distinction is not entirely valid for the Middle Ages) secular rather than religious. Though ordinances and indentures requiring the presence of guilds in the procession often expressed pieties of one sort or another, certain documents refer perhaps more realistically to the fierce competitiveness among the guilds:

> To the Worshippe of God And in sustentacion of the procession of Corpus Xpi playes in the Towne of Newcastle vpon Tine after the laudible and ancient custome of the same Towne and in auoideing of dissencion and discord that hath been amongst the Crafts of the said Towne as of man slaughter and murder and other mischiefs in time comeing which hath been lately attempted amongst the fellowshipp of the said crafts of the Tailor of the same Towne and to induce love charity peace and right.[38]

Similarly, bloody riots broke out during the Chester Corpus Christi procession of 1399.[39] Craft guild rivalry—coupled with civic pride, economic self-interest, and religious piety—was a force strong enough to insure the trundling of expensive pageant wagons through the city streets for a documented time span of two hundred years and more.

In many cities the Corpus Christi procession became the most important *civic* riding of the year. The procession developed during an era in which the public display of persons and objects—in processions, ridings, royal entries and progresses—was a principal instrument in the exercise of temporal power.[40]

The prominence of Corpus Christi as the occasion of civic and guild ostentation was certainly related to its calendar day. Historians of medieval drama have long recognized that Corpus Christi was essentially a summer festival and that the activities of the day—processions, pageants, and plays—were more suited to summer weather than to the bitter days of Christmas. But in the fourteenth and fifteenth centuries Corpus Christi was more than just summer: it was, for all practical purposes, midsummer.

By the beginning of the fifteenth century a discrepancy of nine days had accrued between the Julian calendar and true astronomical time; by the beginning of the sixteenth century, the Julian calendar was ten days out. For John Donne, writing at the turn of the next century, St. Lucy's day (13 December) was the darkest day of the year. The lightest day of the year during the fifteenth century fell on 12 or 13 June (Old Style). But Midsummer day (the Nativity of St. John the Baptist) was celebrated by tradition on 24 June, regardless of the time of the true summer solstice.

The movable feast of Corpus Christi, celebrated on the Thursday after Trinity Sunday, can fall on any date from 23 May to 24 June. In about three years out of every four during the fifteenth century, Corpus Christi was closer to astronomical midsummer day than was the feast of Midsummer itself. Moreover, it fell during the time of year (4 June–5 July New Style) when the English weather is on its best behavior. The long hours of sunlight on Corpus Christi and the relatively fine weather would encourage, or at least permit, an elaborate processional spectacle. So the clergy marched with their colorful habits and with the Host; the civic officials marched with their scarlet robes and gold chains; and the guildsmen marched in their livery, carrying banners and torches. In certain larger cities the guildsmen also mounted a long series of *pageants tableaux,* often on the subject of the history of the world. Many cities were content with pageants alone. Other cities and towns later yielded to a natural desire to perform lengthy dramatic plays on the biblical subjects displayed in the pageants. A cycle lasting several hours might be presented at a single station during the course or at the end of a liturgical procession; however, a dramatic performance lasting half a day or more could be mounted only after the morning procession had reached its destination at the altar of a church.

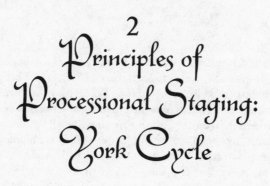

2
Principles of Processional Staging: York Cycle

A Theoretical Analysis of Processional Staging Techniques: York Cycle

One of the most persistent theories about the late medieval English Corpus Christi plays concerns the manner in which they were staged: "Plays were generally performed in a procession of horse-drawn floats, called pageants. At appointed stations along the way, the individual wagon with its carefully prepared scene stopped for the guildsmen to act out their play. Spectators could thus stand in one spot and enjoy an unbroken sequence of scriptural history lasting sometimes a full day or even longer." This account, by David M. Zesmer, goes on to say that not all cycles were performed in this manner but leaves the impression that those which employed fixed stages were the exception.[1]

This traditional hypothesis was first enunciated at length by Thomas Sharp, who drew in turn upon apparently trustworthy descriptions by the early Chester antiquarian Rogers (father or son), and by the Warwickshire antiquarian William Dugdale.[2] Support for the hypothesis has been gleaned from civic records of Coventry, Chester, York, and Beverley.

The mode of production described by Zesmer is usually called "processional" or "perambulatory." But these adjectives are not completely definitive, for several methods of staging plays in the manner of a procession may be imagined.[3] The method which has been

The first section of this chapter is reprinted with slight changes from my "Principles of Processional Staging: York Cycle," *Modern Philology* 67 (1970): 303–20, by permission of the editor and publisher. Copyright 1970, The University of Chicago.

ascribed to the Corpus Christi plays I shall arbitrarily name "true-pro-cessional." It has the following characteristics: (1) The cycle to be presented consists of at least two plays. (2) The plays are presented to at least two audiences. (3) The plays are arranged in serial order and are seen in that order, from beginning to end, by all audiences. (4) The audiences are arranged in serial order, and each play visits all audiences in that order. In a true-processional production, all these conditions must coexist. If a long play is divided into many episodes, this is not in itself evidence of true-processional performance. In the same manner, multiplicity of casts, of audiences, of stations, or mobility of plays, may all be irrelevant unless all are found together.

Students of the drama have generally imagined that a production with these primary characteristics will bring major conveniences to both actors and audiences. Indeed it is argued that true-processional staging was adopted to make originally stationary plays visible and audible to increasingly vast audiences. The plays, according to this way of thinking, originated as liturgical dramas but were driven out of the church. This came as a consequence of what Warton, with masterfully evasive ambiguity, calls their "enormity."[4] From thence the plays traveled to the civic square and finally were mounted on wagons and drawn about the town "for the better advantage of Spectators." [5]

Recently, and for the first time, Martial Rose has tried to imagine how a true-processional production would actually behave, indepen-dent of the wishes of guildsmen or of scholars.[6] He has located a major inconvenience, hitherto scarcely recognized, in the inevitable staggering of beginnings and endings. At the very beginning of any processional production the first play will be shown at the first station. After this, the first play and hence the dramatic cycle will "begin" at each of the subsequent stations in serial order. Spectators at the last station will not see any of the cycle until the first play has been staged at all previous stations. Similarly, the cast of the last play, though the production may begin at four or five o'clock in the morning, cannot begin to play at the first station until all the other plays in the cycle have finished there.

The awkwardness of such a system may be theoretically demon-strated in the visit of Queen Margaret to Coventry in 1457. The queen sat at the first station and there saw all the plays except the Last Judgment, which could not be staged for lack of daylight.[7] Hardin Craig once postulated that Coventry had not only ten plays but also ten stations.[8] If all the plays in the cycle were about the same length, and if the last play could not be given at the first station, then not only did the last cast perform no play that year, but the last audience also saw no play. But this is an impossible situation: Craig's assumptions must have been wrong.[9]

Even if the queen had been permitted to see the entire cycle, the last cast would still have had to play all remaining stations in order that all audiences, including the last, should see all the plays in order. Staggered beginnings and endings therefore naturally result in a greatly protracted production.

An equally serious consequence of true-processional production is entirely overlooked by Rose. In his analysis he considers only terminal irregularities and assumes that the internal conduct of the York production would have been entirely orderly.[10] But internal irregularities can be avoided only on the condition that all plays in a cycle are precisely equal in length, distinctly not the case with any of the extant Corpus Christi cycle texts. In the York cycle, for example, the longest play, with 546 lines, is over six times the length of the shortest, with 86 lines. Other pairs of plays show almost as much variation.[11]

Rose overlooks this variable because in preparing to calculate the length of the production, he introduces an averaging operation which, as if by fiat, equalizes the lengths of the individual plays. According to his reckoning, the average play is 273 lines long. But it is permissible to calculate on the basis of the average only if the plays are in fact 273 lines each. Otherwise this Procrustean approach prompts a serious distortion of the evidence.[12]

The actual consequences of irregularity in length may be appreciated by a consideration of three model cases. Let us assume that a "cycle" of two plays is to be produced in true-processional fashion at ten stations. For the moment we shall disregard time taken up by the movement of plays and wagons.

Case I. Play 1 and play 2 are each thirty minutes long. Play 1 begins to perform at station 1. After thirty minutes, it advances to station 2 and begins to play. At the same time, play 2 begins at station 1. The two plays begin and finish simultaneously, and when play 1 moves to station 3, play 2 moves to station 2. Thus they go on their way, advancing simultaneously and at a uniform rate until play 1 has finished at station 10. Play 2 must finally perform alone at station 10, and when it is finished the production is at an end. The total length of the performance, not counting pauses for movement, is five hours and thirty minutes: Play 1 has played ten thirty-minute performances, which makes five hours. When it is done, play 2 performs for another thirty minutes, and is finished.

Case II. Play 1 is fifty minutes long and play 2 is ten minutes long. Play 1 spends fifty minutes at station 1 and advances to station 2. Play 2 then begins to perform at station 1 immediately and finishes in ten minutes. It must wait forty minutes, however, before station 2 has been cleared by play 1. At every station play 2 must wait until play 1 is finished. When play 1 is finished at the last station, play 2 then performs there for ten minutes, and the cycle is done. The total length of the production is eight hours and thirty minutes: Play 1 spends fifty minutes at each of ten stations, making five hundred minutes, or eight hours and twenty minutes. When it is done, play 2 performs alone for an additional ten minutes.

Case III. Play 1 is ten minutes long and play 2 is fifty minutes long. Play 1 begins at station 1. After ten minutes play 1 advances to station 2 and play 2 begins at station 1. Play 1 again finishes in ten minutes and clears station 2. But whether or not play 1 advances to station 3 immediately, play 2 cannot advance to station 2 for forty more minutes. When play 2 advances to station 2 it finds the station clear but again it must perform its full fifty minutes before it advances to station 3. The same situation obtains at each successive station. The total length of the production is eight hours and thirty minutes: Play 1 performs alone for ten minutes at station 1, and after it is done there, play 2 spends fifty minutes at each of ten stations, making five hundred minutes, or eight hours and twenty minutes.

We may observe that, for each of the three cases, if the plays were performed in sequence at a single station, the total length of the production would be one hour. In all cases, playing at the added stations increases production length. In the last two cases the inequality in length between the plays makes for an additional increase. But the full production in case II is exactly as long as in case III. This reflects the usual rule that the total length of a true-processional production is a function of the lengths of the individual plays, *but is independent of their sequence or order.* (But see Appendix A, no. 2.)

From an examination of these model cases it becomes apparent that the movement of the plays may be governed in several different ways. In case I, where the plays are equal in length, the two plays naturally begin and end simultaneously at adjoining stations and can advance, one behind the other, as if in lockstep. Since the second play is always ready to begin as soon as the first play ends, each audience sees an unbroken performance. In case II also, the second play can begin to play as soon as the first play finishes at any station and advances to the next. But if the two plays begin simultaneously, they cannot end simultaneously:

the cast of the shorter play will have to sit on its hands for forty minutes at each station, waiting for the first play to finish. Similarly, in case III the two plays can always begin simultaneously at each successive pair of stations, but then the audience of the first play, at all stations but the first, will have to sit on its hands for forty minutes while the longer second play is finishing at the previous station. Audiences can see an uninterrupted production only if the shorter play waits 40 minutes at each station before it begins. If the short first play performs at each station as quickly as possible, it will finish at the last station after 100 minutes. But the slow second play cannot begin to perform at the last station until 460 minutes have elapsed. The audience at the last station will wait 360 minutes, or six hours, between plays.

In general, three modes of conducting advances may be imagined for true-processional staging:

1. Uniform advances: All plays in the cycle advance from station to station at the same rate, and casts at the several stations all begin simultaneously. (Advances can occur at any preselected time interval, say hourly or half-hourly. The minimum interval or "acting time" will be equal to the length of the longest play in the cycle.)

2. Synchronized advances: All plays performed during any given acting time begin simultaneously, and all advance at the same rate, but as quickly as possible. (This means, in effect, that all plays performing at any given time will advance at the rate of the longest play then being performed. There might be couriers who would observe when all plays performed at any time were finished and who would then run to tell each cast to advance and begin playing at the next station.)

3. Free advances: Each play advances to the next station and begins to play there as quickly as it can, that is (a) as soon as possible after it has finished playing at its present station, but (b) not before the next station has been cleared by the play ahead. (Since this mode fulfills the two *minimum* conditions for a true-processional production, it represents the fastest possible pace.)

Of these three modes of advance, the first may be dismissed as highly inefficient. Audiences who have watched the shorter plays and actors who have performed them must wait out the gaps of time between the end of the play and the end of the longer acting time. The accumulation of these irregularities throughout the day will extend the full production beyond endurance.

The method of synchronized advances incurs many of the same difficulties as uniform advances. The advantage is that acting times are variable in length, and if only shorter plays are performing at a given time (as at the beginning of the York cycle), the pace of the production can be temporarily increased, and the total length consequently reduced. But long gaps for actors and audiences will still occur, especially whenever a longer play has begun to perform. The method of synchronized advances deserves our attention primarily because it is usually imagined that the movement of plays was at least regular.

The free-advance mode dispenses entirely with simultaneous beginnings. Internal movements are more difficult to keep track of, but since this system results in the shortest possible production time, it will be the test case in determining whether a true-processional production of any cycle could be compressed into an allotted time span.

For each of the three modes of advance, it is possible to estimate the total length of an actual production if certain facts can be established, namely, the lengths of the individual plays, the number of plays, and the number of stations. All that is then needed is to discover proper formulas for dealing with these quantities. Because the construction and use of formulas lies beyond the interest of many students of the drama, I have consigned this matter to Appendix A, and will present only the results in the body of this chapter. It seems to me important, nevertheless, to explain how the length of a free-advance production may be determined.

The time required for all plays to finish at the first station is the sum of the lengths of all the plays in the cycle. But after the last play has performed at the first station, it must still perform at all remaining stations before the production is ended. From our study of the model cases, it is clear that plays behind longer plays are impeded in their movement. Only if the longest play comes last can the last play advance each time it has finished. For the moment let us imagine that the longest play does in fact come last. We may do this because of the rule that the total length of the production is the same whatever the order of the plays. With the longest play last, it is easy to see that the cycle will now end after that play has played out its full length at each remaining station. The total length of the production is therefore the sum of the lengths of all the individual plays in the cycle, plus the length of the longest play multiplied by the number of stations after the first. Rose counts as his "last" play not the longest play but an *average* play. It happens that in the York cycle the longest play is almost exactly twice the length of the average. This of course makes Rose's calculations impossibly conservative.

In an actual production, one cast cannot begin at a station the instant the preceding cast finishes. Even if the new cast is "waiting in the wings," it must wait until the first play clears the stage area, and then it must set up its own stage, or draw up its own pageant wagon. Another longer pause occurs as each cast makes its way from one station to the next. The formulas can be adapted to take these two pauses into consideration. In a free-advance production, the briefer interval occurs between all the plays in the cycle as they perform at the first station. The "last play," in addition, will have to make all the long journeys between the successive pairs of stations. The sum of all these intervals is added to the previously calculated total production time to adjust for these more realistic conditions of performance.

Having established the proper formulas, our next task is to discover real values for all the variables. Beginning from a complete text with a minimum of lacunae and other aberrations, we can first state the length of each individual play in terms of its total number of lines. It is always possible, of course, to piece out a play interminably with dumb shows, mimed action, silent gestures, pauses for thought, scene changes, musical interludes, dances, and a host of other dramatic and nondramatic devices. Moreover, counting lines will not directly reveal the actual duration of a dramatic production. But it can tell us the *relative* lengths of two or more plays on the assumption that the duration of a play is proportional to its length measured by lines. On the same assumption, it can tell us the *virtual* length of a true-processional play, that is, the length of a single play at a single station which would begin when the true-processional production begins and end when it ends. The assumption common to these statements is not always valid but is acceptable on the further assumption that texts are uncut and that actors speak their lines quickly, without pause, and at a constant average rate. A line count is thus a valid measure of the *minimum* relative length of a play in production.

Fortunately, the text of the York cycle survives in exceptionally good condition and thus makes line counting relatively reliable. It is true that several leaves are missing from the manuscript, but any missing parts will reduce the number of lines available to count, and will therefore result in a conservative estimate of length. The number of lines in the various York plays are given in the second vertical column of table 5, below. The count is only approximate, not only because of important lacunae, but also because of irregularities of lesser significance. In general, the count follows that of the Smith text. Special cases are discussed in the footnotes to the table.

The plays in the extant York manuscript number forty-eight, omitting the fragment at the end. At different times the plays may have numbered fifty-one and fifty-seven. Evidence of the number of stations also points to variation, from ten to sixteen.[13] Calculating on the basis of forty-eight plays and twelve stations will therefore yield a conservative estimate.

If plays are measured by lines, the lengths of pauses must be stated in equivalent terms. Let us assume as a rough estimate that the equivalent of 20 lines is required for a play "waiting in the wings" to set up on a cleared station, while the equivalent of 100 lines is required to make a journey from one station to the next and to begin playing there.[14]

Using these measurements and the formulas worked out in Appendix A, we are now in a position to calculate the virtual length of the York cycle under conditions which have been regarded as typical for the production of Corpus Christi plays. Our formulas cover all three modes of advance, but they are also general enough to be able to handle special cases in which the production is not true-processional. In addition, it is possible to calculate for an "ideal" text in which (as in Rose's reckoning) all plays are of the same length.[15] Table 1 gives the results of the most important calculations.

Although this table indicates only virtual length rather than actual duration by clock time, it is of value because it makes possible an analysis of the relative lengths of the various modes of production. The relative lengths are shown even more clearly in table 2, which gives the same information in percentages.

From these two tables it is clear that all methods of true-processional production increase the relative length of the cycle over a single-station performance. Both of the methods which require plays to begin simultaneously are extraordinarily inefficient, even in the case of an ideal text. In fact, a production of the ideal text with uniform (synchronized) advances is longer than the production of the actual text with free advances when pauses are considered for both.[16] Certainly any group intending to stage such plays under pressure of time would reject all methods except free advances or some limited modification thereof.

All estimates and calculations for an ideal text are entirely hypothetical. This corresponds to the method used by Rose, which is not generally valid. The calculation is nevertheless useful, for a comparison of the respective lengths for the same mode of advance shows that in every case the ideal text makes for a much shorter production than the actual text. With free advances, the use of an ideal text at twelve stations results in a production about 25 percent longer than a single-station performance, while use of the actual text increases the production by another 25 percent, for a total of 50 percent.

TABLE 1
VIRTUAL LENGTH OF THE YORK CYCLE IN TRUE-PROCESSIONAL PRODUCTION

Advances	Without Intervals	With Intervals
Performance of text at twelve stations:		
Uniform	32,214 lines	38,014 lines
Synchronized	25,069 lines	30,869 lines
Free..	19,281 lines	21,321 lines
Performance of ideal text at twelve stations:		
Uniform or synchronized*	16,284 lines	22,084 lines
Free..	16,284 lines	18,324 lines
Performance of text at a single station:		
Synchronized or free†	13,275 lines	14,215 lines

*With an ideal text, uniform advances are the same as synchronized advances, since all plays are equal to the longest.
†At a single station, synchronized advances are the same as free advances. Since only one play performs at any given time, that play is the longest during its acting time, and the acting time is simply the length of the play.

It may therefore be stated as a rule for avoiding all internal irregularities, and thereby to promote efficiency and brevity, that all plays in a rationally conceived true-processional cycle should be approximately equal in length. We would imagine that the governors of the pageants must have been aware of this and would have exerted great pressure to keep plays to a standard length. Conversely, inequality in length may be taken as partial evidence that a cycle was not intended for true-processional production, especially if time was an important consideration.

Martial Rose has raised the important question whether the York cycle could have been performed in true-processional fashion during the time span allotted to it. This is a particularly fruitful question because we know that the York plays were produced during the course of one day.[17] But to deal with the question of real time, we must

TABLE 2
PERCENTAGE INCREASE IN VIRTUAL LENGTH OVER SINGLE-STATION STAGING*

Advances	Without Intervals	With Intervals
Single station	0.0	0.0
Free, ideal text	22.6	28.9
Uniform, ideal text	22.6	55.4
Free, actual text	47.5	50.0
Synchronized, actual text.........................	88.4	117.2
Uniform, actual text.................................	142.7	167.4

*York cycle in true-processional production, forty-eight plays at twelve stations.

discover some way to translate the one remaining variable, length by lines, into clock time. Experience or experiment will demonstrate that it is difficult to read expressively or to perform a play of the Corpus Christi type at a rate much faster than 1,000 lines per hour. This figure roughly accords with estimates made by other writers on the subject [18] and also has the practical advantage that to convert from lines to lines per hour, we need only move the decimal point three spaces to the left. Thus 1,000 lines can be performed in 1.000 hours. Using this conversion factor, we may, as in table 3, express the estimated real lengths of the various modes of performance. (In the table, minutes have been rounded off to the nearest five.)

According to York city records, players were directed to assemble at 4:30 in the morning on Corpus Christi day.[19] This might mean that the plays actually began at five o'clock. Table 4 shows the time of day at which the York plays would end if they were begun at this hour in the morning. A standard free-advance production, for example, would end after two o'clock the following morning.

Other records indicate that at times the York plays were preceded by a liturgical procession.[20] Any delay of the beginning past five in the morning would result in an equivalent delay of the ending that night or the next day.

From an examination of these tables, and of the calculations on which they are based, we may confidently agree that whether or not the city of York mounted a procession in advance of its cycle play, it could not posssibly have mounted a true-processional production of the extant cycle text in a single day. The only method which would permit the cycle as it stands to begin and end between sunrise and sunset, even on a long June day, is a stationary, nonprocessional production, or a processional production so radically modified that it no longer conformed to the requirement that all plays should be seen at all stations in order.

Excessive length, as a consequence of both terminal and internal

TABLE 3
REAL LENGTH OF THE YORK CYCLE PLAYED AT 1,000 LINES PER HOUR

Advances	Without Intervals	With Intervals
Single station	13 hrs 15 min	14 hrs 15 min
Free, ideal text	16 hrs 15 min	18 hrs 20 min
Uniform, ideal text	16 hrs 15 min	22 hrs 5 min
Free, actual text	19 hrs 15 min	21 hrs 15 min
Synchronized, actual text	25 hrs 0 min	30 hrs 50 min
Uniform, actual text	32 hrs 15 min	38 hrs 10 min

TABLE 4
CONCLUDING TIME OF YORK CYCLE BEGUN AT 5:00 A.M., PLAYED 1,000 LINES PER HOUR

Advances	Without Intervals	With Intervals
Single station	6:15 P.M. same day	7:15 P.M. same day
Free, ideal text	9:15 P.M. same day	11:20 P.M. same day
Uniform, ideal text	9:15 P.M. same day	3:05 A.M. next day
Free, actual text	12:15 A.M. next day	2:15 A.M. next day
Synchronized, actual text	6:00 A.M. next day	11:50 A.M. next day
Uniform, actual text	1:00 P.M. next day	7:00 P.M. next day

irregularities, is the most telling argument against the proposition that true-processional playing is a satisfactory means for mounting a long, episodic cycle play. Other arguments, also arising from irregular play lengths, may be discovered in an investigation into the internal conduct of a production. But to accomplish this we need to know more than our tables have told us so far.

In a system of free advances, the behavior of individual plays is variable for casts and audiences throughout the production. Some plays preceding longer plays can advance at their own rate, but all plays following longer plays are slowed in their progress. Since movement is so variable, and since plays do not regularly begin or end simultaneously, we require some special means to achieve an overview of an entire cycle in action. We can do this by constructing a table of all the advances of all the plays. Since each of forty-eight plays performs at each of twelve stations, and since both beginnings and endings of all plays are of consequence, over eleven hundred salient instants in time are involved, all within a time span of less than twenty-four hours. Fortunately, however, the table can be constructed without the aid of a computer: an adding machine is sufficient.

The rules for determining the significant instants are as follows: In the case of the first station, each play begins after the play which precedes it has finished and cleared the stage. At later stations, each successively longer play, including the first and up to and including the longest, will always begin its journey to the next station the moment it has finished at the last. At the end of its journey, it can always begin to play immediately. But shorter plays will begin to set up at the next station when the play ahead has finished there.

The time lapse at the beginning of the production is zero. The time lapse at the end of the first York play at the first station, measured by lines, is 160. Since 20 lines are required for the second play to set up after the first play is finished, the time lapse for the beginning of the second play at the first station is $160 + 20 = 180$. Similarly, since 100 lines are required for a journey, the first play will begin to perform at the second station after a time lapse of $160 + 100 = 260$. This accumulative reckoning is continued for all plays at all stations. Table 5 gives selected time lapses by lines for a true-processional production of the York cycle at twelve stations, in the free-advance mode.

The calculations represented in table 5 confirm the results achieved by the formula: the virtual length of the production is 21,321 lines. The table provides other information not revealed by the formula. For example, the length of the cycle varies considerably at different stations. At the first station the virtual length of the cycle is 14,214 lines; at the third, 14,987 lines; and at the last, 18,461 lines. By clock time, the cycle lasts about four and a quarter hours longer at the last station than at the first. The reason for this is that the first play, being shorter, can advance much faster than the longest play. For the later audiences, great gaps occur between each successively longer play and the play which precedes it. In the York cycle this occurs seven times at each station after the first. The lengths of the gaps are given in the table for the third and the twelfth stations. Ranging from several minutes to one hour and forty minutes, and longer in every case at the last station than at the third, these gaps prevent the audiences from seeing an uninterrupted production. After the longest play has performed at each station, the gaps, except for pauses to change plays, cease, and all stations finally witness a smooth performance.

Since the system of free advances incurs the problem of gaps and excessive length at later stations, a change in the mode of governing the plays seems desirable. But since free advances offer the benefit of the shortest possible production time, a change to a different system entirely would not provide a satisfactory alternative. The system of free advances itself, however, has three special peculiarities which can be used to advantage. The first is that all plays behind the longest advance with strict regularity, leaving no gaps, except for changing casts, in the presentation of the plays at the several stations. (The actors in shorter plays must wait a certain time between performances [gap P], but the audience sees an unbroken performance.)

The second peculiarity of free advances is that the *order* of the plays is of no consequence to the total length of the production. It is obvious, therefore, that by putting the longest play first, the *entire cycle* would be seen at all stations as an unbroken performance.

This solution to the problem of irregularity in a Corpus Christi cycle is unacceptable, however, because it violates a fundamental require-ment of true-processional staging: that all the plays must be presented in order. But it is possible to make the short first play *behave* like the longest play in the cycle, even if it is not in fact the longest. This is because of the third peculiarity: the movements of the plays ahead of the longest are of no consequence to the total length of the production if the stage has been cleared each time the longest play advances. Subject only to this condition, the first plays are free to move as they will, whether at random or governed by another system after they have performed at the first station.

The longest play in the York cycle must always play its full 546 lines between the time it begins at any one station and the time it begins its journey to the next. The journey requires an additional 100 lines. The first play would therefore behave as if it were the longest play if it advanced at a rate of 646 lines between beginnings. Thus play 1 would begin at station 1, perform its 160 lines, and then leave the stage clear for play 2. After a journey equivalent to 100 lines it would be ready to perform at station 2. But before beginning to perform there it would wait the equivalent of an additional $646 - 260 = 386$ lines, or about twenty-five minutes. This accumulating series of 386-line delays would have the effect of making the cycle begin relatively later at each station, putting the time gaps ahead of rather than within the actual performance. The first play would begin at the last station about four and a quarter hours later than in a system of unmodified free advances. This is clear from an examination of table 6. Except for short pauses to change casts, no gaps occur within the cycle, and the production is uniform at all stations, a virtual 14,215 lines in length.

This system of modified free advances, though it has great advantages, incurs the disadvantage that the first play behaves like the first play in a system of uniform advances. Its slow progress means that audiences gathered early at stations farther along the line will wait longer (up to seven hours) between the start of the production and the time they will see their first play. More problematic is the fact that the first play is required to gauge its progress not by another event which is actually occurring as it performs but by the predicted real length of the longest play in the cycle.

A practical solution to this last problem is to treat the first *group* of plays as a long single play. This is apparently what Maurice Hussey has in mind when he writes, "By allowing two or three plays to be given at the first point before sending the first pageant to the second point the organizers were able to ensure a complete continuity."[21] But Hussey does not indicate whether this procedure is to be repeated at every subsequent station, nor does he discuss the exact number of plays to be

TABLE 5

LINE LAPSES IN A TRUE-PROCESSIONAL PRODUCTION, FREE ADVANCES
(YORK CYCLE AT TWELVE STATIONS)

PLAY NUMBER	LINES	1 Begin	1 End	2 Begin	3 Begin	Gap A*	10 Begin	11 Begin	12 Begin	12 End	Gap A*	Gap P†
1	160	0	160	260	520	520	2,340	2,600	2,860	3,020	2,860	0
2	86	180	266	440	700	20	2,520	2,780	3,040	3,126	20	74
3	96	286	382	546	806	20	2,626	2,886	3,146	3,245	20	64
4	99	402	501	662	922	20	2,742	3,002	3,262	3,361	20	61
5	175	521	696	796	1,071	50	2,996	3,271	3,546	3,721	185	0
6	168	716	884	976	1,236	20	3,191	3,466	3,741	3,909	20	7
7	138	904	1,042	1,164	1,424	20	3,379	3,654	3,929	4,067	20	37
8	151	1,062	1,213	1,322	1,582	20	3,537	3,812	4,087	4,238	20	24
9	322	1,233	1,555	1,655	2,077	314	5,031	5,453	5,875	6,197	1,637	0
10	380	1,575	1,955	2,055	2,535	136	5,895	6,375	6,855	7,235	658	0
11	406	1,975	2,381	2,481	2,987	72	6,529	7,035	7,541	7,947	306	0
12	240	2,401	2,641	2,907	3,413	20	6,955	7,461	7,967	8,207	20	166
13	306	2,661	2,967	3,167	3,673	20	7,215	7,721	8,227	8,533	20	100
14	154	2,987	3,141	3,493	3,999	20	7,541	8,047	8,553	8,707	20	252
15	131	3,161	3,292	3,667	4,173	20	7,715	8,221	8,727	8,858	20	275
16	203‡	3,312	3,515	3,818	4,324	20	7,866	8,372	8,878	9,081	20	203
17	336	3,535	3,871	4,041	4,547	20	8,089	8,595	9,101	9,437	20	70
18	459§	3,891	4,350	4,450	5,009	126	8,922	9,481	10,040	10,499	603	0
19	231	4,370	4,601	4,929	5,488	20	9,401	9,960	10,519	10,750	20	228
20	281	4,621	4,902	5,180	5,739	20	9,652	10,211	10,770	11,051	20	178
21	228	4,922	5,150	5,481	6,040	20	9,953	10,512	11,071	11,299	20	231
22	175	5,170	5,345	5,729	6,288	20	10,201	10,760	11,319	11,494	20	284
23	210	5,365	5,575	5,924	6,483	20	10,396	10,955	11,514	11,724	20	249
24	240	5,595	5,835	6,154	6,713	20	10,626	11,185	11,744	11,984	20	219
25	267¶	5,855	6,122	6,414	6,973	20	10,886	11,445	12,004	12,271	20	192
26	545	6,142	6,687	6,787	7,432	192	11,947	12,592	13,237	13,782	966	0

Play	A*	P					P					P	
27	294	20	6,707	7,001	7,352	7,997	20	12,512	13,157	13,802	14,096	20	251
28	252#	20	7,021	7,273	7,666	8,311	20	12,826	13,471	14,116	14,368	20	293
29	301	20	7,293	7,594	7,938	8,583	20	13,098	13,743	14,388	14,689	20	244
30	398	20	7,614	8,012	8,259	8,904	20	13,419	14,064	14,709	15,107	20	147
31	546	22	8,032	8,678	9,324	9,890	22	13,846	14,492	15,138	15,684	31	0
32	407	20	8,598	9,005	9,671	10,317	20	14,412	15,058	15,704	16,111	20	139
33	389	20	9,025	9,414	10,080	10,726	20	14,839	15,485	16,131	16,520	20	157
34	485**	20	9,434	9,919	10,585	11,231	20	15,248	15,894	16,540	17,025	20	61
35	350**	20	9,939	10,289	10,955	11,601	20	15,753	16,399	17,045	17,395	20	196
36	300	20	10,309	10,609	11,275	11,921	20	16,123	16,769	17,415	17,715	20	246
37	416	20	10,629	11,045	11,711	12,357	20	16,443	17,089	17,735	18,151	20	130
38	408	20	11,065	11,473	12,139	12,785	20	16,879	17,525	18,171	18,579	20	138
39	454	20	11,493	11,947	12,613	13,259	20	17,307	17,953	18,599	19,053	20	92
40	149	20	11,967	12,116	12,782	13,428	20	17,781	18,427	19,073	19,222	20	397
41	194	20	12,136	12,330	12,996	13,642	20	17,950	18,596	19,242	19,436	20	352
42	198	20	12,350	12,548	13,214	13,860	20	18,164	18,810	19,456	19,654	20	348
43	278	20	12,568	12,846	13,512	14,158	20	18,382	19,028	19,674	19,952	20	268
44	224	20	12,866	13,090	13,756	14,402	20	18,680	19,326	19,972	20,196	20	322
45	194	20	13,110	13,304	13,970	14,616	20	18,924	19,570	20,216	20,410	20	352
46	311	20	13,324	13,635	14,301	14,947	20	19,138	19,784	20,430	20,741	20	235
47	160	20	13,655	13,815	14,481	15,127	20	19,469	20,115	20,761	20,921	20	386
48	380	20	13,835	…	…	…	20	19,649	20,295	20,941	…	20	166
End	…	…	…	…	14,861	15,507	…	20,029	20,695	…	21,321	…	…
Cycle length	…	…	14,215	14,215	14,601	14,987	…	17,689	18,075	…	18,461	…	…

NOTE: Stations 4–9 omitted.

* Gap A is the length of time (in lines) during which an audience has no play before it, between the given play and the one preceding. The minimum gap is equal to the time required to set up a stage from the "wings," in this case, twenty lines. For play 1 it is the time between the beginning of the production at station 1 and the moment the cycle begins at the later station.

† Gap P (constant at all stations) is the length of time between performances for actors. I have imagined that the actors, unlike the audiences, will be busy during the setting up of the stage.

‡ Miss Smith prints only 59 lines. I have added the 144 lines this play shares with the next.

§ This play is displaced in the manuscript. I have returned it to its proper position. Hence the roman numerals in the printed text will not always be in accord with my arabic numbers.

¶ In the Smith text this play has only 209 lines, but is missing a leaf. (I have estimated and restored the missing lines.)

In the Smith text this play has only 187 lines, but is missing a leaf. Miss Smith estimates that sixty-five lines have been lost, and I have restored them.

** In each of these two plays one leaf is missing, but I have not tried to restore the lines.

TABLE 6
LINE LAPSES, MODIFIED (646-LINE) FREE ADVANCES
(YORK CYCLE AT TWELVE STATIONS)

		STATIONS				
PLAY NUMBER	LINES	1 Begin	1 End	2 Begin	3 Begin	Gap A
1......... 160		0	160	646	1,292	1,292
2......... 86		180	266	826	1,472	20
3......... 96		286	382	932	1,578	20
4......... 99		402	501	1,048	1,694	20
5......... 175		521	696	1,167	1,813	20
6......... 168		716	884	1,362	2,008	20
7......... 138		904	1,042	1,550	2,196	20
8......... 151		1,062	1,213	1,708	2,354	20
9......... 322		1,233	1,555	1,879	2,525	20
10....... 380		1,575	1,955	2,221	2,867	20
11....... 406		1,975	2,381	2,621	3,267	20
12....... 240		2,401	2,641	3,047	3,693	20
13....... 306		2,661	2,967	3,307	3,953	20
14....... 154		2,987	3,141	3,633	4,279	20
15....... 131		3,161	3,292	3,807	4,453	20
16....... 203		3,312	3,515	3,958	4,604	20
17....... 336		3,535	3,871	4,181	4,827	20
18....... 459		3,891	4,350	4,537	5,183	20
19....... 231		4,370	4,601	5,016	5,662	20
20....... 281		4,621	4,902	5,267	5,913	20
21....... 228		4,922	5,150	5,568	6,214	20
22....... 175		5,170	5,345	5,816	6,462	20
23....... 210		5,365	5,575	6,011	6,657	20
24....... 240		5,595	5,835	6,241	6,887	20
25....... 267		5,855	6,122	6,501	7,147	20
26....... 545		6,142	6,687	6,788	7,434	20
27....... 294		6,707	7,001	7,353	7,999	20
28....... 252		7,021	7,273	7,667	8,313	20
29....... 301		7,293	7,594	7,939	8,585	20
30....... 398		7,614	8,012	8,260	8,906	20
31*......546		8,032	8,578	8,678	9,324	20
48....... 380		13,835	...	14,481	15,127	20
End		...	14,215	14,861	15,507	...
Cycle length		...	14,215	14,215	14,215	...

NOTE: Stations 4–9 omitted.
*All plays after the longest move exactly as in a production with unmodified free advances (table 5); hence plays 32–47 are omitted here.

TABLE 6 (Continued)

STATIONS

10 Begin	11 Begin	12 Begin	12 End	Gap A	Gap P
5,814	6,460	7,106	7,266	7,106	386
5,994	6,640	7,286	7,372	20	460
6,100	6,746	7,392	7,488	20	450
6,216	6,862	7,508	7,607	20	447
6,335	6,981	7,627	7,802	20	371
6,530	7,176	7,822	7,990	20	378
6,718	7,364	8,010	8,148	20	408
6,876	7,522	8,168	8,319	20	395
7,047	7,693	8,339	8,661	20	224
7,389	8,035	8,681	9,061	20	166
7,789	8,435	9,081	9,487	20	140
8,215	8,861	9,507	9,747	20	306
8,475	9,121	9,767	10,073	20	240
8,801	9,447	10,093	10,247	20	392
8,975	9,621	10,267	10,398	20	415
9,126	9,772	10,418	10,621	20	343
9,349	9,995	10,641	10,977	20	210
9,705	10,351	10,997	11,456	20	87
10,184	10,830	11,476	11,707	20	315
10,435	11,081	11,727	12,008	20	265
10,736	11,382	12,028	12,256	20	318
10,984	11,630	12,276	12,451	20	371
11,179	11,825	12,471	12,681	20	336
11,409	12,055	12,701	12,941	20	306
11,669	12,315	12,961	13,228	20	279
11,956	12,602	13,248	13,793	20	1
12,521	13,167	13,813	14,107	20	252
12,835	13,481	14,127	14,379	20	294
13,107	13,753	14,399	14,700	20	245
13,428	14,074	14,720	15,118	20	148
13,846	14,492	15,138	15,684	20	0
19,649	20,295	20,941	...	20	166
20,029	20,695	...	21,321	...	...
14,215	14,215	...	14,215	...	...

performed as a group, nor what the consequence of such a system would be for the total production time. The point is that the combined length of the first group of plays must equal or exceed the length of the longest play in the cycle. In the York cycle, the sum of plays 1 through 4, including pauses, is 501 lines, less than the longest play. The sum of plays 1 through 5 is 696 lines, more than the longest play, even counting its journey. If play 1 were to begin at the next station each time play 5 ended at the last, then the rest of the plays in the entire cycle would perform at each station at the same 696-line intervals, and, as Hussey surmises, complete continuity would result for each audience, though not for any of the casts. The primary disadvantage is that this practice would usually result in a "composite" play longer than the longest play in the cycle, and the increase in length would be reflected twelvefold in the total length of the production.[22] A refinement might be introduced by alerting the first play to begin before the last play of the group had quite finished. A courier could wait until this play had progressed to a certain point and then run to tell the first play to begin. In any case, it would be impractical to group or "bunch" plays indiscriminately: for example, so that they might be performed by common casts. In fact long plays, whether single-episode or bunched, are inimical to brevity of production. The bunching in the N-Town cycle and in what remains of the Coventry cycle is a strong argument against the possibility that either was intended in its present form for true-processional production at many stations.[23]

One of the obvious difficulties in dividing a single long action like the history of the world into many parts presented by different casts is that the number of actors required for the entire production would quickly climb to astronomical heights. The York cycle, for example, would require over three hundred actors. If doubling were permitted, the number could be reduced considerably. But in a true-processional production, doubling is strictly limited by the fact that so many plays are performed simultaneously. Disregarding the question of doubling within a single episode, an actor in a true-processional drama can take a second role in any play which begins at the first station *after* his first play has finished at the last. An analysis of the York cycle performed at twelve stations will show that an actor could double in three plays during the course of a free-advance production, and in two plays with modified free advances. (See Appendix B.) These numbers might be increased if an actor chose his plays with particular care, but it is doubtful whether such arrangements would be permitted by the authorities.[24] The conduct of an actual performance would not be entirely regular or predictable, and so in practice a very large margin would have to be made for error.

Assuming even the strictest discipline and the most rational behavior on the part of all casts and pageant masters, true-processional production fails to recommend itself as a satisfactory method of staging a play. The inconvenience to the actors, to the audience, or both, is considerable. Nor does the burden of the inconvenience rest equally on all. Casts of early plays and short plays in the cycle have relatively little to do and plenty of time for the small efforts required. But casts of long plays must perform at a fast rate, and the slightest delay will provoke the most unfortunate consequences. Depending on the system adopted, some audiences may have a long wait for the play to begin, or will have to endure great gaps of dead time within the cycle during which no plays are performed for them. Movement is complex, and in many cases crucial: efficient use of the time available can be gained only by perfect management of advances, in some cases requiring accurate prediction of an event still in the future. Any error in prediction will be compounded, and the production time may well be extended. Casts with little to do may be difficult to keep together. Opportunities for doubling, in a production which by its episodic nature entails a vast proliferation of speaking parts, are severely limited, and any error in assigning parts will result in disaster. Finally, even with the most efficient system for governing advances, the production, at least at York, is long beyond endurance. Even if the York cycle begins promptly at five o'clock in the morning, and even if there is no hitch in an event encompassing 576 separate dramatic presentations, the last play could not possibly finish at the last station before two o'clock the next morning.

This all seems an exorbitant price to pay for audibility, particularly when other cities in England and on the Continent gave plays which could be viewed without such inconvenience. The idea of true-processional production at many stations, like a Rube Goldberg invention, may be a credit to the ingenuity of its creator, whoever he may have been, but is of no great credit to his rationality or sense of efficiency.

PROCESSIONS, PAGEANTS, AND PLAYS IN THE LATE MIDDLE AGES

Stripped to its most basic elements, the Corpus Christi procession generally consisted of a group of ecclesiastics who carried the Host from one church through the town and back again, or else to another church. In most cities, Continental as well as English, civic officials, guildsmen, and even ordinary citizens swelled the ranks of the marchers (see

frontispiece). The extraordinary pomp and lavish spectacle which often
became attached to the procession is exemplified in a description of the
pre-Reformation rites of Durham:

> The Auntient solemnytie of procession vpon corpus christi
> day within the church and citie of durham, before the sup-
> pression of the said abbey Churche.
> There was a goodly prossession vpon the place grene on the
> thursday after Trinitie sonndaie in the honour of corpus Christi
> daie the which was a pryncipall feast at that tyme. The baley of the
> towne did calle the occupacions that was inhabiters within the
> towne euery occupation in his degre to bring forthe ther Baner
> with all the lightes apperteyninge to there seuerall Banneres and
> to repaire to the abbey church Doure euery banner to stand a
> Rowe in his Degree from the abbey church Dour to Wyndshole yett
> [gate]; on the west syde of the waye did all the Banneres stand, and
> on the east syde of the way dyd all the Torges [torches] stand per-
> teyninge to the sayd Bannares.
> Also there was a goodly shrine in Sancte Nicholas church,
> ordeyned to be caryed the sayd daie in Prossession cauled Corpus
> Christi shrine all fynlye gilted a goodly thing to behould, and on
> the hight of the sayd shrine was a foure Squared Box all of chris-
> tall, wherin was enclosed the holy sacrament of thaulter and was
> caryed the said daie with iiij preistes vp to the place grene; and all
> the hole prossession of all the churches in the said towne goyng
> before ytt and when it was a litle space within Wyndshole yett yt
> dyd stand still; then was Sancte Cuthbert Banner browghte fourth
> with two goodly faire crosses to meete yt; and the prior and covent
> [convent] with all the whole companye of the Quere [choir] all in
> there best copes dyd meet the said shrine sytting on there kneys
> and prayinge. The prior did sence yt and then caryinge yt forward
> into the abbey church the prior and covent with all the quere
> following yt. It was sett in the quere and solemne seruice don
> before ytt and Te Deum solemnly songe and plaide of the orgayns
> euery man praysinge god; and all the Banneres of the occupacions
> dyd followe the said shrine into the church goyng Rownde about
> Saincte Cuthbert fereture [shrine] lyghtinge there Torches and
> burning all the service tyme. then yt was caryed frome thence with
> the said prossession of the towne back againe to the place from
> whence it came and all the Baneres of the occupacions following it,
> and setting yt againe in the church, euery man maiking his prayers
> to god did departe, and the said shrine was caryed into the
> Revestrie where yt Remayned vntill that tyme Twelvemonthe.[25]

Although this description is dated 1593, it corresponds in all essential respects to the pre-Reformation processions celebrated by other towns where the occupational guilds marched.[26] The Host was everywhere the most important object in the procession. In Durham, as in many other cities, the Sacrament was displayed in a splendid shrine. The affair was thus partly ecclesiastical. But a secular official summoned the craft guilds. These marched in order and carried torches and the banners of their crafts.

In many cities the marching craftsmen also carried or pulled spectacular pageants in the Corpus Christi procession. Sometimes the pageants were on random subjects, but often they displayed ordered scenes from sacred history. Pageants of either sort were not, however, unique to Corpus Christi. Many cities presented pageants in annual civic marches or for special civic occasions. The two chief methods of displaying these pageants are exemplified by civic or ecclesiastical processions on the one hand, and by royal entries on the other. In the procession, pageants moved through the streets past stationary audiences. In the royal entry, the spectators, that is, the king and his entourage, moved past stationary pageants.

The royal entry is a well-documented phenomenon, dating from at least 1313, when Philip IV welcomed Edward II of England into Paris. On this occasion the Life of Christ, from Nativity to Resurrection, was presented at different stations, along with scenes of the Last Judgment and such secular subjects as Reynard the Fox.[27] Sometimes such pageants included action, dialogue, or a formal speech. But many were mute. In 1424, when the duke of Bedford entered Paris, he saw "a very beautiful mystery of the Old Testament and the New . . . and this was done without speech or gesture, just as if [the actors] were images upon a wall [et fut fait sans parler ne sans signer, comme ce feussent ymaiges enlevez contre ung mur]."[28]

The phrase "sans parler" is found in descriptions of several French pageants,[29] though in the royal entry short speeches would not significantly hinder the progress of the procession. It is quite otherwise with processions of pageants which move past multiple stationary audiences, whether the spectators line the streets or assemble at designated viewing stands or stations. Speeches can indeed be given in such a procession, but not if they are long enough to force the pageants to a lengthy halt.[30]

This rule is exemplified in a well-known directive for a Corpus Christi procession issued in Draguignan, southern France, in 1558:

Le dit jeu jora avec la procession comme auparadvant et le plus

d'istoeres et plus brieves que puront estre seront et se dira tout en
cheminant sans ce que personne du jeu s'areste pour eviter
prolixité et confusion tant de ladite prosession que jeu, et que les
estrangiers le voient aisement.[31]

Hardin Craig's insistence that "the interpretation of this is doubtful" is
a result of his understanding this *jeu* as a mimetic performance.[32] If we
take *jeu* instead to mean a procession of pageants introduced by
speeches, the interpretation becomes clear:

> The said play shall go with the procession as in previous times, and
> there shall be as many stories (episodes) [as possible] and these
> shall be as short as possible, and they shall be spoken during the
> march, and no one in the play shall come to a stop—all this in
> order to avoid prolongation and confusion both in the procession
> and in the play, and in order that visitors will be able to see it [the
> play] with ease.

The requirements here are similar to those we have established for a
rational true-processional drama: the episodes must be as numerous
and as short as possible. The additional restriction against coming to a
stop at all means that the episodes must have involved brief presentations, perhaps on the order of Lydgate's verses, rather than true
mimetic plays.

Apart from Lydgate's "ordenaunce of a precessyoun of the feste of
corpus cristi made in london," no processional speeches have survived
from the English Corpus Christi plays. However, the 1391 *ludus de
corpore Christi* from Innsbruck, the earliest surviving Corpus Christi
play, answers almost precisely to the putative form of the early English
processional plays. The Innsbruck play is 756 lines in length, and
consists of thirty speeches ranging from 6 to 96 lines each. Each
speaker delivers his lines in a single monologue: Adam speaks first,
then Eve, then twelve apostles alternating with twelve prophets, then
the three Magi, and finally a pope.[33] In this play the speeches were
apparently all delivered at a single station during the course of the
procession (a *transitus figurarum*), rather than at each of many
stations, as scholars imagine for York and for other cities in England.[34]

Most other German-language Corpus Christi plays (called *Frohnleichnamsspiele*) are from the late fifteenth or sixteenth century, but
many of these, particularly those from Zerbst, Bozen (Bolzano),
Freiburg im Breisgau, Künzelsau, and Ingolstadt, betray similar
processional origins.[35] As subsequent English dramatic Corpus Christi
cycles retained the history-of-the-world structure of the early English

processional pageants, so subsequent *Frohnleichnamsspiele* frequently retained a strong emphasis on the prophet sequence seen first in the Innsbruck Corpus Christi play.

The examples of Draguignan and the *Frohnleichnamsspiele* suggest that we are on the right track in looking to pageant processions as one possible source of cycle dramas, but the same examples introduce a problem of terminology. The English word *play*, like the French *jeu*, the German *Spiel*, or Latin *ludus*, is usually taken to signify mimetic drama. In fact the word is ambiguous and can also mean simply a pageant procession, with or without speeches.[36] In the course of this investigation I will interpret and use *play* in its original, indefinite sense. A pageant play may consist of mute *tableaux*, pageants introduced by short speeches, or a brief mimetic action: the latter two I shall call *presentational* pageants. On the other hand, I shall use the words *cycle, dramatic,* or *cycle drama* to signify a full dramatic representation. I am not concerned in this study with the distinctive characteristics of the dramatic genre. As I have framed my questions and hypotheses, the only difference between a presentational pageant and a cycle drama lies in the length of time required for the respective productions. Presentational pageants are short; cycle plays are long. In most cases the difference will be self-evident. I will discuss ambiguous cases as they arise.

We have now broken some ground, and, I believe, some ill-considered theories concerning the staging of Corpus Christi plays. My argument, however, has been essentially negative, demonstrating what the York cycle in particular could not have been rather than what it was. We shall now try to discover what really did happen at York.

3
York

The Corpus Christi Play Prior to 1426

During the Middle Ages York was second only to London among all English cities in temporal power, and second only to Canterbury in ecclesiastical prestige. Richard II granted the city the right to elect a mayor, and in 1392 he granted a charter which stipulated that the city was to be governed by a lord mayor and aldermen. In 1396 the burgesses won the right to elect sheriffs. In the fourteenth century York had a large number of trade guilds; one of the most prominent, the Weavers, had received its charter from Henry II.[1]

Modern students of medieval drama have regarded York as the prime example of an English city whose Corpus Christi festivities included a true-processional cycle. This has not seemed so clear to other scholars. Francis Drake, who published important civic documents in 1736, did not attempt to explain those which touched on the Corpus Christi pageants.[2] But Robert Davies, who wrote in the mid-nineteenth century, remarked that a single day "would not have sufficed for the performance of so numerous a series of separate pageants, had every one been accompanied by dialogue." He suggested: "Perhaps some of them were little more than short pantomimes or tableaux vivans [sic], or what Dr. Percy describes, 'a kind of dumb shows intermingled with a few short speeches.' "[3] Early in the present century H. F. Westlake, historian of medieval guilds, wrote: "It must be supposed that considerations of time would prevent any but the shortest speeches by the players, for twelve 'stations' were fixed on the route, at each of which the mystery was presented."[4]

38

Robert Davies did not know the York cycle text, but L. Toulmin Smith, E. K. Chambers, and Hardin Craig, who did, were not put off by its formidable length. They persisted in their belief that the Corpus Christi cycle at York was staged in the true-processional manner at twelve or more stations.[5]

The misplaced confidence of these imposing philologists has led to a neglect of historical evidence, and in particular to a misrepresentation of the early York lists of pageants. In 1415 and again a few years later, perhaps in 1420, Roger Burton, city clerk of York, drew up a long list of the pageants of the play of Corpus Christi (*Ordo paginarum ludi Corporis Christi*). Miss Smith printed the 1415 list in the introduction to her *York Plays*. But Martin Stevens has recently noted that both original lists include important items not printed by Smith. The evidence was available all along in Drake's *Eboracum* and in Maud Sellers's edition of the *York Memorandum Book,* but no theater historian before Stevens had noticed it.[6]

Smith faithfully transcribed the series of pageants from the 1415 list, beginning with the Creation and ending with the Last Judgment. But after the Last Judgment the 1415 list goes on to name ten different craft guilds, each of which was to march with from two to eight torches; it then states that "fifty-eight citizens had torches after the same fashion on the day of Corpus Christi." These included "the better sort of citizens, and after them the twenty-four [the city council], the twleve, the mayor, and four torches of Mr. Thomas Buckton [the mayor]." The ?1420 list includes similar items, in less extensive detail.[7] It is self-evident that these ordinances are for a procession and not for a lengthy true-processional play. If the guilds had presented dramatic pageants at each of twelve or more stations along the processional route, the chief citizens of York could not have begun their march until late in the day and would then have been forced to remain at the end of the march for some six hours while the pageants still performing ahead of them made their ponderous way through the city.

In 1426 a friar named William Melton demanded a reorganization of the traditional York festivities on Corpus Christi. The surviving account of this request, preserved in the civic Memorandum Book, confirms the nondramatic nature of the pageants in the early York Corpus Christi play. The memorandum begins with an account of "a certain sumptuous play, exhibited in several pageants, wherein the history of the Old and New Testament [was played] in diverse places of the said city on the feast of Corpus Christi." This play was represented "by a solemn procession" which began "at the great gates of the priory of the holy Trinity in York, and so going in procession to and into the cathedral church of the same; and afterwards to the hospital of St. Leonard in York, leaving the aforesaid sacrament in that place. [See fig. 1.] Preceded by a vast number of lighted torches, and a great multitude of priests in their proper habits, and followed by the mayor and citizens with a prodigious crowd of the populace attending." From this it seems that the Host, borne and accompanied by an entourage of priests, went at the head of the procession; then the craftsmen with their torches; then the processional nondramatic Corpus Christi play; and finally the mayor and the chief citizens.[8] This document, together with the lists of 1415 and ?1420, demonstrates that the pageants were an integral part of an otherwise normal liturgical procession until at least 1426.

It is not beyond the realm of possibility that the pageants, having made one sweep through the town in the morning, made a second advance through the town in the afternoon, this time with dramatic plays. But neither the processional lists nor the 1426 memorandum allows for such an event, and in any case this would have offered a much restricted span of time for mounting a true-processional cycle. On the other hand, actions of some duration were presented on the pageants during the course of the march. The list of 1415 contains detailed descriptions of the individual pageants, many of which involved actions and even speeches. A typical example is the Coopers' pageant: "Adam and Eve with the tree between them, the serpent deceiving them with an apple; God speaking to them and cursing the serpent, and an angel with a sword expelling them from Paradise."[9] A cycle of actions such as this, presented at many stations, may in some sense be regarded as true-processional drama. The "plays" must have been extremely brief, however, quite unlike the half-hour-long plays in the Passion sequence of the extant York cycle manuscript.

In 1399, long before these lists were drawn up, the York commons complained to the council that "the play and pageants of Corpus Christi day, which put them to great cost and expense, were not played as they ought to be, because they were exhibited in too many places, to the great loss and annoyance of the citizens, and of the strangers repairing to the city on that day." As a consequence of this complaint the council stipulated that the play should be given at twelve stations only, beginning "At the gates of the priory of the Holy Trinity in Mickelgate" and ending "upon the Pavement."[10] If the processional route was of a given length (from the priory to the Pavement), it could make no

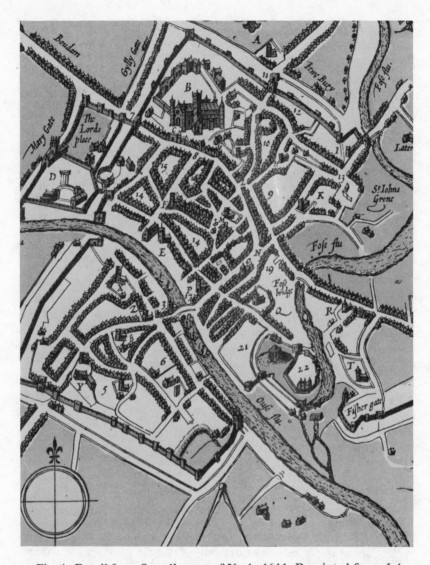

Fig. 1. Detail from Speed's map of York, 1611. Reprinted from *John Speed's England,* edited by John Arlot, Part 4 (London: Phoenix House, 1953, rpt. 1954), by permission of the publisher. Relevant key markings include *B*, St. Peter's (the minster); *E*, St. Martin's, Coneystreet; *F*, St. Helen's; *N*, St. Cross (Pavement); *T*, St. George's; *Y*, Trinity Abbey; 8, Petergate; 13, St. Anthony's hospital; 14, Coneystreet; 16, Stonegate. Common Hall is immediately to the left of St. Martin's. St. Leonard's is to the left of no. 15.

difference how many spectator stands were allowed if the pageants moved silently past the stations. If the extra stations lay beyond the normal terminal point, of course, the procession would last longer because the route would be longer. But the emphasis of the document is upon the exhibition of the pageants rather than the length of the route. We may infer therefore that the pageants halted at each place to make a presentation. But the halts cannot have been of a length to permit the acting of lengthy dramatic episodes.

The vast York cycle text survives, however, and its relationship to the crafts' plays cannot be denied. We are forced to the conclusion, therefore, that in the course of the fifteenth and sixteenth centuries York had two distinct Corpus Christi plays: the procession of pageants on the one hand; and the dramatic cycle on the other. The cycle must have been presented at a single site within the city after the conclusion of the pageant procession.

THE YORK PAGEANT PROCESSION TO 1426

The earliest date recorded for Corpus Christi festivities at York is 1376. A list of rent receipts in the Memorandum Book includes the item, "De vno tenemento in quo tres pagine Corporis Xpi ponuntur, per annum, ijs." Pageant houses imply valuable pageant wagons, no doubt intended for use in the Corpus Christi procession. Another early entry, traditionally assigned to 1378 but in fact of uncertain date, establishes a fine of which one portion was to be paid "a la pagyne des ditz pestours [Sheathers] de Corpore Xpi." This shows that the pageants were in the hands of the guilds. Also undated but from late in the fourteenth century is an order for a fine to be paid for the "sustentacion del lumer de Corpore Xpi." The "lumer" is the torch borne in the Corpus Christi procession.[11]

These records, and many others like them, indicate that the Corpus Christi procession with its lights and pageants was well established at York during the last quarter of the fourteenth century. We do not know the year the procession or its pageants began. An order from 1394 is often looked to for help in establishing the date: "Eodem die concordatum est quod omnes pagine Corporis Xpi ludent in locis antiquitus assignatis et non alibi, sed vt sicut premunientur per maiorem ballios et ministros suos."[12] This shows that the pageants were presented at assigned stations in 1394. But "antiquitus assignatis" only establishes a precedent and does not denote a particular span of time. The order anticipates the 1399 controversy over the multiplication of stations.

The controversy of 1399 resulted in a redesignation of stations and in an order that banners of the play with the arms of the city were to be issued on the eve of Corpus Christi (*in vigilia Corporis xpi*) and returned on the morrow of the feast. The banners marked the stations where the play was to be exhibited.[13] The mayor and council also issued "billets" whenever the pageants were to be mounted. The first reference to billets occurs in a Chamberlains' Roll of 1397/8. An ordinance of the Shearmen from 1404 reveals that when the craft received its billet (*la bille*), the masters of the craft came together in a certain place by a designated time, and there made provision for their pageant, their play, and their livery.[14]

The well-known "Proclamation of the play of Corpus Christi to be made on the eve of Corpus Christi" was yet another instrument of civic authority. This proclamation was probably read aloud by the sheriffs or their sergeants. It forbade "hynderyng of the processioun of Corpore Cristi," and instructed "men that brynges furth pacentes that thai play at the places that is assigned therfore and nowere elles":

> And that menn of craftes and all othir menn that fyndes torches that thai com furth in array and in the manere as it has been vsed and customed before this tyme noght haueyng wapen careynge tapers of the pagentz. . . . And that all maner of craftmen that bringeth furthe ther pageantez in order and course by good players well arayed and openly spekyng . . . and that euery player that shall play be redy in his pagiaunt at convenyant tyme that is to say at the mydhowre betwix iiij[th] and v[th] of the cloke in the mornyng and then all other pageantz fast folowyng ilkon after other as ther course is without tarieng.[15]

Though the play and the procession are named separately in this proclamation, the play must be understood as the procession of pageants within the ecclesiastical procession. This interpretation is substantiated by the order that men of the crafts and others were to carry "tapers of the pagentz": burning candles or torches could have had no place in a lengthy dramatic play performed outdoors during the daylight hours. The pageants were not mute: those players who spoke were to do so openly and quickly, and the pageants were to be presented "fast folowyng ilkon after other as ther course is without tarieng." The starting time of the procession, "at the mydhowre betwix iiij[th] and v[th] of the cloke in the mornyng," was not remarkable in an age when a summer's working day began at four o'clock.

While craft guilds were responsible for torches in the procession and for the pageants, a religious guild, the fraternity of Corpus Christi, was responsible for the Host borne at the head of the procession. The York

Corpus Christi guild was not officially founded until 1408, long after the procession itself had been inaugurated. The first ordinances of the guild refer to the festival and procession as "antiquitatis ordine." They also inform us that all the chaplains of the new guild were to go in procession on Corpus Christi day, and that at least two of the chaplains were to carry white staves for the rule of the procession. Ten large torches were to be borne before the Host. In 1415 the guild, probably following normal practice, paid 3d to have its torches borne from Trinity Hospital to the monastery of the Holy Trinity, at the starting point near Mickelgate bar.[16]

The general history of the Corpus Christi festival at York, the details of the Melton affair, and the particular history of the Corpus Christi guild, all prove that the procession on Corpus Christi was both liturgical and civic in character and that the pageant wagons were displayed in the same marching procession as the Host. Unfortunate as it seemed to the citizens of York, conflict between the ecclesiastical and civic interests was inevitable. The stational route of the pageants, first recorded in 1399, was identical with the route of the liturgical procession from the starting point in Mickelgate to the minster. After leaving the minster, the liturgical procession headed northwest along High Petergate in the direction of St. Leonard's, where the Host was finally deposited. The pageants, on the other hand, which could not have entered the minster, veered off to the southeast along Low Petergate, ending at the Pavement.[17] Those citizens or visitors who had not seen the pageants by the time they reached the minster had to choose between attending the pageants at a later station or attending divine services. It may have been precisely this competition for the sympathies of the spectators which caused Melton to launch his crusade. Melton may have been especially concerned because the mayor and aldermen, who marched behind the pageants, were necessarily prevented from attending services.

A few years before 1426, perhaps in 1422, the Painters, Stainers, Pinners, and Latoners noted in a petition to the city council that "the play on Corpus Christi . . . is regularly delayed because of the great number of pageants." They offered to combine their two pageants into one, "understanding that they can perform the matter of both pageants together in one pageant, and that they are able to present their play to the listening people by speeches."[18] But combining two out of fifty or more pageants could not have had a very significant effect on the total length of a spectacular procession. This may explain why in 1426 Melton insisted on a complete divorce between the pageants and the liturgical procession. According to the document in the Memorandum Book, the council agreed with Melton, and assigned the play to Wednesday, the eve of Corpus Christi.[19] Evidently, however, the council's order was never put into effect.

THE CORPUS CHRISTI PROCESSION AFTER 1426

It is certain that the liturgical procession continued on its proper day for many years after 1426. In 1428 the Marshals and Smiths agreed to "bryng furthe thair bather playes and vphald thair torches in the procession of Corpus Xpi day." An agreement between the city and Corpus Christi guild made on 16 January 1431 required the guild to march in the liturgical procession each year "on the feast of Corpus Christi if the weather permits; otherwise on some subsequent festival day when it is more convenient; through certain streets and places of the said city." This last provision is reminiscent of the civic orders for the exhibition of pageants through the streets of the city and suggests that the pageants were still part of the procession. Provision is made for marching at another festival date in case of inclement weather, but in good weather the procession was to be held as usual (*a tempore et per tempus cujus contrarij hominum memoria non existit*) on the day of Corpus Christi.[20]

In 1437 the Mercers prepared torches and wax for the procession "on Corpus Christi day," and spent a sum "for the makyng of the dwrres [doors] of the pagent hous." In 1439 as in 1440 the guild paid "for beringe of vj torches on Corpus Christi day," and in 1443 the Marshals and Smiths agreed that "al the lightes and torches" were to be maintained "in the processioun vpon corpus Xpi day." They also made provision for "the Pageant . . . in the play of Corpus Xpi."[21] From 1426 to at least 1443, then, the liturgical procession, with the torches borne by the crafts, continued on Corpus Christi day.

Evidently the pageants also continued on their original day. The Chamberlains' Roll for 1433 contains a payment to players [*ludentibus*] in "the pageant of the Coronation of the Virgin on the feast of Corpus Christi" and another payment for the repair of the pageant. Similar payments occur in the roll for 1442, in the surviving rolls from the 1450s, and in other rolls into the sixteenth century.[22]

In 1476 the York council drew up an order for "the Procession on the Friday after the Feast of Corpus Christi." The council agreed "that all other citizens and inhabitants of this city belonging to guilds and crafts, and carrying torches or having torches carried for them shall yerely take part in the said procession."[23] Contrary to Melton's earlier recommendation the liturgical procession of Corpus Christi was itself displaced, to the day after Corpus Christi. This is confirmed for the next year (1477) by the account roll of the Corpus Christi guild, in which the general procession is noted as having occurred "in crastino Corporis xpi."[24]

Surviving accounts do not permit us to establish precisely when the liturgical procession was shifted from Corpus Christi day to the Friday after, but we may hazard a guess. In 1468 the council awarded 6s 8d to a certain Augustinian friar for preaching in the minster "in crastino ad festo," that is, on Friday after Corpus Christi. Later rolls show that a preacher was regularly hired to give a sermon at the conclusion of the procession, and we may surmise that the same thing occurred in this year. The next earlier roll, for 1463, includes no such payment among expenses for Corpus Christi.[25]

An undated "Torchys ordinaunce how they shall goo in ordyr," from the second half of the fifteenth century, shows that the new procession was very much like the old, except that it had no pageants. The crafts retained their places in the line of march, as did the civic and ecclesiastical officials: "Item ilkon of the xxiiij [ti] and of the aldermen ilkman a torche; Item for Corpus Xpi gild."[26] New ordinances of the Corpus Christi guild from 1477 provided that the guild was to march "in solempni processione Corporis cristi."[27] This was the solemn liturgical procession, celebrated on the morrow of the feast.

In 1449 Thomas Spofford, a Yorkman who had been appointed bishop of Hereford, presented a new and spectacular shrine to the York guild of Corpus Christi. More jewels were added year by year until by the time of the Reformation it had become encrusted with a wealth of stones. An inventory taken in 1546, nearly the last year of the shrine's existence, set its value at £ 210 18s 2d.[28] The ever-increasing splendor of the shrine is a measure of the continuing popularity of the liturgical procession. A colorful picture of the event occurs in a civic order of 1544:

> Item it is further agreyd . . . that for the honour of god and worship of this Citie the master of Corpuscrysty gyld and the prestes beyng of the same gild with all other prestes that goyth procession vppon fryday the Morro after Corpuscrysty day shall goo in the sayd procession in Coopes of the best that can be gottyn within the sayd Citie and that every howseholder that dwellith in the hye way ther as the sayd procession procedith shall hang before ther doores and forefrontes beddes and coverynges of beddes of the best that thay

can gytt and strewe before ther doores resshes and other suche
flowers and strewing as they thynke honeste and clenly for the
honour of god and worship of this Citie; And this to be fyrmely
kepte hereafter.[29]

The confident tone of the last order is belied by ensuing events. In 1546,
against mounting pressures, the guildsmen drew up a description of
their activities and properties, placing the most favorable construction
on their financial dealings and acts of charity. They declared that they
were "bounde to kepe a solempne processyon, the sacrament beynge in
a shryne borne in the same thorough the cytye of Yorke, yerly the
Friday after Corpus Christi day; and the day after to have a solempne
Mass and Dyryge." But this did not speak to the guild's credit in 1546:
it was dissolved the following year.[30]

CORPUS CHRISTI PLAY FROM 1426 TO THE REIGN OF MARY

The Corpus Christi pageant vehicles evidently continued in the York
liturgical procession for as long as the procession was still mounted on
Thursday, perhaps until the 1460s. Evidence of subsequent dramatic
performances during this period is scarce, but the council's payment to
players in 1433 suggests that some of the pageants, including the
council's own Coronation of the Virgin, may have been mounted as
independent plays after the conclusion of the procession. In 1442 the
chamberlains recorded a payment "pro ludo de vyne yerde" among
expenses for Corpus Christi. This play does not occur in the extant text,
however, and may have been unrelated to the pageant cycle. In the
1450s certain references to plays and players begin to appear. In the
mid-1460s the Mercers' "costes payd aboute the paijand" included 10d
"payd to Wylliam Clark and his players for rehersyng." This is a
certain sign of true drama.[31] In 1476 the York council issued its famous
ordinance:

> . . . yerely in the tyme of lentyn there shall be called afore the Maire
> for the tyme beyng iiij of the most Conyng discrete and able
> playeres within this Citie to serche here and examen all the plaiers
> and plaies ⌐and¬ pagentes thrughoute all the artificeres belonging
> to corpus xpi plaie; And all suche as thay shall fynde sufficant in
> persoune and Conyng to the honor of the Citie and worship of the
> saide Craftes for to admitte and able and all other insuffcant
> persounes either in connyng voice or persoune to discharge
> ammove and avoide.

And that no plaier that shall plaie in the saide Corpus Xi plaie
be conducte and Reteyned to plaie but twise on the day of the
saide playe and that he or thay so plaing plaie not ouere twise the
saide day vpon payne of xls to forfet vnto the Chaumbre asoften
tymes as he or thay shall be founden defautie in the same.[32]

This assertion of civic authority over pageants, actors, and plays
implies that the Corpus Christi play was essentially a civic as opposed to
an ecclesiastical endeavor. The last paragraph of the order, which
accepts the possibility of doubling in as many as three plays, implies
that the dramatic play was given at a single station after the procession
had finished.

Other documents from this period have been taken to support the
hypothesis of true-processional playing, but a careful analysis will show
that these documents may just as well concern the procession of
nondramatic pageants on Corpus Christi day. The Spuriers' and
Lorimers' ordinances of 1493/4, for example, declare that "euery
maister of the said craftes opon corpus xpi day yerly shall attend vppon
the paiaunt frome the mateir of play be begune at the furst place vnto
such tyme as the said play be played and finished thrugh the toun at the
last playse."[33] But this means no more than that the guild masters must
personally accompany the pageant from station to station along the
processional route until the procession is finished. This interpretation is
also applicable to an ordinance of the Armorers dated 1475: "Item that
alle the maisters of the same crafte frome nowefurth yerely on Corpus
Xpi day in the mornyng be redy in thair owen propre personnez euery
one of thayme with ane honest wapyn to awayte apon thair pagende
maisters ande pagende at the playnge and settyngefurth thair saide
pagende at the firste place where they shall begyn; Ande so to awayte
apon the same thair pagende thurgh the Cite to the play be plaide as of
that same pagende."[34]

Ordinances of this kind remained in force for more than a century.
The rules of the Plasterers and Tilers, redrawn in 1572, still stipulated
"that the artyficers of the said craft shall goe with their pageantes
aforesaid throughe the Citie as other occupacions and artyficers
dothe."[35] The ordinances could not however guarantee perfect order,
and occasional difficulties arose, as in 1554: "That for that the Girdlars
on Corpus Christi day did not forthwith folowe with their pageant in
dewe course accordyng to thordynences and proclamacions thereof but
taried an wholle hower and more in hyndrans and stoppyng of the rest
of the pageants folowyng and to the disorderyng of the same; it is
therfor aggreed . . . that the said Girdlars shall pay for the said defalt xs
to the chambre vse."[36] It need hardly be noted that failure to march on

time is as disruptive for a procession of pageants as for a true-processional play.

The pageants on Corpus Christi continued, with an occasional interruption, into the reign of Queen Mary and beyond. The council's perennial concern for good order in the procession is expressed in the numerous directives from the 1550s and 1560s concerning "billets." In 1551, for example, the council ordered "that the billettes shalbe mayd and delyueryd for the playng of Corpuscrysty play." On 16 December 1562, during the early reign of Elizabeth, "it is nowe further ordeyned and aggreed . . . to be dewly abserved for euer that at the same tyme that it shall happen the billettes to be gyven forth for playeng of Corpus Xpi play even than alsoo the Shirefes of this Citie for the tyme beyng to haue warnyng gyven to prouyde for rydyng with harnessed men on Corpus Xpi day and Mydsomer even accustomed."[37]

"Billets" for the play are mentioned in the House Books every year from 1549 to 1555, and frequently thereafter. No mention of billets occurs between 1405 and 1549, perhaps because their use was thoroughly routine. The reason they became a matter of particular interest in 1549 is evident from the order of that year: "agreyd that billyttes shalbe delyuerd to the officers for the playng of Corpuscrysty play to be playd holy except the assumpcion of our Lady and Coronacion of our Lady ⌈and⌉ dieng of our Lady as it was the Last year."[38] In some manner the billets functioned as a method of control over the play: most likely, a pageant could not be given if its billet was withheld. That the billets were not merely orders newly published each year is evident from a memorandum of 1550, a plague year: "And in consideracion of the seyd playg it is agreyd that the common offycers of this city shall furthwith tayke in to theyre handes the byllettes that was delyuered furth for corpus Xpi play and the sayd play for the seyd consideracion to be sparyd and not to be played this yere."[39] Evidently the billets were documents of permanent value. The possibility that they contained speeches for the pageants will be suggested by our later inquiry into the Wakefield Corpus Christi play.

In the course of our investigation we have touched briefly on the York cycle play but have been mostly concerned to demonstrate that the pageant wagons of the Corpus Christi play were a more or less self-sufficient phenomenon, vehicles in an outdoor civic procession displayed with brief actions to waiting spectators. We have yet to discover where and for whom the cycle plays were performed. Before taking up this question it will be useful for us to look into other civic plays and pageants which were contemporary with the Corpus Christi procession and play.

OTHER PAGEANTS AND PLAYS IN LATE MEDIEVAL YORK
The Sheriffs' Riding: Yule and Yule's Wife

We have noted that in 1396 York was granted the right to elect its own sheriffs. These officers are not listed among the dignitaries who marched in the Corpus Christi liturgical procession. Their absence may be explained by the fact that (at least in the early sixteenth century) the York sheriffs conducted a riding of their own. A memorandum of 1517 mentions a traditional sheriffs' riding held "affore Christenmes," and suggests that the riding was usually followed by a dinner. From a nearly contemporary record we learn that the riding was held annually "betwixt the feastes of Seynt Mighell Archangell and the Natyvyte of our lorde," that is, between 29 September and 25 December.[40] Often the riding was held near the feast of St. Thomas the Apostle, which falls on 21 December.

One of the more amusing events connected with the sheriffs' riding was the presentation of Yule and Yule's wife, a tradition which aroused the wrath of the archbishop of York and others in 1572. From this episode we learn that "yerely vpon St Thomas day before Christmas, twoo disguysed persons called Yule and Yules wif [rode] throughe the Citie very vndecently and uncomely drawyng great concurses of people after theym to gaise, often tymes comyttyng other enormyties." The York council agreed "that no disguysed persons called Yule and Yules wif nor yet the Sheryffes Seriantes shall ryde this yere nor any yere frome hensforth on Saynt Thomas day before Christmas; And that comandement herof shalbe forthwith gyven frome my Lord Mayour to the Sheryffes accordyngly."[41] Evidently it was the sheriffs' very own sergeants who were primarily involved in the pageant.

As it happens, a further investigation of these customs will help to confirm the processional nature of the Corpus Christi pageant play. In 1536 the sheriffs were ordered to march with the aldermen and to bear torches with them in the procession of Corpus Christi, held on the morrow of the feast. The presence of the sheriffs in this procession was entirely unusual and was ordered only because the Corpus Christi play was not held that year.[42] An ordinance of 3 May 1537 shows that the sheriffs usually rode on Corpus Christi day: "Item it is agreyd that master Shyrryffes of this Citie shall Ryde vppon Corpuscristy day with men in hernesse accordyng to the ancyent custome of this said City."[43] It seems in fact that the sheriffs rode along with the Corpus Christi play, perhaps at the head of the procession of pageants. This is strongly suggested by a council resolution of 12 May 1569: "And nowe apon certayne reasonable consideracions . . . it is thought requysete . . . that the shewe of harnessed men of this Citie *at Corpus Xpi play* shall be spared and not had for this yere" (emphasis mine).[44]

St. George Procession

The York St. George procession, which may have been a Protestant innovation, can be traced back only to 1546: "Memerandum this yere dyd Saynt George day fall vppon good Fryday and therfore thay dyd not ryde with Saynt George this yere . . . Also Corpuscristi day and Mydsomer day fell bothe vppon one day."[45] (In 1546 Easter fell on its latest possible date. Apparently this did not have any important effect upon Corpus Christi activities. We are not told whether the sheriffs marched on Midsummer eve at the watch as well as on Midsummer day with the pageants.) Our principal information concerning the St. George riding is from the Chamberlains' Book of 1554/5, a long list of expenses incurred by the council for various elements of a civic spectacle, including a St. Christopher, a dragon, and a "pagyant." These were fabricated from canvas and lath, but a king, a queen, a "May," and St. George were all represented by human actors in costume. Though a "play" and "playing" are mentioned in the accounts, this was probably a lively processional riding and not a dramatic play. If a play with dialogue was mounted, it must have occurred in St. George close, in the southern part of the city near Skeldergate.[46]

Creed Play and Pater Noster Play

Late medieval York sponsored two plays of little-understood scope and subject matter in addition to the better-known Corpus Christi play. On 12 May 1495 the York council recorded an order which concerned the Creed play and the Pater Noster play:

Item it is agreid . . . that the master and kepers of corpus Xi gilde shall cause the Crede play to be plaid this yere that is to say the furst bone [banns] to be cryed on whissonmonday the next at maudleyn day and the play on seynt Bartylmewe euyn acordyng to the warnyng gyfyn to the said maister be the maire on Philypp day and Jacob, or els to pay xx li to the Chambre . . .

Item it is agreid that the master and bredren of the Gild of Seinte Anthonyes forsomuch as thay may not this yere conuenyently bryngfurth the play called the pater nostre play acordyng to the wurship of this Citie therfor thai shall pay to the vse of the Commonaltie [blank] and to prepar thame therfor aganst the next yere.[47]

Evidently it had been expected that the Pater Noster play would go this year, but for some reason the guild of St. Anthony was unable to bring forth its play. As a consequence the guild was fined, and another guild, Corpus Christi, was ordered to present its Creed play instead. St. Anthony's guild was ordered to ready the Pater Noster play for the following year.

Creed play. Two weeks after this order was issued, the masters of the Corpus Christi guild "graunted to play the crede play this yere and every tent yere successiuely as apereth by a writtyng remanyng with the said maister and kepers the tenour wherof ensuyth on the next syde folowyng and entiled in the booke of the cred play." Following this occurs an entry in Latin which has hitherto been entirely overlooked: "Et prima pagina & ostencio in festo apostolorum philippi & iacobi secunda in crastino penticostali."[48] From this we learn as a certainty what was only guessed before, that the Creed play, like the Corpus Christi play, consisted of a sequence of separate pageants. The dates, however, are confusing. The first pageant is indicated for SS. Philip and Jacob, which is 1 May, eleven days prior to the date of the order. In the order itself 1 May is stipulated as the time the mayor was to give the warning. Evidently the order was entered into the book long after the council had met to make its decision.

Records show that the Creed play was normally produced once during the middle years of each successive decade, usually late in the summer. The play is first heard of in 1446, when it was deeded to the Corpus Christi guild in the will of William Revetour: "Lego fraternitati Corporis Christi in Eboraco quemdam librum vocatum Le Crede Play cum libris et vexillis eidem pertinentibus." Both books and banners are mentioned in this codicil, providing us with our earliest evidence that the Creed play, like the play of Corpus Christi, was a dramatic play mounted at the conclusion of a marching procession. Revetour deeded to the Guild of St. Christopher a separate playbook on the subject of St. James, "in sex paginis compilatum." This may have constituted one episode in the long play, or it may have been a separate play altogether.[49]

In 1495 the guild of Corpus Christi concerned itself with the register of the Creed play:

> . . . in the year of Our Lord 1455 this book was renewed and revised, and then written anew, compiled from an ancient, worn copy which William Revetour . . . gave and willed in his testament to the said fraternity, at the urging of Johannas Foxe, his executor; and he did this on the condition that this incomparable play should be shown publicly every tenth year in various places throughout the

said city of York, to the spiritual benefit of the gathered hearers,
and also that the inhabitants of these places should remunerate
the worshipful guild for the costs and expenses of the play.[50]

The playbook had been much used, both before 1455 and probably
after that year. The public showing in many places was foreseen as a
method of recovering the costs of the play. Unlike the Corpus Christi
play, however, formal stations were never established for the Creed
play: in fact, as we shall see, the stations were canceled whenever the
Creed play took the place of Corpus Christi.

The dual nature of the Creed play as procession and as drama is
confirmed by an extensive inventory of the properties of the Corpus
Christi guild made in 1465. First is listed a "liber vocatus Originale,
continens articulos Fidei Catholicae in lingua Anglicana, nuper scrip-
tus, appret. x[li]. Et alius liber inveteratus de eodem ludo, cs. Et alius
liber de eodem, Anglice vocatus *Crede Play*, continens xxij quaternos."
The "original," of which the guild had several copies in different states
of repair, was thus a large volume of twenty-two quires, that is 176 leaves
or 352 pages, perhaps comparable to the Corpus Christi play text.[51]
Following the brief list of playbooks in the 1465 inventory is a long list
of processional appurtenances, including seventeen large banners, four
small red silk banners, nine pennants, twenty-four "sokketts" or
extension poles for the banners, a miter, a royal crown and scepter,
twelve scrolls adorned with the articles of the faith, two bishop's miters,
a key for St. Peter along with two pieces of one tunic, four more
pennants, ten diadems for Christ and the apostles, a mask, and nine
other chevrons. In addition are listed forty torches, three "judas"[52]
torches, thirty-four banners for the torches, and twelve "castella"
splendidly adorned.[53] That these belonged to the Creed play is particularly obvious from the twelve banners of the Creed. It is equally obvious
that most of this equipment was intended for a marching procession
and not for a true-processional dramatic play twenty-two quires in
length. Among the marchers were men costumed as Christ and the
twelve Apostles.

In 1483 the Creed play was mounted for the visit of Richard III to
York. It was given, as usual, in late summer. On Saturday, 6 September, the council agreed that "for the honor of thys cite . . . all my
maisterz the aldermen and all the xxiiij[ti] shalbe with my lord the mair
to atend apon the Kynges gude grace to morou at seyng of the creid
play."[54] Margaret Dorrell and Alexandra Johnston have recently uncovered another reference to this event, and have been most generous in
granting me permission to cite it here. It is from the Chamberlains'
Rolls in the York Minster Library, for the year 1483:

Et pro firma Camere supra portas clausi ubi domini Decanus et
Confratres sui ludum Corporis Xpi (iijs iiijd) et ludum vocatum Credplay (iijs iiijd) audierunt, vjs viijd.[55]
(And for rental of the chamber above the gates of the minster close
where the lord dean and his brothers heard the Corpus Christi
play and the play called Creed play, 6s 8d.)

This entry, which we shall examine again when we raise the question of
the site of the dramatic plays, reveals that both the Corpus Christi play
and the Creed play were mounted in 1483, and suggests that the
minster officials sat above the minster gates to observe the presentations and speeches of the pageants.

It is not known whether the Creed play was given again in 1485 or
1486, but this seems doubtful. It was performed, as we have seen, in
1496. On 10 February 1505 the council "agreed that my lord shall send
for the maister and vj kepers of corpus Xpi gild and to comaund and
charge theym vpon payn of xx[li] that the said master and kepers and
gild to be leved to the Common Well and proffyte of this Citie this yere
tofore the fest of lammese next ensuyng herafter of thayr cost and
charge to bryng furth the crede play."[56] (During this same year the
council gave orders concerning the Drapers' pageant, though there is
no evidence that the Corpus Christi play was presented then.)[57] Civic
books for 1515 make reference to neither Corpus Christi nor any other
play, but the Creed play was performed in 1525 and, under unusual
circumstances which we shall examine later, in 1535. On 16 March
1545 the council "agreyd that my lorde Mayour shall call before hym
the master of Corpuscristi gyld and to take an order as towchyng playng
of the creyde play as he shall thynke good for the mooste profett and
advauntage of the sayd Citie."[58] No further records concerning the
Creed play exist for this year, and perhaps the threat of war from the
French and Scots prevented the anticipated celebration. On the other
hand, the Creed play may have been performed once late in the reign of
Henry VIII. An undated letter from the king cautions against the
repetition of circumstances which led to a civic rising:

Wheras we understand by certain report the late evil and seditious
rising in our ancient city of York, at the acting of a religious interlude of St. Thomas the Apostle, made in the same city on the 23rd
of August now last past; and wheras we have been credibly informed that the said rising was owing to the seditious conduct of
certain papists who took a part in preparing for the said interlude,
we will and require you that from henceforward ye do your utmost
to prevent and hinder any such commotion in future, and for this
ye have my warrant for apprehending and putting in prison any

such papists who shall, in performing interludes which are founded on any portion of the Old or New Testament, say or make use of any language which may tend to excite those who are beholding the same to any breach of the peace.[59]

Judging from the time of year, we may conclude that this was not the Corpus Christi cycle. But the Creed play may have contained pageants on the various apostles, and the late summer date—St. Bartholomew eve—agrees with the normal time of its production.

Pater Noster play. The third anciently established York play, Pater Noster, was probably the oldest of all. It is mentioned in Wyclif's *De officio pastorali* of ca. 1378: "herefore freris han tauȝht in englond the paternoster in engliȝsch tunge, as men seyen in the pley of ȝork, and in many othere cuntreys."[60] But if the play originated with the friars, by 1389 it had come into the hands of a religious guild. In 1388 Richard II demanded an accounting of all guilds and brotherhoods in England. The reports submitted in 1389 constitute our most complete source of information on fourteenth-century English guilds.[61] Among the respondents was the York Pater Noster guild:

> As to the beginning of the said gild, be it known that, once on a time, a play, setting forth the goodness of the Lord's Prayer, was played in the city of York; in which play all manner of vices and sins were held up to scorn, and the virtues were held up to praise.

Certain citizens of York, feeling that the play should be continued, formed a fellowship whose chief purpose was to mount dramatic productions. The document goes on to delineate the responsibilities of the members on the day of performance:

> Also they are bound, as often as the said play of the Lord's Prayer is played in the city of York, to ride with the players thereof through the chief streets of the city of York; and, the more becomingly to mark themselves while thus riding, they must all be clad in one suit. And, to ensure good order during the said play, some of the bretheren are bound to ride or to walk with the players until the play is wholly ended.

Once again, as with the Creed play and the Corpus Christi play, we discover that the chief role of the guild members was to participate in a procession or riding which accompanied the play and players through the streets of York; but once again it seems doubtful that a long dramatic play could have been performed during the course of a mounted procession. Like the Corpus Christi guild, the Pater Noster guild owned certain "properties needed in the playing of the before-named play; which properties are of little or no worth for any other purpose than the said play. And the gild has one wooden chest, in which the said properties are kept."[62]

In 1399 John Downom and his wife squared an old debt to the Pater Noster guild by incurring certain debts "in diuersis expensis circa ludum Accidie ex parte Ric. Walker."[63] Since the play in question bore the name *Accidie,* or Sloth, it seems probable that Pater Noster was a long play on the seven deadly sins, divided into many parts.

We have no information concerning the production of the Pater Noster play during the first half of the fifteenth century, but something is known of the history of the guild. Between 1410 and 1424 the York guild of the Holy Trinity was forced to disband because it had never obtained a royal license. The guildsmen subsequently associated themselves with St. Anthony's guild, and by the 1440s these were joined in turn by the Pater Noster guild. The resulting guild, which took the responsibility for the Pater Noster play, was ordered to take the name of St. Martin, but in practice it continued to go under the name of St. Anthony.[64]

In 1464 the Pater Noster playbooks were willed to William Balle, Master of St. Anthony's guild, by William Downham, guild chaplain.[65] The play continued in the hands of St. Anthony's guild during this time, though a misinterpretation of documents has led scholars to believe that the responsibility for Pater Noster play passed temporarily into the hands of the Mercers' guild. The editor of the guild's chartulary dated the entry in question 1488 and understood it to indicate that the Mercers were to "chuse iiij pageant masters on the Friday next after Midsomerday . . . and they iiij shall bring forth the paternoster play and recyve all the ornements that belang thereto."[66] Alexandra Johnston, who has examined the entry carefully, writes:

> The entry in the Merchants' chartulary has nothing to do with the paternoster play. The entry is overwritten, bound backwards, and consequently misdated. Ultraviolet light shows the original reading is "thair play" (i.e. the Corpus Christi Doomsday play), not "paternoster play," and the real date is 1443. Bluefront, who is named as one of the constables or wardens, died in 1446 and the only year that Thomas Scauceby was master before 1446 was 1443.

The Pater Noster, like the Creed play, was traditionally produced in late summer. We have already seen that in 1496 the Creed play was mounted in place of the Pater Noster play on St. Bartholomew eve, and that St. Anthony's guild was ordered to be prepared the next year to mount the Pater Noster play.

The customary relationship between the Corpus Christi and Pater Noster plays is clarified by an order made in Easter week 1536: "agreyd . . . that Corpuscristy Play shalbe sparyd for this yere and not playd for somuche as pater noster play aught by course to be playd this yere; Therfore It is agreyd that the sayd pater noster play shalbe playd vppon Lames day next."[67] Since the two plays were not mounted at the same time of year, there could have been no direct conflict between them. Nevertheless, they were by rule not produced in the same year. On 20 June 1536 the initial order was slightly modified: "Item it is agreyd that pater noster play shalbe playd vppon sonday next after Lames day."[68]

The documents we have now examined may give us confidence that our basic understanding of the nature and performance dates of York's chief plays and pageants is correct. The St. George pageant, Yule and Yule's wife, the Corpus Christi play, the Creed play, and the Pater Noster play all began with a procession. The pageant spectacle, whether this consisted of costumed figures, pageant wagons, banners, or torches, was accompanied by councilmen, sheriffs, or members of a craft or a religious guild. (Lammas, the day of the late summer plays, was also a day of the sheriffs' riding.) The processions were normally mounted on festival occasions: St. George day, St. Thomas day, Corpus Christi day, or Lammas (also called St. Peter ad Vincula). St. George and Yule and Yule's wife were probably annual events, perhaps introduced in the course of the sixteenth century. The more ancient plays of Corpus Christi, Pater Noster, and Creed, on the other hand, alternated with one another. In any ten-year period the Corpus Christi play would normally be given eight times, the Pater Noster and Creed plays once each. But each of these three plays was normally given only at its proper time. Exceptions were infrequent, and occurred only under the most pressing circumstances. St. George and Yule and Yule's Wife were perhaps merely processional. The other three events—Creed play, Pater Noster play, and Corpus Christi play—also involved lengthy dramatic productions. Of these three, only Corpus Christi involved craft guilds, processional stations, and wheeled pageant wagons. But if all three dramatic plays were mounted in an identical manner—and we shall see later that this was indeed the case—then it becomes apparent that none of them, including the dramatic play of Corpus Christi, could have been mounted on the pageant wagons.

CORPUS CHRISTI, CREED, AND PATER NOSTER
PLAYS FROM THE END OF QUEEN MARY'S REIGN

The presentation of Corpus Christi play and other processional spectacles was undertaken with ardor in York during the reign of Mary, but the good fortune of civic entertainments ran out even before her death. In 1558, during her last year, York suffered hardships brought on by plague, economic collapse, and a levy of troops.[69] One consequence was the suppression or at least moderation of the traditional sumptuous feasts given by the mayor for the more prominent citizens of the town:

> First the festes dynars and bankettes made by the sayd mayour to his bretherne thaldermen and others of the privay counsell of this Citie etc in the tyme of Lent, on Saynt George day after procession, on mydsommar even, the day of Election of the maistr of Saynt Thomas hospitall and the day of thaccomptes takynge of the same, and alsoo apon Saynt Blasy day [the election of the mayor] to be clerly dischardgd and leaft of.

> Item lyke dynars and banketes made to the ladyes on palmesonday, Wytsonday, Corpus Xpi day, Saynt Stephene day and mydsommar even to be alsoo dischardged. . . .

> Item that the players and suche as taketh peyne on procession etc on saynt George day to be payd for their labour of the chambre costes.[70]

The traditional banquet for the mayor and aldermen on Corpus Christi did not fall under this order. The play of Corpus Christi was dealt with a week later: "The play of Corpus Xpi for this yere apon good and reasonable considerations is thought best and alsoo aggreed to be spared and leaft of playeng ⌐for this yeire¬ the tyme instant beynge bothe trowblous with warres and alsoo contagious with sykenesse."[71]

However, on 20 April the council decided that Corpus Christi should not go unrecognized:

> agreyd . . . That John Branthwate master of St antonys and his kepers shall furthwith provyd for the playng of one play callyd the Pater noster play this yere and the charges therof to be borne of the money to be gatheryd by the occupacions of this Citie of there pagyant money and that the furst bayn or messynger shall ryde in dyvers streetes within this Citie appon St George day next and the other messynger to ryde in like maner vppon Whitson Monday to thentent that the contry may haue knowelege that the sead play shalbe playd appon Corpus Xpi day next; master holme Alderman haith promysed to speke with the said master of St Anthonys for the same purpos.

> Item it is agreyd in consyderacion abouesayd that this yere St George play shall be lefte and not playd and the provision of thynges alredy boght and mayd for the furnytour therof shall be

payd of the Chambre costes and broght in to the Chambre to be
kepte agaynst a nother yere.[72]

The plans to mount the Pater Noster play on Corpus Christi were
carried out, for on 8 July the council agreed "that Ametson paynter
shold haue for paynteng of certayne bannar clothes for patre noster
playe, liijs iiijd of the money gathered of pagiant sylver."[73]

The production of the Pater Noster play on Corpus Christi was
unprecedented, but substitutions of one play for another became the
rule during the early reign of Elizabeth as the city council maneuvered,
with some success, in an attempt to mount plays and processions in the
face of increasing official hostility. The story is fascinating in its own
right as an example of civic resourcefulness. More important for us, the
complex permutations of processions and plays show clearly once more
that each of the "plays" consisted of a processional spectacle followed
by a more or less independent dramatic production at a single location
within the city.

No plays are recorded for 1559 and 1560, the first years of Elizabeth.
But on 27 March 1561 the York council agreed "that Corpus Xpi play
shalbe played this yere with good players as hath ben accustomed
Except onely the pagiantes of the dyenge assumption and Coronacion
of our Lady."[74] On 7 May the council agreed "that the Shirefes of this
Citie that nowe be shalle this yere on Corpus Xpi day in decent wise
ryde with a competent nombre of men in harnes ⌐and¬ with weapons
for the Citie wourship as hath ben laudably accustomed; And lyke
rydyng to be on midsomar even; And the said Shirefes to haue warnyng
for makyng preparacion accordyngly."[75] But the earlier order for the
play was revised in a policy statement issued by the council on 30 May:
"And for soo moche as the late fest of Corpus Xpi is not nowe celebrat
and kept holy day as was accustomed, it is therfor aggreed that on
Corpus even my lord mayour and aldermen shall in makyng the
proclamacion acoustemed goe about in semely sadd apparell and not in
skarlet."[76] This decision to ride in dark clothing and on the eve rather
than on the morrow of Corpus Christi was obviously designed to
eliminate suspicion that the Romish festival was being celebrated.[77]
The fate of the play and riding on the day of Corpus Christi is
unknown, but the suppression of the feast no doubt precluded both.

The mayor and aldermen, not content with the apparent demise of
the plays, resorted to various machinations to have them revived. On 3
March 1562 the council:

Aggreed that the play comonly called Corpus Xpi play shall this
yere apon reasonable consideracion be played on St Barnabe day

thapostle; And thystories of the old and new testament, or elles the
Crede play if apon examinacion it may be shalbe played; And
billettes therapon to be gyven forth as hath ben accustomed.[78]

This document shows definitively that the Corpus Christi (processional)
play was one thing, and the (dramatic) histories of the Old and New
Testaments another. The processional pageants were to be mounted in
any case, and the usual billets for the pageants were to be delivered to
the several masters of the guilds. The procession was to be followed by
dramatic plays, either the play of the Old and New Testaments (the
Corpus Christi cycle), or else the Creed play.

Concern for the matter of the Creed play ("if apon examinacion it
may be") is a sign of Reformation pressure. Another sign is the removal
of the play from the suppressed Corpus Christi day, 28 May, to St.
Barnabas's day, 11 June, also a Thursday in 1562, but two weeks later.
On 16 April, in a mood of restored confidence, the council agreed "that
Corpuscrysty ⌐day¬ play shall be playd of the day accustomyd viz. apon
Corpuscrysty day."[79] On 10 May the council agreed "that the Shirefes
shall haue commandement immediatly to prepare for their rydyng with
harnessed men on Corpus Xpi day and mydsomar even accustomed."[80]
The old play was given as usual, and the alternative play and day were
avoided. The Corpus Christi play was given again in 1563, but in 1564
York was troubled by the plague,[81] and the plays were evidently
suppressed.

The 1565 records of St. Thomas Hospital note that "Mr Symson
brought nowe in the auncient booke or regestre of the Crede play to be
saffly kept emonges thevidens as it was before."[82] The Corpus Christi
guild, which normally produced the play, had been disbanded in 1547,
but the Hospital of St. Thomas, which had been associated with the
guild from the fifteenth century, continued under the care of the city
council.[83] This shows that in 1565 the Creed play was returned to the
care of the Hospital. But it is doubtful that a production of the play was
actually contemplated in that year. In the same year the York
Innholders agreed to an ordinance which included the provision "that
what yere it shall chanse the play accustomed at Corpus Xpimas to be
omitted and not played then the occupacion of Inholders for that yere
shall not be compelled to pay any pagiant money to the Chamber use no
more than other craftes of this citie shall doo."[84] This testifies to a lapse
of confidence in the Corpus Christi play as a traditional event.
Evidently the provision was operative in both 1565 and 1566, for no
evidence of a production survives from either year.

On 18 March 1567 the council "Aggreed nowe that Corpus Xpi play shall be played this yere and billettes made forth with spede and accordyngly."[85] The play was mounted as usual, but the repercussions were immediate. Less than three weeks later the council was compelled to undertake a reformation of the texts:

> Aggreed that the pageantes of Corpus Xpi suche as be not allredy Registred shalbe with all convenyent spede be fayre wryten by John Clerke in the old Registre therof viz. of vyntenors the archetricline of thyranmongars, Marie Magd wasshyng the Lordes feete and of the Tylars the latter part of their pageant, Of the Laborars the purificacion of our lady, and of the Cappers to be examined with the Registre and reformed; And John Clerke or other takyng peyne to be honestly recompensed for their peyns.[86]

The principal objection was, as usual, to plays with Marian themes.

The York council must have felt threatened by this censorship of their Corpus Christi play, for in 1568 they decided to mount the Creed play instead. The resolution, made on 13 February, is worth quoting in full as it gives a lively picture of the work which went into the production of a civic play.

> Alsoo . . . it was aggreed . . . that in steade of Corpus Christi play this yere the Crede playe shalbe played; And the same to be provided for and brought forth by thoversight and ordre of the Chambrelaynes; And first the original or regestre of the sayd Crede play to be goten of the mastr and brethrene of St Thomas hospitall whoo haue the custody therof.
>
> And after expert and mete players found owte for the conyng handlyng of the sayd playe, than euery of theym to haue their partes fair wrytten and delyuered theym ⌜in tyme⌝ soo that they may haue leysure to kunne euery one his part; And the sayd Chambrelaynes further to see all maner the pageantes playeng geare and necessaries to be provided in a readynes; And as occasion shall requyre to aske advise and ayde abowt the same.
>
> Item it is further aggreed . . . that all suche the craftes and occupacions of this Citie as are chardged with bryngyng forth of the pageantes of Corpus Xpi shall gather euery of theym their accumstomed pageant money and pay it to the Chambrelaynes handes towardes the chardges of bryngyng forth the sayd Crede playe; And warnyng to be gyven to euery of theym accordyngly.[87]

The chamberlains were to oversee the entire production. New individual parts were to be written out, and expenses were to be met by a contribution from the pageant-producing guilds.

But the elaborate plans of the council proved unfruitful. Within two

months of this decision the council received an advice from Matthew
Hutton, dean of the minster, that "the Creyd play is not meet to be
playd for that he seyth many thynges therin . . . he cannot allowe
bycause they be dysagreying frome the Senceritie of the gospell and for
other causes." The council "therefore agreyd to haue no play this yere
and the bookes of the Creyd play to be delyveryd in agayn."[88] Neither
the Creed play nor its procession is ever heard of again.

On 27 April, soon after the council learned that the Creed play had
been suppressed, "my L Mayour declaryd . . . that dyverse commoners
of this Citie were muche desyerous to haue Corpuscristy play this yere;
whereunto these presens wold not agree, but that the booke thereof
shuld be perused and otherwaise amendyd before it were playd."[89] But
though Corpus Christi did not occur until 19 June, there was apparently
insufficient time (and official good will) to mount a production.

In 1569 the Corpus Christi play was successfully shown, but not on
its proper day: "Item it is nowe further aggreed that Corpus Xpi play
shalbe played this yere on Tewisday in Witsone weeke; And that
billettes accustomed shalbe immediatly made forth for preparation to
the same."[90] Orders were made for the joint production of pageants by
several guilds, which suggests that objectionable pageants were eliminated. On 26 May, "nowe was appoynted places for hearyng Corpus
Xpi play on Wytsonᶠdayˡ Tewisday next."[91] This year there were
fourteen places.

The removal of the play from Corpus Christi to Whittuesday, the day
of the procession of aldermen, did not forestall criticism, for on 23
March, long before Whitsuntide, the council had to deal with the
reluctance of the sheriffs to dress in crimson gowns for any occasion
whatsoever.[92] This extreme recalcitrance can be attributed to a Reformation hostility to all holiday festivals, and to the traditional conserva-
tism of the plays. As it turned out, the sheriffs escaped the force of the
ultimatum, for on 12 May the council decided "apon certayne reasonable consideracions . . . that the shewe of harnessed men of this Citie at
Corpus Xpi play shall be spared and not had for this yere."[93] Among
the "consideracions" may have been the fact that the councilmen
normally marched on Whittuesday, so that the pageants would still be
accompanied by a march of civic officials.

The last year the Corpus Christi play was presented in the traditional
manner was 1569. When it next appeared the circumstances of
production were radically altered. On 14 April 1572 immediately after
confirming a royal order to suppress "all unlawfull games," the council
agreed "that my Lord mayour shall send for the maister of St

Anthonyes and he to bryng with hym the booke of the play called the
Pater noster play, that the same may be pervsed amended and
corrected; And that my said Lord mayour shall certifie to theis presens
at their next assemblie here of his pleasure to be taken therin."[94] By 14
May the mayor had made his inquiries: "Item it is aggreed . . . that the
play commonly called Pater Noster play shalbe played this yere on the
Thursday next after Trynitie Sonday nexte comyng."[95] Once before, in
1558, the Pater Noster play had been given on Corpus Christi. Now, in
1572, the name of the festival is suppressed and replaced by the
euphemism, "Thursday after Trinity Sunday." The sheriffs were also to
ride, along with armed men supplied by the aldermen.

The combination of the Pater Noster play and sheriffs' riding may
have been half a century old, but now a new element was added to the
mix. On 2 June, the Monday before Corpus Christi Thursday, the
council agreed "that the pageant maisters of suche pageantes of
certayne occupacions of this Citie as shalbe occupied in Pater Noster
play or for the Shew this yere, and alsoo twoo other honest men of the
same occupacions shall goo togithers with their owne pageant and
attend apon the same and see good ordre kepte." At the same time the
council drew up a list of stations for the procession, "for hearyng of
Pater Noster play."[96] Stations are never otherwise mentioned in
connection with either the Creed play or the Pater Noster play. This is
almost certainly because the processional parts of these plays consisted
of persons marching with banners rather than spectacular wheeled
pageants designed for presentation at stations. On the other hand,
these were the very same stations which are mentioned again and
again in resolutions and in chamberlains' accounts concerning the
Corpus Christi play from the late fourteenth century onward. The 1572
procession thus included the Corpus Christi craft pageants[97] (which
could easily be mounted in a matter of days if no cycle plays needed to
be rehearsed), and probably the processional banners from the Pater
Noster play, along with the sheriffs and men in armor. But the dramatic
play given after the procession was the play of Pater Noster.

For all this resort to euphemism and unprecedented combination of
processions and plays, the council's action did not go undetected. By 30
July the archbishop informed the council that the playbooks were to be
brought in for inspection. The council agreed "that his grace shall haue
a trewe copie of all the said bookes even as they weare played this
yere."[98] But once the archbishop secured the books, he would not
relinquish them again. In 1575, when Pater Noster would normally
have been produced, the council made tentative plans for the play.

Evidently it was to be given in late summer as of old, for the decision
was taken on 17 June, after Corpus Christi was past:

> agreed that Christopher Learmouth shall [have] paid hym forth-
> wyth by Nicholas Haxvppe master of St Anthonies, xxs for making
> iij play bookes perteyninge [to] the said hospitall of St Anthonies
> whiche iij bookes were now Delyured to the said Nicolas to be
> saiflie kepte to thuse of the saide hospitall.

> And wheras certayne of the same bookes ar in my L Archebisshopps
> handes it is agreed that the same shalbe required to be restored
> agayne.[99]

Three weeks later, on 8 July, the council appointed a delegation which
was to:

> goe and requier of my L Archebishop his grace all suche the play
> bookes as perteyne this Cittie now in his graces custodie and that
> his grace will apoynt twoe or thre sufficiently learned to correcte
> the same wherein by the lawe of this Realme they ar to be
> reformed; And if ther leysure will serve, to goe about the premisses
> before lammas next.[100]

Michaelmas was named as the absolute deadline for beginning negotia-
tions with the archbishop, but such a late date would preclude
mounting the play during the course of that year. Hence the council
expressed its wish that the matter could be settled before Lammas. The
Pater Noster play is not named in any of the records for 1575, but this
was the play "perteyninge [to] the said hospitall of St Anthonies" and
was one of two plays commonly given at Lammas.

All attempts to revive the old plays after the 1572 joint production of
the Corpus Christi pageants and the Pater Noster procession and play
were unsuccessful. On 8 April 1579 the council agreed "that Corpus
Xpi play shalbe played this yere; And that first the booke shalbe carried
to my Lord Archebisshop and Mr deane to correcte if that my L
Archebisshop doo well like theron."[101] No other record exists from this
year, so no doubt the archbishop and dean did not "well like theron."
The next year's effort was even less spirited:

> And nowe the Commons did earnestly request of my L Mayour and
> others this worshipfull Assemblee that Corpus Xpi play might be
> played this yere; Wherapon my L Mayour answered that he and
> his brethern wold considre of their request.[102]

From the absence of further records it is clear that the considered
judgment of the council was that there should be no play. This year,

1580, was the last in which a revival of the old plays was even contemplated.

THE SITE OF YORK'S DRAMATIC PLAYS

The 1572 joint production of the Pater Noster play and the Corpus Christi pageants occurred on Thursday, 5 June. On that same day the council took the following action as it was "Assembled in the Chambre at the Common Hall gates":

> Alsoo it is further aggreed . . . that forasmoche as Mr William Bekwith and Mr Christopher Harbert Aldermen of this Citie this present day haue disobeyed the commandement of my Lord Mayor whan as he did the same day in this place commande the said Mr Bekwith and Mr Harbert to assocyate and assist his Lordship at the tyme of playeng of the Pater noster play whoo than and there refused the same and wolde than haue departed frome this place; Wherapon the said Mr Bekwith and Mr Harbert by thadvise and consent of this worshipfull presens are nowe comanded to warde, there to abide duryng my Lord Mayour pleasure.[103]

The circumstances of these arrests were as curious as the festivity. In 1572 Christopher Harbert paid 3s 4d for the right to control the thirteenth station,[104] and must therefore have been sympathetic to the nondramatic procession of pageants. Yet he was so opposed to the "playeng of the Pater noster play" that he tried to leave the chamber where the mayor and aldermen were gathered, and was thereupon arrested. Moreover, he refused "to assocyate and assist his Lordship *at the tyme of playeng,*" which distinctly implies that the play was being performed in "this place" at the time of the arrest.

This is only one of numerous documents which suggest that Pater Noster, Creed, and Corpus Christi dramatic plays were performed in the chamber at Common Hall gates during the course of the fifteenth and sixteenth centuries. The most unambiguous of the early records comes from the Chamberlains' Roll for 1478:

> And in expenses incurred this year by the mayor, aldermen, and many others of the council of the chamber at the feast of Corpus Christi, *seeing and attending to the play in the chamber of Nicholas Bewyk according to custom,* together with 40s 4d paid for red and white wine given and sent to knights, ladies, gentlemen, and noblemen then present within the city, *and 9s for the rent of the chamber.*[105] (Emphasis mine.)

Taken on its face, this document clearly states that the mayor,

aldermen, and common council met in Nicholas Bewyk's chamber to
see and to govern the (Corpus Christi) play.

An examination of other entries from the Chamberlains' Rolls and
Books—none of them previously published—will put this interpretation beyond doubt. In 1486/7 the mayor and council saw the play "in
camera Thome Cokke," and paid 4s for the rent of the chamber. In
?1499 they saw the play "in hospico communis Guihald," that is, in the
inn pertaining to Common Hall. In this year they paid 5s for the rent of
the hall. The same *hospicium* is named in the rolls for 1501, 1506, 1508,
1518, 1520, and probably in several other rolls from this period which
are now illegible. Forty years later, in 1561, the officers paid a total of
£9 8d, "hearyng Corpus Christi play ageynst the common Hall gates."
In another year, perhaps 1566, they paid £4 4s 4d "at the place ther as
they hard the seyd play of corpus xpi."[106] These late entries in English
are merely translations of the earlier formulas in Latin: but they add
the important information that the play which the mayor and his
council watched was the play of Corpus Christi.

Entries in the Chamberlains' Books show that the officers of the city
attended a banquet as they watched Corpus Christi play within the
chamber. The "Expenses at the feast of Corpus Christi" which survive
from the fifteenth century are not broken down into individual items,
but they do show that the mayor and his officers regularly spent
upwards of 40s on themselves at Corpus Christi. In 1453 the expenses
included 12d spent on a gallon and a half of wine.[107] Sixteenth-century
accounts are itemized in overwhelming detail. The earliest, from 1520,
is a huge list under the usual heading, "Expense in festo Corporis xpi."
The list contains over thirty entries for food alone and concludes with
certain charges for the chamber:

> Item in regardo ijbus custodibus porte, viijd.
> Item in regardo Thome Sadler pro le hingyng Camere, xxd.
> Item in lez naylez pro eodem, iiijd.
> Item in regardo filie dicti Thome Sadler pro suo diligenti labore,
>   ijd. . . .
> Item pro conduccione Camere Thome flemyng, vjs viijd.[108]

These entries show that the chamber was decorated for the occasion by
Thomas Sadler, who was assisted by his daughter. The mayor and his
officers paid 6s 8d to Thomas Fleming for the "conduccione," or hire,
of the chamber. Nearly every year from 1520 to 1525 Thomas Sadler
received 20d and upwards "pro le hyngyng camere." "Hanging the
chamber" by itself implies decorating the chamber with tapestries.

Thomas Sadler's work almost certainly entailed this function, but in 1521 the chamberlains also paid 2d "in emendacione de lez firmez." A "form" in general is a bench, but it could also be part of a platform or a stage for plays, perhaps a stage made up of a series of backless benches placed one against the other. The 1522 entry shows that the "forms" were part of the hanging of the chamber: "Item in regardo Thome Sadler pro le hangyng Camere domini maioris et fratrum suorum scilicet cum lez nayles & formes, ijs ijd ob." In 1525/6 the chamberlains paid 2d "In footyng de lez formes & Trestyls."[109] "Trestles," of course, were sometimes used as legs for portable tables. But we shall see independent evidence from Norwich and Edinburgh that forms and trestles were also used in the construction of demountable stages for indoor plays.

Later entries are even more circumstantial. In 1538 the chamberlains paid 6s 8d "to Thomas flemyng for the Chambre that my lorde and his bredryn stondyth in of Corpuscristy day to here the playe accustomyd therfore," and in 1542 they paid 3d "for nayles that was occupyed in the hangyng of the Chambre at Thomas Flemynges where as my lorde mayer and his Bredern hard the sayd play [of Corpus Christi]." In 1554 they paid the standard fee of 6s 8d "to Rychard Aynlay for easment of his Howses and Chambres vppon Corpuscrysty day to my Lorde maior and his bredren."[110]

Other entries in the chamberlains' records and in the House Books show that the Pater Noster and Creed plays were performed under identical circumstances. In 1558 the York council agreed "that this yere pater nostr play beyng playd on Corpus xpi day, dynar with brekfast and supper shalbe prouyded by the Chambrelaynes for my sayd Lord mayour aldermen and xxiiij[or] as hath ben accustomed at Corpus Christi play in the Chambre at the Commonhall yates."[111] This extremely important document has hitherto been obscured by Angelo Raine's transcription of "at Corpus Christi play" as "on Corpus Christi day."[112] The document shows that the officers took their meals at the play, and that the Pater Noster play was modeled in its production after the Corpus Christi play: or perhaps the reverse is true, since Pater Noster long antedated the Corpus Christi play.

The Creed play was also performed in the chamber, though some of the documents which reveal this involve obscurities of one kind or another. On 27 March 1484, the year after Richard III saw the Creed play, the council "agreid that Thomas Gray maister of Saint Christophir Gyld shall have the Canves that lys in the Chambir that remaynyd of the Shew made late to the king to make hallynges of in the Commun

Hall to be stend and payntid of the cost of the master of the gyld."[113] The language is confusing, but it seems that the canvas was used originally to hang the chamber (at Common Hall gates), and that Richard saw the Creed play there.

The Corpus Christi play, with both pageants and drama, was given as usual in 1525,[114] but on 28 July of the same year the council "agreed for the honour and worshipe of this Cety that all my lorde maire3 and brederen shiriffes and xxiiij ti shall attend of my lorde maire att the commen Halle vppon Sunday next and ther to here the Crede play."[115] This is the only document which might be taken to suggest that the dramatic Creed play was performed in or at Common Hall itself. The more probable meaning is that the mayor, sheriffs, and council sat outside Common Hall to watch the Creed procession. Though the Creed procession may thus have been accompanied by speeches, it did not entail either pageant wagons or a complete series of stations.

Alexandra Johnston and Margaret Dorrell have supplied me with a transcription from the York Chamberlains' Books which to my mind strongly supports the argument that the dramatic performance of the Creed play was given principally for the chief civic officials of York. Once again this is for 1525: "Item paid to Thomas the Master of Corpus Cristi [guild] for the Crede Play that was playde before my Lorde Mayer and his brederin, iiijs."[116] This payment was evidently for the play which, as we have seen from the Chamberlains' Rolls, the mayor and his men watched as they sat in the chamber at Common Hall gates.

It was unusual to mount the Creed play in the same year as the Corpus Christi play, and it was also unusual to produce the Creed play at the beginning of August. The production of a decade later was even more out of the ordinary. In 1535 the council "agreyd to spare the sayd play of Corpuscrysty," and canceled the "Lesys of [the stations for] Corpuscrysty play," "for that the play was not playd forsomuche as creyd (play) was then playd by the order of my lord mayer and his bredren."[117] This shows that the Creed play replaced the Corpus Christi play on Corpus Christi day itself. In the same year the council paid 2s "to the fower offycers for rysshis and nayls and for hynggyng of the (Chamber next) Common Hall vppon Corpuscristy day." The council also paid 6s 8d "to 'Mr' Thomas flemyng for the Chamber that my lorde Mayer and his Bredren stude in of Corpuscristi day and the fryday after to here the play."[118] This is of interest not only because it proves that the Creed play was performed under the same circumstances and in the same chamber as the Corpus Christi play, but also because it reveals that the Creed play was a two-day event.

A half-century before 1535 the Corpus Christi play was once performed at the usual time for the Creed play. The pageants had been scheduled as usual for Corpus Christi in 1487, but the army of Northumberland came to York and remained until noon of Corpus Christi day. Because of the congestion in the city the council postponed the play until 7 July, "the Sonday next after the fest of Saint Thomas of canturbury. And than after it was differd to the sonday next after the fest of Saint petre callid Advinculo, because of the Kinges cvmyng hidder." In the event, "On Weddynsday after in the feast of thadvincle of Saint peter the play of corpus X^i by the Kinges Commaundement was played thrugh the citie and his grace hering the same in conyng-strete at thomas Scot house."[119] Though this entry is slightly ambiguous, it seems fairly clear that the Corpus Christi pageants were first shown in procession through the streets, and that the king subsequently retired to Scot's house in Coneystreet to observe the dramatic performance.

New Civic Theater in the 1580s

The events of 1487, 1535, and those during the reigns of Mary and Elizabeth, show that York was capable of adapting its civic spectacles to meet all manner of political exigencies. This is shown again in the 1580s, when York attempted to revive its defunct civic theater. The city council brushed aside the citizens' attempts to restore the Corpus Christi play, but in 1580 agreed "that ther shalbe a shewe of Armor by the Cyttizens of this Cyttie on St Bartholomewe day next at one of the clocke after none accordinge to the auncyent vsage of this Cyttye; and the sheriffes to ryde that day with ther foote clothes. . . . And so frome hensforth yerely vpon May day and Midsomar even."[120] The ridings on May Day, Midsummer eve, and St. Bartholomew's day (24 August) were evidently Reformation equivalents of the earlier ridings on Corpus Christi, Midsummer, and Lammas. Orders were given during the next several years for similar ridings,[121] but these were confined to Midsummer eve, the one festival of the three which was entirely above suspicion.

On 3 June 1584 the city undertook a decisive new effort to revive its ancient festivities. The old bottle, however, was to be filled with new wine:

A bill or supplicacion was exhibited . . . by one Thomas Grafton Scholemaister wherby he desireth that for the furtherance of midsomer shewe, he may be licensed to set forth certane compiled

speaches and also to haue one pageant frame for that purpose,
which speaches and matter is referred first to Mr Sheriffes to se
and pervse, and if vpon triall maid therof the said Sheriffes do
thinke the same matter to be worthie the publishinge, then the said
Grafton to procead according to his request, Orels not.[122]

A civic show in general was a marching procession which involved not
only a riding of men in armor but the discharging of guns and cannon.
We learn from an ordinance of this year that gunpowder had been
purchased for similar purposes every year "within these fower yeres last
past to helpe to sett forthe the shewe for the worshipp of this cyttie."[123]
This brings us back to 1580, the year the citizens fought and lost their
last battle for a revival of the Corpus Christi play. Grafton was now
proposing to elaborate on the Show by preparing a pageant with
speeches, on the model of the old Corpus Christi processional play.

On 19 June the council issued orders for the Show and play. They
first made provision for armor, and then went on to deal with the
processional events:

> Also it is agreed that the Shewe shall bygynne betwene iiij[or] and fyve
> of the clocke on midsomer even next and to be endid by xj of the
> clocke; And than the play to begynne at one of the clocke at after
> noone; And warning to be gyven thereof accordinglie.
>
> And now places ar appoynted to heare the playe as followeth
> [Eight places are named, including "iij[d] place at my lord maiors
> doore; the iiij[th] place at the comon hall yates."]
>
> Also it is agreed that aswell the chardges of the lord maior alder-
> men Sheriffes and xxiiij[or] etc hearing the play at the common hall
> yates as also the chardges the lady maioris and the ladies etc
> hearing the play at my lord maiors doore on mydsomer even next
> shalbe borne of the cyttie chardges and the Chamberlaynes to have
> warning to make provision accordinglie.[124]

In 1580, when the Show went without a play, it was scheduled for 1:00
P.M. Now the Show is scheduled to begin between four and five o'clock,
the time of the ancient Corpus Christi play, and the play is to begin at
1:00 P.M. In earlier days the riding of the sheriffs was apparently
integral with the pageant procession. The Show of the 1580s, however,
involved not only the sheriffs but citizens in armor. Thus for many of
the chief citizens it was a participatory rather than a spectator event. As
a consequence, the processional play had to be scheduled for a different
hour, and we learn that the mayor, aldermen, and the sheriffs
themselves watched the play from a station at the Common Hall gates.

The ladies sat at the preceding station, situated before the house of the current lord mayor.

Thomas Grafton's bill, in his own hand, written on 25 June 1584, survives in the York Chamberlains' Book. Its heading gives us a brief insight into the subject matter of the processional play: "A note of the Charges laide oute for and concernynge the settinge forth of the Pageaunte and the forerydinge Champions in their apte and requisete manner." Evidently the pageant had a martial theme, accompanied as it was by "Champions" (probably from myth or history) mounted on horses. Other expenses included payments for the repair of the pageant, for drummers and ensign bearers, for the repair of an ensign accidentally torn by "the two hand sworde players," for trumpeters, and for "Cuthberte our musityan."[125]

At the conclusion of Grafton's processional play the mayor and his councilmen retired indoors for a banquet. A list of expenses in the Chamberlains' Book includes an expenditure of 18d "for Rishes to the chamber," and 6s 8d "to Thomas Colthirst for Rowmes in his house for my L maior and aldermen on mydsomer even accordinge to his lease."[126]

The banquet of 1584 was not evidently accompanied by a dramatic play, but this lack was made up the following year. On 4 June 1585 the council made provisions for a show of armor on Midsummer eve and agreed at the same time "that Mr Grafton shall proceed with one Interlude which he preferred into this Courte to be examined."[127] On 22 June the council met in the Ousebridge chamber, "when and where the interlude latelie presented by Mr Grafton and set over by this court to be examined, was now openly redd over and pervsed; And it is agreed that the same shalbe plaid on midsomer eve next."[128]

Immediately after approving the "Interlude" for Midsummer eve the council "agreed that the play shalbe plaid" at eight stations, as in the preceding year. All stations were assessed 3s 4d "except the pavement, which is to pay nothing in respect that the ladies are to be placed at Mr aldermen harbertes howse." The preceding station was "at Mr alderman beckwith dore." Harbert and Bekwith were the two men arrested in 1572 for refusing to attend the Pater Noster play in the chamber at Common Hall gates. More important for our argument is the distinction between Grafton's "Interlude," which was certainly a dramatic production, and the "play" which was to be shown in the streets.

The festivities of 1585 evidently lasted two days, for the occupations were assessed "for and twowardes the chardges of the play on mydsomer even and day," and the chamberlains laid out a large sum, over ten pounds sterling, for "Chardges of the shew and play on mydsomer even and mydsomer day." This list includes payments to the Skinners, Tailors, Cooks, Innholders, and Bakers, for charges of their pageants. It also includes a payment to the choirmaster "Mr Wormemall for his payns and his boys in synginge."[129] Grafton once again submitted a bill which detailed some of the particulars of his pageant: "for armes paintinge aboute the hearse in the firste pageant, a crowne for the angell, spangells for his shirte, the mendinge of the Queenes crowne, paintinge of the childe one of the furyes bare, with some other trifells . . . more for Cutberds paines and his boyes the musityans . . . 5 visards . . . Mr Wormall for the lending of the Queristers, and prickinge of the songes . . . charges I my sealf have bene at ether at my howse with my players or elsewhere."[130] Most of these expenditures must have been for the pageant play, but the last entry may have been for the dramatic interlude. The details of the pageant, especially the queen and the child which the Furies bore, are consistent with our earlier suggestion that the pageant may have had a classical motif.

Once again the chamberlains paid the "Expenses of my L maior and aldermen and Ladies on mydsomer day at the play." These included 6d "paid for baking (demen) and settyng vp the glasse in Mr colthirst house," 18d "for Reshes and drissing the chamber," and the usual 6s 8d "to Mr Colthirst for his house Rome at the [dramatic] play."[131]

THE CHAMBER AT COMMON HALL GATES

Though the chamber where the three civic plays were given their dramatic performances is named variously in different documents, we can determine that all references are to a single place, the chamber at Common Hall gates in Coneystreet. The tenants of the chamber, so far as we know them, were Nicholas Bewyk, Thomas Cokke, Thomas Scot, Thomas Flemyng, Richard Aynlay, and Thomas Colthirst. Certain biographical information survives concerning four of these men. Nicholas Bewyk, who leased the chamber for the production of 1478, was a vintner of considerable means.[132] A parishioner of St. Martin's, Coneystreet, upon his death in 1479 he left a piece of valuable plate to the church.[133] In 1475 Bewyk paid 8s for the rights to the eighth station for the Corpus Christi processional play.[134] This was the last station in Coneystreet, the ninth station being situated in Stonegate, which intersects with Coneystreet near Common Hall gates. Nothing is known about the next two tenants except that Thomas Cokke's name is mentioned in the same manner as Bewyk's, while Thomas Scot's house is identified as being situated in Coneystreet. Thomas Flemyng's name,

as we have seen, occurs in all relevant Chamberlains' Book entries
between 1520 and 1542. The Chamberlains' Roll for 1520 names the
hospicium communis Guyhald as the site of the plays: Flemyng was
clearly the tenant of this inn. He was a joiner who in 1541 was charged
by the York council with constructing a scaffold at Mickelgate Bar for
the royal entry of Henry VIII.[135] Like Bewyk, Flemyng was a parishioner of St. Martin's, Coneystreet (Flemyng died in 1545).[136] Also like
Bewyk, Flemyng held the lease for the eighth station for the Corpus
Christi processional play (1524 and 1527).[137] Richard Aynlay, who
leased the chamber in 1554, died in 1575, leaving certain items of
clothing to Thomas Colthirst, who was his son-in-law and his successor
as tenant of the chamber where the mayor sat to watch the plays.[138]

The leases of processional stations for 1524 and 1527, both of which
contain Flemyng's name, will completely dispel any remaining suspicion that the mayor and his officers sat inside or outside the chamber
at Common Hall gates to watch a true-processional dramatic play being
performed in the streets. These two leases record the fact that the
mayor and his men watched the processional play not from the eighth
station at Flemyng's house (the chamber), but from an earlier station,
number six. Thus the 1527 lease, entitled "Dimissio ludi Corporis
Xpi," lists the following information for the sixth, seventh, and eighth
stations:

Sextus locus dimittitur coram maiore & sociis suis etc., [blank]
Septimus locus dimittitur Raginald Beysley pro iijs iiijd.
Octauus locus dimittitur Thome Flemyng, ijs.[139]

The Chamberlains' Book for 1538 reveals the exact site of the mayor's
station: "Item the sext place at the Common hall where my lorde
Mayor and his bredren ar accustomyd to be wherefore that place goith
free." Entries for 1542 and 1554 convey an identical message, except
that in these years three stations had been added earlier along the route
so that the mayor's station at Common Hall was now number nine.[140]
Thus the mayor and his men began the day by watching the processional pageants from in front of Common Hall proper and afterward moved
to the chamber for the production of the dramatic plays. The chamber
was near Common Hall but far enough away to allow for another
station, the seventh, to be situated between.

The York Guild Hall, or Common Hall, was part of a construction
program which began in 1445 and ended in 1459. Common Hall is set
back by the River Ouse a considerable distance from Coneystreet, near
its intersection with St. Helen's Square, the lower reach of Stonegate

Street. Common Hall is now approached by a passageway which leads off Coneystreet directly through the north end of the eighteenth-century Mansion House.[141] Between Mansion House and Common Hall is a rather spacious courtyard.

The exact site of the chamber at Common Hall gates is a matter for conjecture. The chamber and gates were not set back by Common Hall but fronted on Coneystreet. Since the Corpus Christi processional play passed by the chamber on its way from Common Hall into Stonegate, the chamber must have been situated to the *north* of the gates. We have already discovered that the chamber survived until at least 1585. It probably survived until January 1724/5, when Common Hall gates and two adjoining buildings were demolished. The event is recorded in the diary of Thomas Hammond: "Two large houses, one on each side of the Common Hall Gates in Coney Street were pulled down in order to be rebuilt into one large house for the Lord Mayor."[142] The medieval chamber at Common Hall gates was evidently the northernmost of these two houses. Thomas Hammond's statement that this was a large house perfectly satisfies our expectation that the building was of sufficient size to have enclosed a chamber of generous proportions.

Even in the early eighteenth century, the building still served as an inn. In 1722/3 it is called "the Cross Keys at the Comon Hall Gate."[143] In January of the following year, 1723/4, the corporation committee dealing with leases of civic properties decided that James Young, lessee of the "Cross Kieys in Conney Street," should be granted only yearly leases because the passage to the Guildhall was "generally dirty by reason of the said Cross Keys being a publick house," and also because of "the Citys Intention of (sometime) Building a House there for the Lord Mayor."[144] Thus the Cross Keys must have been the former inn at Common Hall gates while James Young must have been the eighteenth-century successor of Nicholas Bewyk, Thomas Flemyng, Richard Aynlay, and Thomas Colthirst. The ground floor of the house south of the gates was evidently the former chapel of St. Christopher guild. According to Drake, who wrote in 1736: "The chapel of the Gild of St. Christopher stood to the street, almost facing Stone-gate; which was turned into a dwelling house, and long continued so, till *anno* 1726. it was pulled down, with another adjoining, in order to build the present mansion-house for our lord mayors."[145] This leaves the large house immediately to the north of the Common Hall gates as the evident site of the chamber at Common Hall gates.

Speed's rather generalized map of 1611 (fig. 1) is useless for establishing the site and proportions of the chamber. Much more useful is William Archer's survey of ca. 1685 (fig. 2). Archer's survey is not

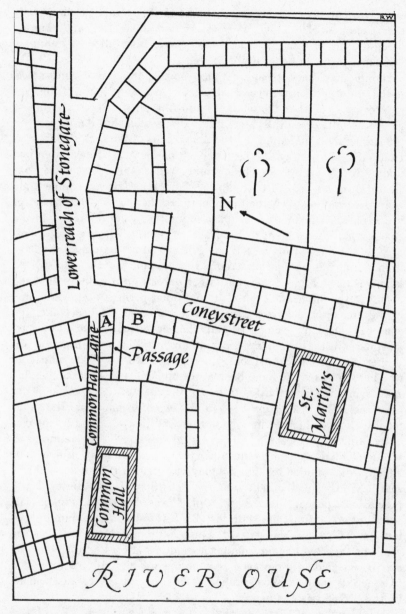

Fig. 2. Detail after William Archer's plan of York, ca. 1685. From the York City Library, published by permission of the Library. Identifying names added. The chamber at Common Hall gates was probably on the site marked *A*, though *B* is also a possibility.

entirely accurate: for example, Common Hall is actually built directly over Common Hall Lane, whereas Archer shows the lane running alongside the Hall. Nevertheless, the general disposition of buildings and lanes seems to be accurate enough.

Hammond's diary strongly implies that Common Hall gates stood in the center of the frontage of the present Mansion House. If this was indeed the case, then the chamber abutting on the north side of the gates was situated on the parcel I have designated with the letter A on the Archer map. Judging from the dimensions of the present Mansion House (54-foot frontage, 58 feet deep),[146] parcel A must have been just under 20 feet on a side. The chamber indeed may have been considerably larger than this. The inn at Common Hall gates apparently comprised more parcels than one, perhaps the entire strip of land of which parcel A is a part. This may be inferred from references in the chamberlain's documents to a plurality of rooms ("Howses and Chambres"; "Rowmes in his house").[147] But of course the play must have been mounted in a single large room. It is possible that the long strip of land was divided into fewer and larger parcels until 1585, or that the chamber was situated above the ground floor, perhaps occupying some of the area over the passageway itself. Whatever its exact site, the chamber must have been an intimate theater indeed, by our standards.

Apparently the chamber was part of an inn which was ultimately the property of the city council but which was leased to private managers who in turn leased the room back to the city on special occasions. This may be inferred from the description of the chamber as "the Inn of the Common Hall" (*hospicium communis Guyhald*); and from the statement for 1584, which we have seen, that Colthirst was paid by the city "accordinge to his lease." In 1585 Colthirst was evidently reimbursed through a remission in his rent rather than in cash: "Mr Colthirst shall haue vjs viijd allowed for that the play was plaid at the comon hall this year 1585 to be allowed in his rent."[148] The "play" in this context is the processional pageant. In 1584 this "play" was shown at Common Hall gates but not at Common Hall; in 1585 it was shown at Common Hall but not at Common Hall gates.[149] Thus Colthirst in 1585 lost whatever profit he expected to gain from his lease of a station, and the council's action was evidently designed to recompense him for his loss. The banquet, as we have seen, probably with the Interlude, was held in Colthirst's chamber as usual.

The chamber at Common Hall gates may have been part of the construction program of 1445–59, or it may have been considerably older. Although the site of the banquet is nowhere indicated prior to

1478, we can perhaps extrapolate back as far as 1433, when the council spent the subsequently standard sum of 6s 8d "pro firma camere maioris et proborum hominum eodem die [Corpus Christi]." An identical sum occurs for 1468, and the heading, without a specified sum, occurs for 1475.[150] This same procedure might bring us all the way back to 1397 and Richard II's visit to York. At that time the council spent 18s 8d "in bread, ale, wine, flesh, and firewood for the mayor and for other worthy persons on [Corpus Christi] day at the play."[151] Here, however, we must take care: it is quite possible, even probable, that the council sponsored a festival banquet on the occasion of the processional play years before the advent of the dramatic play.

The year 1433 antedates the completion of the Common Hall by more than ten years: this may explain why the York council established the practice of watching plays in a private chamber rather than in a more spacious public building. Having once set a precedent for private indoor productions, the mayor and council probably saw no reason why this successful arrangement should not continue.

It is not certain what play may have been performed in the chamber in early years. The mayor and council paid players in their 1433 Coronation of the Virgin pageant, as we have seen, but it is not possible to insist on this account that the entire cycle was performed in the chamber that year (or, indeed, in any year). In 1442, as we have noted, the mayor and his men paid for a *ludum de vyne yerde*, also on Corpus Christi. Perhaps it was not until the 1450s or even the 1460s that the cycle as a whole was performed in the chamber.

The 1524 and 1527 leases of stations, together with the chamberlains' accounts of the same period, demonstrate beyond reasonable doubt that the mayor and his officers watched the pageant procession from in front of Common Hall but moved to the chamber at Common Hall gates for the dramatic play. Explicit statements from individual documents and the cumulative force of all relevant documents from the York House Books, Chamberlains' Rolls, and Chamberlains' Books have pressed me to the unanticipated conclusion that the dramatic plays were performed *within* the chamber. Two interpretations of the documents other than the one I have offered are worth entertaining: that the officers sat inside the chamber to watch a stationary performance which occurred directly outside the chamber in Coneystreet; or that the dramatic performance in the chamber was only one of several (two or three, but not as many as twelve) which followed the conclusion of the morning procession. Thus, for example, whereas I have interpreted the minster Chamberlains' Roll of 1483 as signifying that the

dean and his brethren sat above the minster gates to watch the
Corpus Christi and Creed processions, it might be argued that a
dramatic performance of the plays was given inside (or outside) this
chamber as well as inside (or outside) the chamber at Common Hall
gates.

None of the alternatives I have just suggested contradicts the major
propositions I have urged here: that the extant York cycle text could
not conceivably have been mounted intact at twelve stations in the true-
processional manner; that the Corpus Christi play, the Creed play, and
the Pater Noster play of York consisted of spectacular processions
followed by distinct dramatic plays; and that the mayor of York and his
council sat before Common Hall to watch the processions, but sat
inside the chamber at Common Hall gates to watch the dramatic plays.

The alternative hypotheses, while not inconsistent with my major
arguments, present practical (to say nothing of evidential) difficulties of
their own. That thirty-seven men could comfortably watch an outdoor
play while crowded against the windows of a medieval chamber is
doubtful. The possibility of multiple performances, even two or three,
raises all the lesser organizational problems of a true-processional
production. On the other hand, we shall discover from our investiga-
tions of other cities, particularly Lincoln, King's Lynn, Ipswich, and
Edinburgh, that Corpus Christi plays were frequently mounted indoors
for the exclusive benefit of a handful of powerful officials.

The idea that a Corpus Christi cycle was produced indoors may seem
unacceptable to those who have been taught to believe in extravagant
outdoor productions on pageant wagons. But an indoor production
seems entirely logical in the case of York. The principal civic officials
were accustomed to celebrating the Corpus Christi festival with a
formal breakfast, dinner, and supper. At 4:30 A.M., perhaps after
breakfast, they went to their scaffold in front of Common Hall to observe
the pageant procession and the riding of sheriffs which accompanied or
preceded it. The procession, with its many pageants each presented as a
brief action, must have lasted several hours. The dramatic cycle
therefore could not have begun until later in the morning. But if it
began toward noon, it must have lasted until near midnight. Even at
astronomical midsummer, plays would not have been visible out of
doors after about 10:30 P.M.[152] An indoor production therefore seems to
have been a necessity: the comforts of the mayor and aldermen would
be better served where weather could be no concern and where hunger
could be relieved by a sumptuous feast even during the course of the
play.

The Text of the York Cycle

The text of the York cycle contains nothing which might contradict the idea of an indoor performance. From the dramatic dialogue we may infer the usual stage properties: a mountain, houses and scaffolds, a tree, a throne, beds, and so forth. Stage directions are almost entirely lacking, and where they occur imply almost nothing concerning staging. An exception is a stage direction in the Transfiguration: "Hic descendunt nubes Pater in nube" (Here let clouds descend, the Father in the cloud).[153] This clearly indicates a cloud machine for ascending to and descending from heaven. The machine is used again at the Ascension, where Jesus cries:

> Sende doune a clowde, fadir! for-thy
> I come to thee, my fadir deere.

Since both plays were performed on the same stage, the same machine could have been used on both occasions.

The York cycle is singularly lacking in references to riders mounted on horseback. A messenger does tell Herod that he has seen three kings "Rydand full ryally," but the kings themselves, as they enter or leave the stage area, make no mention of horses. The use of an ass is distinctly indicated for Abraham and Isaac, the Flight into Egypt, and the Entry into Jerusalem. It is not impossible that a real ass was brought indoors for the performance: an ass is a docile creature which might easily have been led in on these three occasions. On the other hand, it is conceivable that a fabricated beast was used in place of a real one. We shall see that fabricated horses were used by the Magi in an indoor play at Canterbury.

A curious feature of the York cycle text is the extraordinary irregularity of the various plays in the cycle. The massive length of the longest plays has constituted one of our most powerful arguments against the hypothesis of true-processional production. The very short plays at the beginning of the cycle, on the other hand, might not be incompatible with pageants moving in a liturgical procession. Indeed, these may represent the general nature of the York processional play in its early years, before it was revised and extended by the genius of the York Realist, whose work is generally dated around the middle of the fifteenth century.[154]

York Stations and Pageant Wagons

The stations which were crowded into the vicinity of Common Hall

must have confounded any attempt to extend the speeches of the
pageants into lengthy dialogue. The sixth station at Common Hall was
in effect a double station: the mayor and his officers sat on one side of
the street (or courtyard), while the other side was leased to a private
individual.[155] The seventh station must also have been situated in the
yard, and the eighth station, before the chamber at Common Hall
gates, must have been situated in Coneystreet. Some of the stations
were certainly within earshot of one another. Short presentations could
have been managed in such a way as to avoid simultaneous speeches by
pageants at successive stations: full-length Corpus Christi plays could
not have been managed without intolerable interference.

The location of Common Hall must have presented difficulties even
to processional pageants: the only access was through the narrow
passage (about 6 feet wide) and the procession with its wagons had to go
first in and then out the passage, doubling back on itself for a space.
The narrow passage clearly limited the size of the pageants.

New evidence concerning the nature of one pageant seems to confirm
our belief that the pageants were not suitable as stages for dramatic
plays. Alexandra Johnston and Margaret Dorrell have recently published and analyzed a newly discovered indenture of the York Mercers
which contains an inventory of the Doomsday pageant, dated 1433.
Johnston and Dorrell believe that the plays were performed on the
pageants, but they express concern over the superabundance of angels
on this particular wagon. Close analysis of parts of the inventory will
show that this "Pagent with iiij wheles"[156] was indeed largely devoted to
angels, and to other items suitable to a tableau heaven:

> iiij Irens to bere vppe heuen; iiij finale coterelles [cotter-pins] and a
> Iren pynne; A brandreth of Iren that god sall sitte vppon when he
> sall fly vppe to heuen with iiij rapes at iiij corners; A heuen of Iren
> with a naffe of tre; ij peces of rede cloudes and sternes of gold
> langing to heuen; ij peces of blu cloudes payntid on bothe sydes; iij
> peces of rede cloudes with sunne bemes of golde and sternes for the
> hiest of heuen with a lang small border of the same wurke; vij grete
> Aungels halding the passion of god; Ane of thame has a fane of
> laton and a crosse of Iren in his hede giltid; iiij smaler Aungels
> gilted holding the passion; ix smaler Aungels payntid rede to renne
> aboute in the heuen; A lang small corde to gerre the Aungels renne
> about.[157]

These items all suggest a mechanical pageant or *tableau vivant* instead
of the rather empty, stagelike vehicle which would be required for a
dramatic performance. The mechanism by which God is raised to

heaven is reminiscent of stage devices required for the dramatic play. Equally spectacular, but distinctly less suitable for drama, is the figure of Christ, represented here not by a costumed actor but by a fabricated Passion or Crucifix borne by seven great angels and several small angels, all of whom are likewise fabricated. Heaven here is not a raised platform but a wheel of iron with a nave, or hub, of wood, suspended on an iron "pynne," or axle, and given motion by a long thin cord, which probably ran over a pulley fastened to the wheel.

To add to the problem, the pageant had cloths along three sides, and another cloth, probably a backdrop, at the rear. Now the "back" of the pageant must have been situated either at one side or the other of the wagon, or at the front, or at the back. If it was at the front or the back, the pageant would have been suitable as a processional wagon, but not as a stage for a lengthy dramatic action which was to be presented to audiences seated along the sides of the streets. If the "back" was on one side or the other of the wagon, then the play could be seen by an audience on one side of the street but not by an audience on the other side. A play could not easily have been presented to both sides of the street at once, as the pageant evidently was at Common Hall before the mayor. Unless all audiences were situated in the same position relative to the pageant wagon, difficulties of projecting a play adequately would arise even if there were no backdrop. The evidence from the indenture brings this dilemma more forcefully to view and may remind us how problematic any attempt at processional production of plays must necessarily have been.

4
Wakefield

I have suggested that we must exercise great caution in using records from one city to effect an interpretation of Corpus Christi activities in another city. But the civic records of Wakefield and York, like parts of their dramatic cycles, are sometimes nearly identical,[1] a consequence of geographical proximity and of unquestioned cultural dependence of Wakefield on York. The Wakefield records, which are exceedingly sparse, attain significance for both cities when read in light of what we know of York.

EVIDENCE FROM THE BURGESS COURT ROLLS

The Wakefield Burgess Court Rolls for the years 1554 and 1556 are the only extant records from that town which bear directly on the Corpus Christi play.[2] The second of the two rolls is for the meeting "nexte after the feaste of Saynte Michaell tharchanngell in thirde and fourte yeare of the Reignes of oure Soveraigne Lorde and Ladye Kinge Philyppe and quene Marye 1556."[3] The 1556 inquest was thus held during Michaelmas, the last quarter of the year. The 1554 document is not so clearly dated, but tradition and internal evidence suggest that this session also occurred late in the year.[4]

The 1556 record includes orders for the conduct of the play and also a list of expenses. The orders must anticipate a production in the coming year, 1557, while the expenses must be for the 1556 production.

Reprinted in revised form from "Informal Notes of Seminar 17," and from my "The Wakefield Corpus Christi Play: Pageant Procession and Dramatic Cycle," *Research Opportunities in Renaissance Drama* 13-14 (1971-72): 209-33, by permission of the editor and publisher. Copyright 1972, by Northwestern University Press.

Similarly, an order in the 1554 document must anticipate a production in 1555, while a demand for an accounting of expenses must refer to the 1554 production. Evidently the pageants were shown every year from 1554 to 1557.

The 1556 roll includes a list of expenses under the heading, "The summe of the expens of the Cherche mester for the Corpus Christi playe, xvijs xd":

Item payd to the preste, xijd.
Item payd to the mynstrells, xxd.
Item payd to the mynstrells of Corpus Christi playe, iijs ivd.
Item payd for the Corpus Christi playe and the wrytynge of the spechys for yt, iijs viijd.
Item payd for the Baner for the mynstrells, vjs viijd.
Item payd for the ryngyng the same day, vjd.
Item payd for garlonds on Corpus Christi day, xijd.

The sum of the individual items is 17s 10d, which proves that "the summe of the expens . . . for the Corpus Christi playe" is indeed a heading for the list, and not a separate item. None of the seven items on the list bears any necessary relation to the dramatic cycle. All may be regarded as elements of a liturgical procession which included pageant wagons and other festive spectacles. Certainly the "garlonds" are appropriate to a procession, and the "Baner" and the "ryngyng" also.[5] A priest would naturally be paid for liturgical duties. It is true that two different payments were made to the minstrels, one unspecified and one for "Corpus Christi playe." But these may well have been for the ecclesiastical entourage on the one hand, and for the processional pageants on the other.

It has always been assumed that the payment "for the Corpus Christi playe and the wrytynge of the spechys for yt" refers to the dialogue for the dramatic play. The same thing is assumed concerning the speeches which are mentioned in the first Burgess Court order for the same year:

Item a payne is sett that everye crafte and occupacion doo bringe furthe theire pagyaunts of Corpus Christi daye as hathe bene heretofore used and to gyve furthe the speches of the same in after holydayes in payne of everye one not so doynge to forfett xls.

The first part of this order appeals to an ambiguous precedent, which might be either a procession of pageants or a dramatic play. The second part is not only ambiguous but perplexing. Why should speeches be given "in after holydayes," that is, after Corpus Christi is past?

Martial Rose has interpreted this to mean that the dramatic plays were presented after Corpus Christi, over a period of several days.[6] But in the York records concerning the billets for Corpus Christi play, "give forth" means "hand over" or "deliver up" rather than "speak aloud." The billets were papers of enduring value, collected each year after the play, that is to say, "give[n] furthe . . . in after holydayes." The playbooks for the dramatic plays, on the other hand, would not have been turned in after the performance. Evidently, then, the Wakefield "speches," and very possibly the York "billets" as well, were stanzas of verse delivered aloud at stations along the processional route. We may regard it as proof of this hypothesis for Wakefield, I think, that the "Cherche mester," who supervised the procession on behalf of the council, listed the cost of having these speeches written along with other costs of the procession such as garlands, banners, and ringing of bells. Analogous evidence for the hypothesis comes from the example of Thomas Grafton, the York schoolmaster who in 1584 was "licensed to set forth certane compiled speaches and also to haue one pageant frame for that purpose."[7]

The first order of 1556 is followed by additional "paynes":

Item a payne is sett that everye player be redy in his pagyaunt
at setled tyme before 5 of the clocke in the mornynge in payne
of every one not so doynge to forfett vjs viijd.

Item a payne is sett that the players playe where setled and no
where els in payne of no [sic] so doynge to forfett xxs.

Item a payne is sett that no man goe armed to disturb the playe or
hinder the procession in payne of everye one so doynge vjs viijd.

The order for all players to be ready in their pageants at the same time in the morning makes no sense for a true-processional dramatic play, but is quite proper for a procession of spectacular tableaux. A nondramatic procession beginning at 5:00 A.M. could easily be finished in time for morning mass. The dramatic play could then begin later in the morning or early in the afternoon.

The Burgess Court also ordered, as at York, "that the players playe where setled and no where els." This has been taken to support the theory of processional staging for both cities, but the order is perfectly compatible with the theory that the pageants were briefly presented at specified stations along the processional route by means of short expository speeches. The order not to "disturb the playe or hinder the procession" probably refers respectively to the procession of pageants and the ecclesiastical entourage, both of which went in the Corpus Christi procession.

MATTHEW HUTTON AND THE SUPPRESSION
OF THE WAKEFIELD CORPUS CHRISTI PLAY

The Wakefield pageants and dramatic cycle both survived until the 1550s.[8] On 27 May 1576 Dean Matthew Hutton, who had earlier suppressed the York civic plays, issued an order which yields ambiguous information on the demise of the Wakefield play:

> This daie vpon intelligence geven to the saide Commissioners that it is meant and purposed that in the towne of Wakefeld shalbe plaied this yere in Whitsonweke next or theraboutes a plaie commonlie called Corpus Christi plaie which hath bene heretofore vsed there; Wherein they ar done tundrestand that there be many thinges vsed which tende to the Derogation of the Maiestie and glorie of god the prophanation of the Sacramentes and the maunteynaunce of superstition and idolatrie; The said Commissioners Decred a lettre to be written and sent to the Balyffe Burgesses and other the inhabitantes of the said towne of Wakefeld that in the said playe no Pageant be vsed or set furthe wherein the Maiestye of god the father god the sonne or god the holie ghoste or the administration of either the Sacramentes of Baptisme or of the lordes Supper be counterfeyted or represented; or any thinge plaied which tende to the maintenaunce of superstition and idolatrie or which be contrarie to the lawes of god or of the Realme; Which lettre was sent accordinglie and was subscribed with the handes of the said Dominus Hutton and of others of the Counsell and commission.[9]

Evidently Wakefield had decided to follow the earlier example of York in shifting or disguising its play in order to suppress traditional associations with Corpus Christi.[10] Thus the prohibition is not tied to a specific day but rather refers to the play scheduled for "Whitsonweke next or theraboutes." It is not clear whether the anticipated event was a procession of pageants, a dramatic play, or both. Thus we cannot be certain that the Wakefield cycle survived even into the reign of Elizabeth. In York the pageant procession outlived the cycle, and the same may have been true at Wakefield.

We have argued that nearly all the extant records concerning Wakefield, even the 1556 Burgess Court record twice mentioning speeches, concern the pageant procession rather than the dramatic cycle. No other documents concerning the Wakefield play are known. To understand how the cycle plays were staged, we are therefore entirely dependent upon the internal evidence available in the single surviving manuscript.

STAGING REQUIREMENTS OF THE WAKEFIELD CYCLE TEXT

The Wakefield cycle, in its present rather mutilated form, contains something over 12,000 lines of verse. Martial Rose estimates that in its complete form it contained about 15,000 lines.[11] Even without both Shepherds' plays, the cycle would have lasted over fourteen hours at one station. The longest plays of the cycle run some 750 lines each. If the equivalent of 100 lines were allowed for journeys, each additional station would require the equivalent of 850 lines, or almost one hour's time. This consideration militates against any extensive true-processional production, even one beginning early in the morning.

Martial Rose, who argues for a single-station production, states that within the Conspiracy-Crucifixion portion of the cycle, the plays sweep on from one to the next, forming a single unit like the N-Town Passion.[12] But each play in the Conspiracy group has its own distinct beginning, in which Pilate threatens the audience into silence. If there were no distinct breaks between the plays, such prefatory admonitions would be superfluous. But though the episodic nature of the cycle suggests that the plays derived from a sequence of craft pageants, it cannot be taken as evidence for true-processional staging. More mundane evidence, drawn from allusions in the dialogue, supports the argument for single-station production.

At the end of the Crucifixion play, as the burial of Christ approaches, Joseph says, "Bere we hym furth vnto the kyrke, / To the tombe that I gard wyrk."[13] As sacred history this is nonsense, for the tomb of Christ was not in a church. Possibly the play was performed outside an actual church, and Christ's body, after being taken down from the cross, was conveyed into the church. This would allow the actors to dispose of the body and would clearly suggest a burial.

The cycle contains other references to a church, particularly in the Purification, where Simeon goes "to the kyrk," and there hears "Oure bellys ryng by thare oone." Real bells were used for the play (stage direction: *Tunc pulsabunt*), and nothing would have been so impressive or convenient as the bells of the Wakefield parish church, now the Wakefield Cathedral.

The story of the Wakefield parish church and its bell tower may lend some interest to this suggestion. Sometime around 1315 the central bell tower of the old church collapsed, with considerable damage to the church fabric. A new church was completed in 1329, but reconstruction of the bell tower was delayed for nearly a century. Henry Bowet, archbishop of York, personally encouraged the project in 1409, and work was still in progress in 1420. The tower was set about 12 feet to the

west of the nave entrance, but during the course of the fifteenth century
the church was almost entirely rebuilt, and extended until it joined the
tower. The Wakefield citizens must have been consciously proud of the
new tower, which soared 247 feet into the air.[14] In such circumstances a
playwright might naturally call attention to "Oure bellys."

Other evidence from the Wakefield cycle supports the idea of a
single-station production. Noah refers to "this greyn," Abraham to
"this playn," Primus Tortor of the Buffeting to "a yerde," and the
same character in the Talents refers to "this place." In the Scourging,
Secundus Tortor exclaims:

> we are worthy greatte lose
> that thus has broght a kyng
> from sir pilate and othere fose
> thus into oure ryng.

Evidently the actors brought their Christ from the *locus* of Pilate into
the central *platea* of their playing area.

Although this evidence points to an outdoor performance near the
church, none of the arguments for the place of production may be
finally convincing.[15] Since most of the Wakefield documents concern
the presentational pageants rather than the play, perhaps the wisest
course is to confess how little we know concerning the staging of the
Wakefield dramatic cycle.

5
Beverley

FOURTEENTH-CENTURY PAGEANT PROCESSIONS

Several marching pageants were mounted each year in fourteenth-century Beverley, another near neighbor of York. Two were simple in form, sponsored by religious guilds. The Guild of St. Mary, founded on 25 January 1355, presented appropriate costumed figures in its annual procession:

> Every year, on the feast of the Purification of the blessed Mary, all the bretheren and sisteren shall meet together in a fit and appointed place, away from the church; and there, one of the gild shall be clad in comely fashion as a queen, like to the glorious Virgin Mary, having what may seem a son in her arms; and two others shall be clad like to Joseph and Simeon; and two shall go as angels, carrying a candle-bearer, on which shall be twenty-four thick wax lights. With these and other great lights borne before them, and with much music and gladness, the pageant Virgin with her son, and Joseph and Simeon, shall go in procession to the church. And all the sisteren of the gild shall follow the Virgin; and afterwards all the bretheren; and each of them shall carry a wax light weighing half a pound. And they shall go two and two, slowly pacing to the church; and when they have got there, the pageant Virgin shall offer her son to Simeon at the high altar; and all the sisteren and bretheren shall offer their wax lights, together with a penny each. All this having been solemnly done, they shall go home again with gladness.[1]

This constitutes an extraordinarily detailed example of an early costumed procession which culminated in a dramatic performance.

88

The guild of St. Helen, founded 3 May 1378, also mounted a procession on its patronal feast day:

> . . . a fair youth, the fairest they can find, is picked out, and is clad as a queen, like to St. Elene. And an old man goes before this youth, carrying a cross, and another old man carrying a shovel, in token of the finding of the Holy Cross.

Like the procession of St. Mary's guild, this was accompanied by music. At the altar of St. Helen in the church of the Friars Minor, the procession came to a conclusion with a mass, but not, apparently, with a play.[2]

The religious fraternities of Beverley probably had neither the opportunity, the resources, nor the desire to develop their pageants into lengthy dramatic plays. The craft guilds, on the other hand, did succeed in making at least a major thrust in this direction. This occurred, as at York, in conjunction with the procession on Corpus Christi day.

The Castles of the Guilds on Cross Monday

The typical craft guild of late fourteenth- and fifteenth-century Beverley supported a castle, a light, and a Corpus Christi pageant or play. Since town and guild records give such prominence to the crafts' "castles," it will be helpful to begin with an accounting of these before we move on to a discussion of the pageants on Corpus Christi.

The government of medieval Beverley was in the hands of twelve worthy citizens called governors or keepers. In 1411 "most of the aldermen and stewards of the crafts in Beverley . . . submitted themselves to the award of the aforesaid twelve keepers, as well in respect of the erection of castles as for the maintenance of the Corpus Christi Play":

> Whereon the aforesaid keepers thus gave their award: that all and singular of every craft, who were accustomed to have and set up wooden castles in honour of God and of St. John of Beverley, or in future shall have them, shall henceforth for ever set up and cover them in an ornamental fashion [*et ornate cooperiant castra sua*], under a penalty of 6s 8d . . .[3]

These wooden structures were covered with colorful fabrics: in the 1441 ordinances of the Bowyers and Fletchers each guildsman is ordered to appear "with a fit bed-covering [*cum cooperatura lecti habili*]" for the castle.[4]

According to an ordinance of 1416, the Tanners were to "raise upe on castle of tre vpon monday in the Rogacion weeke . . . and the sayd brether of tanneres to sytt in the same castell at the hour of prime [6:00 A.M.] and the tyme of procession in clothynge all of on suyt as nygh as yt maye be hade and gotten; And also brether shall ryd at after noyn in the saym suyt as other craftes doo after ther old auncyent and laudable custom."[5] The Rogation days are the Monday, Tuesday, and Wednesday before Ascension Thursday. Thus on Rogation Monday, called Cross Monday, the craftsmen sat in their castles to watch the ecclesiastical perambulation in the morning, and in the afternoon the craftsmen themselves went in the processional riding.

The Treasurers' Account Roll for 1502 shows that the twelve keepers of Beverley also had a castle for the Rogation procession. On Cross Monday they spent a total of 15s 11d for various items of food; for repairing their ornamental "cover" with a piece of silver; for two minstrels; for nails for the castle; for bearing the castle out and in; and for erecting the castle and arraying it. The keepers paid 4d each toward their expenses, and let the remaining 11s 11d fall to the city treasury.[6]

THE LITURGICAL PROCESSION ON CORPUS CHRISTI DAY

The foundation deed of the Beverley Corpus Christi guild is dated 1352, but guild ordinances date back still further, perhaps to 1330. As at York, the Beverley guild consisted in large part of priests and was founded for the purpose of fostering the liturgical procession on Corpus Christi.[7] The craft guilds also marched in the procession, and were required to carry torches according to the usual custom. In 1430 great dissension arose "between the aldermen and stewards of divers crafts as to the carrying of wax lights or torches yearly heretofore in the procession of the revered feast of Corpus Christi." The town aldermen and the stewards of the crafts agreed "that every year in future on Corpus Christi day the stewards of each craft underwritten shall pass with their light in the said procession in their order in the form underwritten, and no one else of their craft with them, under the penalty below stated; but yearly in future with their aldermen shall hold, keep, and behave themselves in honourable and decent wise behind the most holy Body of Christ [the Host]." At the end of this agreement appears a list of crafts in their marching order:

Next the clergy of the Corpus Christi Gild, the Gild of the Blessed Mary, the Gild of S. John of Beverley, the Mercers, Drapers, Butchers, Bakers, Carpenters, Smiths, Tailors, Skinners, Dyers, Turners, Weavers, Shearmen, Fullers, Seamen, Shoemakers, Barbers, Glovers, Coopers, Fishers, Tilers, the Gild of S. Helen,

the Gild of Pater Noster, the Gild of S. John the Baptist, the Gild
of S. John in May, and the Gild of S. Peter of Milan.[8]

Thus the craft guilds were sandwiched between religious fraternities,
among which were the guild of the Blessed Mary and the guild of St.
Helen.

New ordinances of 1498 summarize the organization of the liturgical
procession on Corpus Christi. The twelve keepers ordered:

> that the forsayde xij for tyme beyng shall go yerly in processyon on
> corpus xpi day, or of the morne after as itt shall happyn, a fore all
> the aldermen; And euere man of the other two bynkes to go with
> thare alderman of ther occupacyon in thare clothyng belongyng to
> ther brodyrhed . . .
>
> The ordor of the processyon on corpus xpi day.
> In primis the xij Gouernors.
> Item Alderman of Merchauntes . . .[9]

The aldermen of nineteen other companies follow after the alderman of
the Merchants. The religious fraternities are not mentioned, however,
either because their presence was taken for granted, or because they
had been dropped from the procession.

The presence of the twelve keepers in the liturgical procession, along
with the aldermen and torchbearers of the crafts and, in early years, the
religious fraternities, makes it certain that pageants were not performed dramatically in this context. Indeed, all evidence points to the
conclusion that the pageants were presented in another procession later
the same day.

THE CORPUS CHRISTI PROCESSIONAL PLAY

The earliest reference to Corpus Christi pageants in Beverley
documents comes from 1377, when the governors "consented in the
Gild Hall that all tailors of Beverley should appear in person at the
making of their account of the expenses of the pageant of the play of
Corpus Christi [*pagine ludi Corporis Christi*], and on the castle and
feast on Monday in Rogation days."[10] From 1390 comes a general order
"that all craftsmen of the town of Beverley, viz. mercers and drapers
[and thirty-seven additional named guilds] have their plays and pageants [*suos ludos et pagentes*] ready henceforth on every Corpus Christi
day, in the fashion and form of the ancient custom of the town of
Beverley, to play in honour of the Body of Christ."[11] This shows that by
the end of the fourteenth century the town had a complete sequence of

processional pageants and plays. But for now we must reserve judgment
on the nature of the performances.

An agreement from the next year, 1391, is full of significant detail:

> John of Arras, hairer [came] in the Gild Hall before the twelve
> keepers of the town of Beverley, and undertook for himself and his
> fellows of the same craft to play a play [*ludere quemdam ludum*]
> called Paradise adequately, viz. every year on Corpus Christi day
> when the other craftsmen of the same town play, during the life of
> the said John Arras at his own proper cost, willing and granting
> that he will pay to the community of the town of Beverley for every
> default in the aforesaid play, 10s, Nicholas Falconer being his
> surety. And also he undertook to redeliver to the twelve keepers of
> the town, for the time being, at the end of his life all the necessaries
> in his possession belonging to the play [*ludo*] aforesaid, under
> penalty of 20s, viz. j karre, viij hespis, xviij stapiloz, ij visers, ij
> wenges angli, j firsparr, j worme, ij paria caligarum linearum
> [linen stockings], ij paria camisarum [shirts], j gladius [sword].[12]

The "karre" was probably a wheeled pageant wagon. Since no provision is made for images, and since the wings only of the angel are
mentioned, it seems likely that all the roles (except perhaps that of the
serpent) were taken by live actors. It is remarkable that at the end of
Arras's life all the items were to be returned to the keepers, rather than
to the guild of the Hairers. But the Beverley corporation remained more
closely identified with the actual production of the pageants than the
governments of most other English cities.

The very next year, in 1392, Thomas Lorymer, Robert Marshall, John
Lorymer by the Cuckstoolpit, John Lorymer over the Smith's Row, and
their fellows, incurred the displeasure of the aldermen and keepers
because they "failed in their play [*defecerunt . . . in ludo suo*] on Corpus
Christi day."[13] This is the first of a long sequence of fines imposed for
failure to mount plays according to the customary standard.

A 1411 "Order for playing the same Corpus Christi play forever"
strengthens the impression that the pageants of Beverley were not mere
dumb shows. The order notes that in years past only the lesser
commons of Beverley had mounted pageants. Now the worthier commons, "not having liveries every year like others of the other crafts of
Beverley, and not playing in other plays [*alibi non ludentibus*]," agreed
that they would "erect at their cost, maintain and cause to be played, in
honourable and becoming wise, a pageant at the feast of Corpus
Christi." They agreed that they would "have a proper pageant made,
and a proper play to be played on the same [*honestam et honorabilem*

pagendam fabricari faciant, et honestum ludum ludi in eadem]."[14]
Apparently the pageants were not merely tableaux, but were vehicles on
which plays of some sort were performed.

In 1423 the Beverley council paid a friar named Thomas Bynham for
composing the banns of the play. The occasion for the new effort may
be guessed from another entry in the same roll: the earl of Northumberland visited the town on Corpus Christi day in this year, and the keepers
treated the earl, his spouse, and his entourage to a banquet in the home
of William Thyxill, barber.[15] There is no suggestion here, however, as
there is at York, that the Corpus Christi play was performed within a
private chamber.

According to the same document, Friar Thomas's banns were
proclaimed through the town on 4 May, and again on the Friday
following Ascension Thursday, this time by the town waits on horseback. Later, just before the feast of Corpus Christi, the keepers paid
John Driby 2s for painting certain signs, beginning at North Bar, then
at other locations, and ending at "Torentem Beuerlaci." This is
precisely the stational route specified in later town ordinances for the
Corpus Christi play, and there can be little doubt that Driby's signs
marked the stations. In the event, the keepers spent 7s 6d for their
comfort as they "governed all the pageants going through the whole
town." Presumably they sat at the first station near North Bar, as they
always did in later years. In any case, they were not entirely pleased
with what they saw: they fined Roger Penykoke "because he did not
present his pageant at North Bar on the day of Corpus Christi," and
John Sutton "for impeding the play of diverse pageants in High Street
on the day of Corpus Christi."

Minute Book entries for 1449 and 1450 contain itemized assignments
of stations for the Corpus Christi play.[16] The Account Rolls for these
same years include expenditures of some 2s 6d for the keepers and
other officers, "being at North Bar, governing the pageants of the play
of Corpus Christi during the whole day." According to the roll for 1460,
the town paid for officers "sitting near North Bar to watch and govern
the pageants of Corpus Christi play," and for "j scaffolde & emptione
stuffero sue." This scaffold was probably a raised platform from which
the keepers watched the play. Since it was provided with cloth, or
"stuff," it may have looked much like the castles which the guilds
erected for Cross Monday. Indeed, in 1502 the keepers may have sat in
the Carpenters' castle. They paid the Carpenters 4d "for removing the
castle which belonged to the Carpenters, that is to say, on the day of the
play of Corpus Christi." They also paid over 30s "for themselves and

for the stewards of the crafts and for other citizens and nobles assembled with them on the day of Corpus Christi play."[17] These records may be our best evidence for the appearance of the processional stations in York, Beverley, and other places as well (see also frontispiece and fig. 3).

Either the keepers of Beverley kept an exceptionally strict watch over the pageants, or the craftsmen of Beverley were exceptionally careless in their playing, for in nearly every year for which information about the plays survives, records of fines for misconduct survive also. Many penalties were laid down in the 1450s. In 1452 Henry Couper, a weaver, was fined 6s 8d "because he did not know his play [*nesciebat ludum suum*] on Corpus Christi Day." Robert Thornskew was fined the same amount "because the players of the Carpenters' craft did not know their play [*lusores . . . nesciebant ludum suum*]." In the same year the Porters and Creelers were ordered to prepare "one pageant newly made for playing on the day of Corpus Christi next coming [*j pagendam de novo factam ad ludendum super die corporis xpi*]." In 1456 William Hoseham was threatened with a fine "because the players of the pageant of the Dyers' craft were not ready to play their pageant in the first place at the North Bar." Similarly, the Butchers were fined in 1459 because they "came late with their players [*cum lusoribus*] to North Gate for playing their pageant [*ad ludendum pagendam suam*]."[18] This series of fines will remind us that the Beverley play involved live acting on processional pageants, and that it was indeed a true-processional dramatic production of some magnitude.

Although no text of the Beverley play survives, we do know the subject matter of all the pageants. A list of crafts and the pageants they presented, entitled "Gubernacio Ludi Corporis Xpi," is inscribed at the beginning of the Great Guild Book. The list is not dated, but is probably from the early sixteenth century. The pageants in the list conform closely to the York cycle and to the Corpus Christi "proto-cycle." Leach, who has published a corrected version of the Beverley list, counts thirty-five pageants, while I count thirty-six.[19]

Pageant assignments seem to have been unusually stable in Beverley, unlike other cities where crafts changed pageants with some frequency. Thus the Smiths had their Ascension pageant in 1392, the Bakers their Maundy in 1428, the Saddlers their Creation in 1441.[20] The Barbers had their "Sent John Baptyste" as early as 1414. In this case the craft was assigned a pageant for reasons of appropriateness: the Barbers' guild was dedicated to the Virgin and to St. John the Baptist.[21] The Braziers had their Crucifixion in 1425; the Millers their Resurrection of

Fig. 3. Detail from frontispiece showing the viewing stand for a Corpus Christi procession. In Beverley a similar structure was called a "castle."

Lazarus in 1491; and the Goldsmiths their Three Kings in 1455.[22] The Cooks' play, which in 1485 was called "The Redemption of Adam and Eve, called le Coke Pageant,"[23] is the same as the "Haryinge of hell," mentioned in the late list. The Bowyers and Fletchers had their Abraham and Isaac in 1413,[24] and an ordinance dated 1411 credits a number of guilds, including Bowyers, Fletchers, and Coopers, with "Habraham and Isaak" and also with "Fleyng into Egip."[25] In the sixteenth-century list it is the Coopers who are credited with "fleynge to Egippe."

In 1493 one important change did occur. In that year the Mercers and Drapers became separate guilds, dividing their play into "Blak Herod," performed by the Mercers, and "Demyng Pylate," performed by the Drapers.[26] Thus the number of pageants may have been thirty-five rather than thirty-six prior to 1493. The only other known shift occurred around 1520, after the list was prepared. In that year the Painters rather than the Goldsmiths played "Les 3 Kyngys of Colleyn." The Tailors, however, had "Slepyng Pilate," unchanged from the list of pageants.[27]

We may be confident, therefore, that the sixteenth-century list is a relatively accurate reflection of fifteenth-century practice and that some thirty-five pageants were regularly shown in a procession mounted on the afternoon of Corpus Christi. We have also seen that as early as 1423 the pageants were shown at designated stations: in 1449 the number was seven. Assuming that thirty-five pageants were shown at each of seven stations and retaining our provisional estimate of a five-minute journey between stations, we can use our formula for the free advance mode of true-processional production to estimate the duration of the pageants. If the pageants were simply *tableaux vivants,* and if they passed the first station at the rate of one every two minutes, then the entire production would have lasted about an hour and forty minutes. If each pageant stopped before each station for a performance lasting five minutes, the production would have taken about four and a half hours. If each pageant performed for ten minutes, the production would have lasted nearly eight hours: if it began at 1:00 P.M., it would have finished about 9:00 P.M. Any increase in length beyond ten minutes, when multiplied through thirty-five plays and six additional stations, would press the 10:30 P.M. deadline very hard. Ten or twelve minutes therefore seems to be the maximum length we can conceive for the individual pageant presentations. This is the equivalent of 160 to 200 lines of verse, a composition long enough to be called a short play. A cycle of thirty-five plays of this length would total 5,600 to 7,000 lines, not as long as the York cycle, but nevertheless a substantial work.

Possibly, however, the Beverley cycle was much shorter than this. A sequence of thirty-five ten-minute pageant productions would have kept the keepers and their guests occupied at North Bar for over six hours. If the earl of Northumberland witnessed the pageants when he visited Beverley in 1423, as seems not unlikely, then the pageants must have finished in good time so that he could enjoy his banquet at the home of William Thyxill.

If the Beverley pageants were indeed brief presentations rather than plays of moderate length, they may have borne a fair resemblance to the processional pageants of York. Indeed it is difficult to overlook the fact that the York pageants are first recorded in 1376 and the Beverley pageants in 1377, and that both towns had full pageant processions and probably a complete sequence of appointed stations by the end of the fourteenth century. In both towns the pageant procession was severed from the liturgical procession in which the Host was borne. The great difference is that Beverley could accommodate her two processions on Corpus Christi with comfort through the whole of the fifteenth century, whereas at York the day's activities grew to such an extent that not only did the pageants have to be separated from the liturgical procession, but the dramatic plays also had to be separated from the pageants.

PATER NOSTER PAGEANT PLAY

Beverley, like York, also supported a Pater Noster play. This was similar in many respects to the Beverley Corpus Christi play and may shed some light on its nature. Evidence concerning the Pater Noster play is available from two years, 1441 and 1467. The entry for 1441 refers to "the play of Pater Noster, to be played the twenty-third of June." The twenty-third of June is, of course, Midsummer eve, which in 1441 occurred on a Friday, a week and a day after Corpus Christi. Specific pageant assignments are noted: "Viciouse," evidently the chief of sins, was assigned to the "Generosi," or the worthier persons of the town. The Merchants played Envy, while the other six deadly sins were assigned to other groups of craftsmen.[28]

In 1467 the Pater Noster play was performed on Sunday, the day after St. Peter ad Vincula or Lammas.[29] The play was shown at eight stations along exactly the same route as the Corpus Christi play. Eighteen crafts were signatory to the agreement for the play, and eight players [*Lusores*] were named: "Pryde; Invy; Ire; Avaryce; Sloweth; glotony; luxuria; vicious." As in 1441 the Pater Noster play included eight pageants, the seven deadly sins plus "Viciouse." But with only one player per pageant, the play must have been more declamatory than properly dramatic.

Guild assignments follow under the rubric: "Crafts and mysteries are assigned for playing the said play. All these worthies and crafts are assigned for playing the several pageants of Pater Noster as noted below." Forty-three crafts, including the "gentilmen," are named, four or more to each pageant. The gentlemen again sponsored "Viciouse," this time assisted by the Merchants, clerks, and servants ("vadletti"). An alderman was assigned to each pageant. The pageant of Viciouse had two aldermen, Roger Kelk and John Copy.

The second of these two aldermen evidently proved uncooperative, for on 7 August, five days after the production, he was fined 40s "for his rebellion in the pageant of the Merchants' craft of Beverley, against the said players [*dictis lusoribus praestanda*], and for his other rebellions."[30] It is not clear that the rebellion was against other players in the Merchants' pageant: the only other "players" mentioned in the document are the "Lusores" representing the seven deadly sins and "Viciouse."

The information available on the Pater Noster play of Beverley suggests that it was similar to the Beverley Corpus Christi play, and that both were rather unlike the lengthy dramatic plays at York. The verbal presentations at Beverley may have been even more strongly developed than the presentations in the Corpus Christi pageant procession at York. But there is no evidence that lengthy and independent dramatic cycles or plays ever developed from the Beverley processions.

The Early Demise of the Beverley Corpus Christi Play

Beverley was an extraordinarily active promoter of plays, interludes, and musical entertainments in the fifteenth and sixteenth centuries. Several plays mounted by "foreign" players have hitherto gone unnoticed. In 1445/6 the keepers gave 6d in bread and beer "to men of Riston after the proclamation of its play in the corn market," and 9d in the same commodity "to men of Cockyngham after the proclamation of its play in the common market of the town."[31] A large number of similar payments to minstrels and players, recorded in less detail, may be found in the Treasurers' Rolls for these and other years.

It is surprising, therefore, to discover that Beverley's Corpus Christi play came to a sudden end after the performance of 1520, at which the town spent 45s 6d "for expenses of the 12 Governors and other gentlemen [*generosorum*] at the time of the Corpus Christi play this year." But in the same year Richard Trollopp, alderman of the Painters, paid a penalty "because their play of *lez iij Kynges of culleyn* was badly and confusedly played, in contempt of the whole community,

before many strangers"; the Tailors' Richard Gaynstang paid a fine
"because his play of *slepyng pylate* was badly played"; and the
Drapers' William Patson paid a fine because his play was "badly
played," and also because his pageant was not covered with "decent
cloths."[32] This seems to have been a bad year for the plays. Indeed
some important change in the very nature of the Beverley Corpus
Christi play had occurred just before this. No play was mounted the
previous year, but the twelve keepers had spent 7s, "being with Sir
William Pyers, Poet, at Edmund Metcalff's house to make an agreement with him for transposing [*transposicione*] the Corpus Christi
play." To transpose can mean to translate, but here it more probably
means to adapt, to alter, or to modify. The next entry is for 3s 4d "given
to the said William Pyers for his expenses and labour in coming from
Wresill to Beverley for the alteration [*alteracione*] of the same." [33]

It is not clear what Pyers was up to, but it seems that the innovations
may have provoked general displeasure, or were an unsuccessful
attempt to rescue the plays from the antagonism of the craftsmen.
Notices concerning the Corpus Christi play are absent hereafter. It is
true that a translation of the ancient Tanners' ordinances, made about
1539, incorporated a 1494 order providing for a payment of 8d "whan
the playe of corporis xpi ys played in the sayd toune of Beverley; and
yerly whan that play ys note played, vjd."[34] But the order is conditional,
and it is unlikely that the pageants were ever ordered after 1520.
E. K. Chambers took a 1555 reference to the "common place" as signifying "common plays,"[35] but this interpretation is quite invalid. A 1547
ordinance refers to "comon place," signifying Common Hall, the place
where the civic ledger book [lyer] was kept.[36]

6
Lincoln

Many scholars have sought to identify Lincoln as the home of the orphaned N-Town cycle. These include Hardin Craig and, more recently, Kenneth Cameron and Stanley J. Kahrl.[1] Mark Eccles, however, has shown on dialectal and other grounds that the Hegge manuscript must belong to a more southerly county, most probably Norfolk.[2]

Apologists for Lincoln concede that records of guild pageants at Corpus Christi are nonexistent. They argue that the procession on St. Anne's day (26 July) was the occasion of a cycle play and that a *visus* of the Assumption displayed within the cathedral was one of many pageants in the dramatic cycle.

Historians of the Lincoln pageants have been prone to the systematic error of interpreting every record of a play, a pageant, or a *visus* as signifying true drama. Bishop Christopher Wordsworth, who had no special case to make for drama, wrote in 1898 concerning the records of Lincoln Cathedral: "from 1500 to 1531 I find paid to T. Watson (or other), porter of the close, as a reward (regard') for the clock, and for Coronation of [the image of] Mary at the feast of St. Anne, 12s."[3] Virginia Shull, who was on the hunt for drama, objected to Wordsworth's interpretation of the figure of the Virgin as an image: "[this shows] that the true nature of this ceremony escaped him."[4] A close examination of the records will show, however, that Wordsworth was probably closer to the truth: this "play" may have been a mere pageant, and Watson a fabricator rather than a producer of true drama.

LINCOLN CATHEDRAL PAGEANTS AND PLAYS, 1318–1561

Lincoln Cathedral has in its possession an extensive series of records

100

testifying to the production of numerous pageants and sights from 1318 to 1561.[5] These include a play of the Three Kings on Epiphany, a play of St. Thomas Didimus (shown in the nave) in Easter week, a "star and dove" at Pentecost, and a Salutation at Christmas. These plays were all liturgical, however, in Kolve's disciplined sense of that word: they were always performed on their proper liturgical occasions and show no tendency whatsoever to combine into a "cycle." There is some question whether all of these "plays" were even properly dramatic. Certainly the star and dove were merely spectacular. This is shown in an entry in the Account Book for 1395/6: "Item soluti J. Tetford pro reparacione cordarum & aliorum necessariorum pro columba & angelo in festo Pentecostali, ixd." Probably the dove and angel were lowered by a cord from the cathedral vault in imitation of the descent of the Holy Spirit.[6] In any case, there is no reference to spoken dialogue, even in the events which are called plays.

The Account Book for 1458 lists a new pageant along with the customary ceremonies:

> Et in regardo dato Johanni Hanson pro laboribus suis habitis circa Assencionem factam in ecclesia Cathedrali vltimo Anno, xxvjs viijd.

> Et in consimili regardo dato Stephano Bony vicario pro eius laboribus habitis circa visione facta in Choro in die Natalis domini, vjs viijd.

> Et Willelmo Muskham vicario pro eius laboribus circa columbam & vexillam in choro ac orrilogium ultima Anno, iijs iiijd.[7]

The first pageant, as we learn from subsequent accounts, is not the Ascension of Christ, but the Assumption of the Virgin, presented on St. Anne's day. The large payment is for the labor of one individual, and is not distributed among actors. A smaller sum is awarded to Stephen Bony for his work on the Christmas "vision." This word suggests a spectacle (something seen) rather than a dramatic play. Even more suggestive is the payment to William Muskham for an unnamed feast, quite certainly Pentecost. Muskham is paid for the dove and a banner in the choir, and also for work on the clock. The clock is mentioned repeatedly in subsequent entries which also concern a pageant. It is most unlikely that the clock was inspected and repaired on pageant occasions only. More probably the clock constituted part of the pageant spectacle: perhaps it was fitted out with mechanical figures. William Horman, author of *Vulgaria* (1519), seems to have been thinking of such a device when he wrote: "Of all the crafty and subtyle paiantis and pecis of warke made by mannys wyt, to go or moue by them selfe, the cloke is one of the beste.''[8] William Muskham should probably be regarded as a mechanical engineer or a tableau craftsman rather than a producer of dramatic plays.

In 1460 John Hanson was paid 13s 4d for "laboribus & diligencia sua circa assumpcionem & visus factos in ecclesia in festo sancte Anne." This confirms the connection of the Assumption with St. Anne's day, and identifies the Assumption as a *visus*. Hanson was paid each year from 1460 until 1465. In 1463 he was paid 10s, while John Bradley was paid 3s 4d for his efforts "circa le orlege." In 1460, when Hanson's wage was equal to the sum of these two payments, Hanson probably undertook both jobs. We know that Hanson was a chaplain. But the payments concerning the clock suggest that both Bradley and Hanson were responsible for work on spectacular pageants. In 1465 the location of the *visus* is specified: "in Naui ecclesie."[9]

In the Chapter Acts under the date 29 July 1469 appears a long paragraph relating an agreement among authorities of the cathedral to pay the costs and charges of John Hanson "circa visum assumpcionis beate Marie in festo Sancte Anne ultimo p[reterito] in Naui dicte ecclesie factum."[10] A similar entry from 1483, once again in the Chapter Acts, provides our earliest evidence concerning a citizens' procession on St. Anne's day:

> On Saturday, the Chapter Day, June 1483 [certain officials of the cathedral] . . . discussing the procession of St. Anne to be made by the citizens of Lincoln on St. Anne's Day next, determined that they would have the play or ceremony [*ludum siue serimonium*] of the Assumption or Coronation of the Blessed Mary repaired and got ready, and played and shown [*ludificatum & ostensum*] in the procession aforesaid, as usual in the nave of the said church.[11]

This is the "play" which has been regarded by historians of the drama as the cathedral authorities' contribution to a full dramatic cycle presented on the feast of St. Anne. But it is clear in the first place that this pageant was shown in the nave of the cathedral and that it was not actually borne in a procession. In the second place, there is much legitimate doubt whether this was a dramatic play at all. It might just as well have been a spectacular pageant capable of mechanical action. A. F. Leach, who is responsible for most of the above translation and who was on the lookout for dramatic plays, actually transcribed *serimonium* as *sermonium*, and consequently translated the word as "speech" rather than "ceremony." With this error eliminated, we have lost all warrant for necessarily inferring dramatic dialogue.

Short entries for work on the Coronation *visus* on St. Anne's day continue for many years, though the standard fee is reduced to 2s. In 1510, however, a reference to the clock appears once again, and the fee rises sharply: "Et Johanni Baron Janitori clausi ei dati in Regardo pro orilegio et Coronacione beate Marie in festo Sancte Anne et pro laboribus et expensis, xs." Here and in subsequent years the responsibility for the pageant is in the hands of the porter of the close. The Coronation and clock continued to occupy the porter's time, as in 1516: "Et soluti Johanni Barne Janitori Clausi in Regardo pro orilogio & Coronacione marie in festo sainte Anne pro laboribus & expensis cum ijs sibi concessis per Capitulum pro tempore, xijs." Thomas Watson, a new porter introduced in 1528, was also paid for both the pageant and the clock.[12] In 1537 appears an entry which concerns the clock, the king's banner, and a star: "Et soluti Thome Watson Janitori Clausuris in Regardo pro horilogio vexilla Regis et stella in Nocte Natalis domini, vjs." This is repeated every year until 1542. Expenses for the Coronation appear in 1539, 1542, and 1543.[13]

In 1488 the treasurer of the Lincoln chapter was ordered to retain the services of Robert Clarke "pro eo quod est ita ingeniosus in ostensione & lusu vocato assensionem vsitato singulis Annis in festo sancte Anne": because he is so ingenious in the show or play called the (Assumption).[14] On the basis of this document A. F. Leach has identified Robert Clarke as a playwright; by a similar argument R. S. Loomis has suggested that John Hanson was substantially responsible for the N-Town cycle (*Ludus Coventriae*) in its present form.[15]

Ingenuity, however, is not the exclusive possession of playwrights. In 1488 the word *ingenious* could imply mechanical dexterity as well as facility with language.[16] A century earlier, in 1377, a pageant was erected in Cheapside, London, for the coronation of Richard II. This pageant was in the shape of a castle: "In the top of the castle, and raised above and between its four towers, a golden angel was stationed holding in its hands a golden crown. This angel had been devised with such [mechanical] cunning [*tali ingenio factus*] that, on the King's arrival, it bent down and offered him the crown."[17] Another pageant was erected for Richard in London in 1392. This time a youth and a girl descended from a tower "without the aid of any visible steps or ladder. In their descent they were surrounded by clouds and suspended on air—by what machines I know not [*Quo tamen ingenio nescio, crede mihi*]."[18] The frequent references to the clock may suggest that the Lincoln Cathedral Assumption belonged to the same category of spectacle as these London *tableaux*.[19]

The labors of the porter of the close at different times and in different years are neatly summarized by an entry in the Chapter Acts for 1509, expressing the chapter's enthusiasm and offering a reward:

> for the work and lively diligence [*deligencia animata*] continued
> heretofore and to be continued in the future by John Barnes, in
> regard (among other things) to the dove and the clock in Pentecost
> week and the Assumption of the Blessed Mary at the feast of St.
> Anne, and similarly on Christmas day in preparing the star in the
> morning, and in the Passion week with the banner.[20]

Barnes was obviously kept busy with these ceremonies, but for us to
turn this porter of the close into a playwright is too great an apotheosis.
He was, it seems, a fabricator of pageants.

All records suggest that the liturgical elaborations sponsored by the
cathedral at Epiphany, Christmas, Pentecost, Passion week, and St.
Anne's day, were simple or mechanically sophisticated visual displays,
or at most brief dramatic ceremonies in the manner of liturgical plays.
The play of the Assumption is a particularly unqualified candidate for
a pageant in a full cycle play.

THE PROCESSION ON ST. ANNE'S DAY
Evidence from Civic Documents

The 1483 memorandum from the Chapter Acts mentions the citizens' procession on St. Anne's day but reveals nothing of its nature.
Annual entries in civic records are more helpful to our attempt to
understand this event.

St. Anne's guild of Lincoln was founded in 1344.[21] No doubt the guild
mounted a procession from the beginning. But the earliest extant
Minute Book of the Lincoln council, which begins with 8 October 1511,
makes no mention of the procession or its pageants until 27 July 1515.
On that day the council agreed "that wher[as] diuers garmentes and
other heriormentes [ornaments] is yerly boroyd in the cuntrey for the
arryeyng of the pagentes of scaynt anne gyld now the knyght[es] and
gentylmen be freyd with the plage so that the graceman can borowght
non sutch garmentes wherfore euery alderman schall prepare and
setfoorth in the seid arrey ij good gownes and euery scheryf pere a
gowne and euery chaumberlen pere a gowne and the persons with
theym to weyr the same." The council also ordered the underconstables
"to weyt vppon the arrey in pressession bouth to kepe the people from
the arrey and also to take hede of sutch as weyr garmentes in the
same."[22] This order is unlike anything in the civic orders from York,
Wakefield, or Beverley concerning the Corpus Christi play. The council
seems to be primarily concerned with supplying the procession with

costly vestments and ornaments, and with providing adequate protection for them.

St. Anne's procession involved more than a mere display of ornament, however. In 1517 Sir Robert Denyas was appointed St. Anne's priest on the condition that he should yearly "helppe to the bryngyng foorth and preparyng of the pageantes in saynt anne gyld."[23] In the next year the council ordered the underconstables to "wayt on the pageantes on scaynt anne dey by vij of the clok in the seyd procession," and also ordered every alderman to "sendfoorth a seruaunt with a tortch to be lightyd in the procession with a rochet vppon hym abowt the sacrement."[24] The "rochet" is a cloak, in the entries of 1521 and after called "an onest gowne."[25] From these entries we learn that pageants went in the procession. But it is impossible that the pageants could have been used for dramatic plays in the course of the torch-lit march.

By 1519 the festivities on St. Anne's day had become the object of full civic pride: on 18 June of that year the council "agreid that euery man and woman within this citie beyng able schall be broder and syster in scaynt anne gyld and to pay yerly iiijd man and wyf at the lest."[26] In this year also appears the first indication that the pageants were supported by the craft guilds: "Also that euery occupacion schall bryng furth ther pageantes that be longyng to scaynt anne gyld sufficiently."[27]

The plague which proved such a threat to the 1515 procession occurred again in 1521, and once more the alderman who was graceman for the guild could not "gayt sutch garmentes and other honormentes as schauld be in the pagentes of the processyon of scaynt anne day." The council therefore agreed to borrow "a gowne of my lady powes for one of the maryes and thother mary to be arayed in the cremysyng gowne of veluet that longith to the same gyld."[28] Apparently the Virgin was represented by a splendidly dressed person, perhaps by a young girl who received the appointment with honor. The crimson gown of "the other Mary" would be more appropriate to Mary Magdalene. This is the first indication that the procession included living representations of biblical figures.

On 31 December 1521 the council passed two resolutions which are of particular interest to us:

> Also it is agreid that euery alderman schall make a gowne for the kynges in the pageantes in the procession of scaynt anne day.
>
> Also it is agreid that pater noster play schalbe played this yer.[29]

Pater Noster is the first play ever mentioned in any connection with St.

Anne's procession. The connection is slight, however, amounting only to the fact that the two matters were considered on the same day.

The "kynges in the pageantes in the procession" are mentioned again in 1525, along with another group of costumed figures:

> In this present comyn concell it is agreid that thold ordynaunce ordenyd for scaynt anne gyld schall stand in effect that is to sey euery alderman a gowne of sykke for preparyng of the kynges in processyon with a man and a torch to weyt on the sacrement.

> Item euery scheryfpere to haue a man in an honest gowne to go as profyttes in the same procession vppon payn of euery alderman that feylyth to forfyth iijs iiijd and euery scheryfpere to forfyt xijd.[30]

On the analogy of the N-Town cycle, Cameron and Kahrl have claimed that the Lincoln "kings" constituted a walking Jesse tree, and that the pageants of the kings and prophets were later presented as a dramatic play.[31] This goes far beyond what may logically be made of this entry.

According to the order of 1518, the procession was to begin at 7:00 A.M. An order of 1524, which apparently concerns St. Anne's procession, completes our information on the duration of the march:

> Also it is agreid that the ordynaunce for attendance of mr maier to the mynster schall stand in effect and strynght and euery man to be redy to gyf hys attendaunce so that mr maier be at the mynster afore x of the bell.[32]

The march could have lasted no more than three hours, proof in itself that no lengthy cycle was performed en route. Nor could cycle plays be given within the cathedral close at this time. The procession was still bound to enter the cathedral to view the Assumption *visus* and the citizens would certainly not have departed from the cathedral without having heard mass. Furthermore, if the citizens witnessed the Assumption in the morning, it is unlikely that this play was part of a cycle which could only have begun in the afternoon.

In 1525 the council agreed that the crafts and guilds were to "prepare and aparell the pageantes in all preparacion exceppt plate and copz [copes]."[33] We have already noted the council's concern for the "honourments" (ornaments) of the pageants. In 1527 the parish of the church of St. John Evangelist in Wickford refused to lend its share of "stuff of dyuers churchus in this citie fore the furnychyng of the pageantes in the procession."[34] Other "honourmentes" were regularly obtained from the prior of St. Katherine's.[35] Thus the Lincoln pageants served in part for the public display of ecclesiastical treasure.

The Minute Book is silent on the matter of pageants for a dozen years after 1527. Pageants were required for St. Anne's day again on 18 July 1539.[36] On 12 November of that year the council "agreyde . . . that ther schalbe a large door mayde at the layt scowle howys that the pagentes mey be seyt in and euery pagent to pay yerly iiijd and noy schyppe xijd."[37] Noah's ship was doubtless the largest of the pageants. Since the ship evidently constituted the whole of the Noah pageant, it was probably a tableau device rather than a stage for a play. At this same meeting the council ordered that "the stuffe belongynge to sent an guyld schalbe leyd in the chapell of the bryge and the howse wher the saide stuffe lythe to be letton to the use and profyt of the comen chambre." As we are coming to see, this "stuffe" was more on the order of ecclesiastical treasure than stage properties.

An order for the following year, made on 2 June 1540, suggests that the council was determined to make a success of the procession, even though some of the craft guilds had become neglectful:

> Also yt ys agreyde that sent ane guylde schall go forwardes as yt hathe downe tymes paste and that euery alderman schall haue a gowne and a torche and euery scheryffe to fynde a gowne and euery occupacion to brynge furthe theyr pagens accordyng to the old custoume and euery occupacion that haue theyr padgeans broken to make them reddy aȝenste the same dey vppon payne of euery pagent to forfyte xxs.[38]

The procession was mounted again in several subsequent years but was suppressed by official order after the production of 1547:

> Item it is agreid that henry Sapcote alderman schall bryng Inne to the guyldhall the Inventorye of the juelles plate and ornamentes lately belongyng to the procession for Saynt Anne sight and that the same juelles plate or ornamentes schalbe sold to thuse of the comen chambre.[39]

The guild treasure also included "apperell," and we know that one item of apparel was a crimson gown of velvet for a Mary. The plate and copes, however, could not conceivably have been intended for props in a play. Probably they were displayed as a sign of the wealth and merit of St. Anne's guild. The dissolution of the guild meant that the treasure passed back into the hands of its virtual owner, the Lincoln city council.

Evidence from the Cordwainers' Accounts

The Cordwainers' guild of the Blessed Virgin Mary was founded in

1307. According to the guild returns of 1389, the guild brothers
marched with "Mary, Joseph, St. Blaise and two angels," and the
destination of the march was the monastery. This constitutes another
valuable piece of evidence demonstrating the presence of historical
figures in fourteenth-century processions. The guild also mounted a
procession with a candle on major festival occasions. The candle was
placed on the high altar of the mother church at the termination of the
procession.[40] It seems likely that among the processions so celebrated in
later years was the one on St. Anne's day.

Entries in the extant Cordwainers' Account Book, which begin in
1527, contain numerous references to the pageant of the guild.[41] The
book begins with five oaths administered annually to the officers and
members of the guild. The detail and solemnity of these oaths, four of
which contain references to the pageant, are a measure of the serious-
ness with which the guild accepted its responsibilities:

> The outhe of an outbrother or suster
> I shalbe trew brother—or suster—Vnto 'this gild and fraternite
> wiche is founded for the honore of god his moste blissed moder our
> lady saint mare saint Blaice and all the Saintes in heven. . . . I
> shalbe redy yeerly to goo in procession with the graceman brether
> and susters of this fraternite from the chappell of saint thomas of
> the hy brige in lincoln vnto the cathedrall churche of lincoln and
> ther to offer on farthyng as custom is.
>
> The outhe for on brother beyng a cordvaner
> [Nothing concerning pageants.]
>
> The outhe to be geven to the Graceman at his elleccione
> . . . and at saint anne even or day I shalbe personally at the
> dressyng and arrayng of the pageaunt of Bethelem and awaitt of
> the sam in the tym of procession of the gild of the said saint anne
> for the worshipe of this citie: and when the said procession is doune
> then I shall helpe to vnaray and vndresse the said pageant agayn.
>
> The outhe to be geven to the wardons of this gild
> . . . I shall helpe to dresse and redresse the pageauant of Bethelem
> at saint Anne tyd and to goo in procession in saint anne gild with
> master graceman from the place accustomed to the moder churche
> of lincoln and so doune agan.
>
> The outhe to be geven to the Dean of this gild
> . . . I shalbe personally at the dressyng and redressyng of the
> pageauant of Bethelem with master graceman at saint anne tyd
> and to awaitt of the sam with master graceman.[42]

The officers of the guild were thus to assist personally in the preparation of the pageant, and in its disassembly. The guild members,

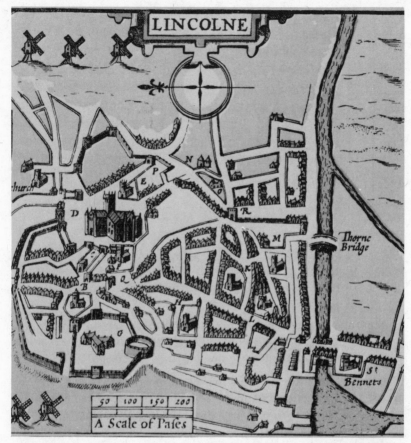

Fig. 4. Detail from Speed's map of Lincoln, 1611. Reprinted from *John Speed's England,* Part 4 (London: Phoenix House, 1953, rpt. 1954), by permission of the publisher. The minster is marked *D.* The chapel of St. Thomas was situated on the High Bridge (bottom right).

together with the officers, marched in the procession. The terminal points of the procession are specified: beginning from St. Thomas chapel on the high bridge, the procession made its way up the hill and finished at the cathedral (see fig. 4). (St. Thomas chapel is the place where "the stuffe belongynge to sent Ane guylde" was to be stored in 1539 and after.)

An inventory of guild properties, dated 1519, eight years before the routine entries were begun, follows immediately after these oaths. It begins with liturgical paraphernalia, and ends with the following items for a pageant:

The pageant of Bethelem.

Item iij[re] lynen clothes stened of damaske warkes for bethelem.

Item a great hed gildyd sett with vii beames and vii glasses for the sam and on long beame for the mouthe of the said hed.

Item iij[re] greatt stars for the sam with iij[re] glasses and a cord for the sam steris.

Item ij angelles with sencers for the sam.

Item on cage for to beir dowes in.[43]

(The last item is in a different ink, and may not belong to the original pageant.) It is impossible to explain this "great hed gildyd," these three "greatt stars for the sam," the three "glasses," or the fabricated angel if we assume that this pageant was a portable stage for a dramatic play. An account of 1527 confirms this observation and provides more information about the nature of the pageant:

Item soluti pro le pageaunt Rome de Bethelem in ecclesia fratrum carmilitiarum, iiijd.

Item soluti pro vno jantaculo facto pastoribus in processione gilde sancte ane, vjd.

Item soluti pro vna corda ad dominationem le pageaunt, jd; et le takytes, jd; et pro vno speculo, jd ob, summa iijd ob.

Item soluti pro emendacione brachij vnius angeli, jd.[44]

The pageant was stored during the year in the church of the Carmelite friars. The shepherds were presented by real persons. The pageant was "governed" by a cord, evidently the "cord for the sam steris" mentioned in the inventory. Thus the stars were probably set in motion by a mechanical device. The "speculum" here may be the same as the "glasses" of the inventory. The pageant incorporated windows as well as mirrors, as indicated by an entry in 1528: "pro faccione de handill pro le wyndows de le pageant."[45]

The Cordwainers' pageant seems to have been dominated by the "hede and the stares," which, as we shall learn, were recorded in 1554. The windows recall a device used in the 1501 celebration for Prince Arthur and Katherine of Aragon:

Therewith cam in a goodly pagent made rounde, after the fachyon of a lanterne, caste owte with many propre and goodly wyndowes fenestred with fyne lawne, wherein were more than an hundred great lights; in the which lanterne were XII goodly ladies disguysid. . . . This lantern was made of so fyn stuf, and so many lights in hit, that these ladies might perfectly appiere and be known thorugh the said lanterne.[46]

Perhaps the Lincoln pageant incorporated a version of the same spectacular device. Of course it was smaller, displayed in the daylight, and shaped like a head with three stars nearby. The glasses and mirrors may have been designed to catch and reflect the light of the sun. Curiously, nothing in the Cordwainers' records points to a Nativity scene. Perhaps the three shepherds merely walked alongside a pageant which represented the Annunciation to the Shepherds, that is, a heavenly glory with a fabricated angel swinging a censer, and with three stars in motion. The three "lynen clothes stened of damaske warkes for bethelem" fit in with this interpretation. But we are still left to wonder why the rejoicing heavens were represented by a gilded head with protruding beams. In any case this strange spectacle was no dramatic play.[47]

An entry in the Cordwainers' accounts for 1530 makes specific reference to players, but in a different context:

Item soluti pro portacione de bethlem, xd.
Item soluti coco nostro, iiijd.
Item soluti certes de players in aula nostra ad conum, iijd. . . .
Item soluti pro le pageaunt de Bethelem standante ad Whittfrerie, iiijd.[48]

The Cordwainers paid a modest sum to their cook for a banquet, and the same amount to players who evidently played *in their guildhall,* probably during the course of a guild banquet on the day of the pageant. Players are mentioned again in 1532, once more for St. Anne's day: "Item paid in expenses for the plaiers, ijd; Item paid to the plaiers aboue all that was getherd, viijd."[49] Here the amount is substantially larger than that paid in 1530. Apparently the players took up a collection of their own, and the additional sum was merely to sweeten the pot. Once again their performance was probably held in the Cordwainers' guildhall.

We should not overlook the payment "pro portacione de Bethlem." Porters are mentioned frequently in the guild records, as in 1537: "Item soluti pro pane et seruicia data portarijs dicte le pageaunt in die Sanct Anne, iiijd. . . . Item soluti pastoribus et portarijs de le pageaunt predicte, xvd (non allocatur)."[50] The shepherds and porters are the only persons paid in connection with the pageant. In fact the pageant may have been quite literally carried and may thus have been quite unlike the wheeled carts of other cities.

Revival of St. Anne's Day Procession in the Reign of Mary

The last entry in the Cordwainers' accounts which concerns their pageant before the reign of Mary is dated 1542. In some late year, perhaps 1554, the Cordwainers made a great effort to rebuild their pageant:

> layng owt for the pachgan at Saint Annes.
> Pamentes.
> Item pade to Spede the caruer for makynge of the paghan, iijs ijd.
> Item pade for nalls and drynke to the carvars, iijd.
> Item pade to Wylliam Lyttyll for panttynge ther of the hede and the stares, ijs.
> Item pade to the sheperds on Santandaye, xviijd.
> Item pade for drynge to the berers of the pagane, iijd.[51]

All details suggest that the old pageant was taken as a model. William Lyttyll was in fact the very man who painted the pageant back in 1537.[52]

The procession was set forward at least one more time. Three separate entries, including the one above, occur together in the book, which may point to three diferent revivals; it is not entirely clear which entry refers to which year:

> layngs owt for the paggane the nyxte ʒere after
> Item pad to the iij shepherdes on SantAnedaye, xviijd.
> Item pade to the berers of the paggan on Santanedaye, ijd.
> Item payde for takxe, jd.
> Item in alle, jd.
> Item for howsrowme for the paggane to Jhonsone, vjd.
> Item for dryngke to the berars of the paggane, iijd.

> Item pade in the seconde and thwrde yere of Ryne of owre Soffarand lawarde and ladye Kynge and qwyene [Philip and Mary, i.e., 1554/5] of Eyngland Fransse Iarlande napylls and so forthe
> Pamentes
> Item pade to Roberte Jonsone on Shant anes daye laste paste for the Rowme of the paggyene all the y[e]re a fore paste, iiijd.
> Item pade for berynge of the paggane of Sant anes daye last to vj felows, ijs.
> Item pade for a Corde to the strys, iiijd.
> Item pade for taks and pacthrede, ijd.
> Item pade for dryncke and brede to the berars, viijd.[53]

An important new item in this entry concerns the number of men who brought the pageant up the hill. Since this required only six "felows," and since the hill is very steep, the pageant could not have been large.

The Minute Books of the Lincoln corporation also document the revival of the procession under Mary. Students of the drama will easily recognize the 1554 entry, which has been crucial to the traditional identification of St. Anne's procession with a putative Corpus Christi processional play:

> [July 6, 1554] first it is agreid that Saynt Anne Guyld with corpus xpi play schalbe broughtfurth and playd this yere and that euery craftesman schall bryng furth ther padgeons as haith ben accustomed and all occupacions to be contributoryes in payment of ther monye towardes the same as schalbe assessed.[54]

> [June 3, 1555] Item it is agreid that saynt Anne Guyld schalbe brought furth and that mr mayor and the scheryffes last beying schall stond in suche sorte and bryng furth the same as haith ben hertofore accustomed and that sir william Smyth shall haue yerely vs of the commen chambre for his paynes that he schall taik aboute the same and also schall haue vs forgeven hym that he owith to this cytye.[55]

At the very least the 1554 entry suggests that the procession of St. Anne's guild and the Corpus Christi play were not one and the same thing. We have already noted the fortuitous connection between St. Anne's procession and the Pater Noster play in 1521. What are we to make of the apparently stronger connection between the procession and the Corpus Christi play in 1554?

DRAMATIC PLAYS AT LINCOLN

Among the Lincoln civic records is a long roll which lists mayors of Lincoln from the thirteenth century to the sixteenth. The part covering the fifteenth and early sixteenth centuries was written late in the reign of Henry VIII. It is not clear on what authority this roll was compiled, but its accuracy concerning mayors and sheriffs during the fifteenth century is impressive. Plays on various subjects are recorded on twelve occasions, beginning in 1397/8 and ending in 1473/4. A. F. Leach has published an inaccurate list of the plays. Here is a corrected version:

1397/8	Ludus de pater noster hoc anno
1410/11	Ludus pater noster
1424/5	Ludus pater noster
1441/2	Ludus Sancti Laurencii
1447/8	Ludus Sancti Susanni
1452/3	Et ludus de kyng Robert of Cesill
1454/5	Ludus de Sancto Jacobo
1455/6	Ludus de Sancta Clara

> 1456/7 Ludus de Pater noster
> 1458/9 Ludus de pater noster
> 1471/2 Ludus Corporis Christi
> 1473/4 Et ludus de Corporis Christi[56]

Pater Noster was distinctly the oldest and most popular of these plays, while Corpus Christi was the latest of all and is listed twice as against five times for Pater Noster. The Corpus Christi play is exceptional here primarily because the subjects or themes of most of the others are revealed in their titles. It is impossible to assert that the Lincoln Corpus Christi play had the same subject as the Corpus Christi plays of York and Coventry. Perhaps it did, but by analogy with a play of St. Lawrence or St. Clara, it may have been brief in comparison to the great cycles.

Pater Noster and Corpus Christi plays are also mentioned in the Account Books of Lincoln cathedral. The earliest such entry coincides with the year of the last entry in the Mayoral Roll: 1473/4. The Account Book entry is for an expense "pro Jantaculo canonicorum in festo corporis xpi," and makes no specific mention of a play.[57] But the next year's accounts make the nature of the event entirely clear. An initial entry "ludentibus lusum corporis xpi hoc anno" is crossed out, but is still fully legible. The subsequent entry remains unaltered: "Et in prandio dominorum canonicorum in festo corporis xpi videntum ludum hoc anno, xvjs ijd."[58] An essentially identical entry occurs the next year. Thus the canons convened an early meal, probably after the morning mass which followed the Corpus Christi procession, for the specific purpose of watching the Corpus Christi play. The next extant record, for 1477, completes our picture of the event: "Et in conuiuio canonicorum existentium ad videndum ludum Corporis Xpi in camera Johannis Sharpe infra clausum, xvijs iijd ob." An essentially identical entry occurs for the year 1478.[59] The account for 1479 is missing but probably contained a similar entry.[60]

Scholars in quest of an outdoor performance on pageant wagons have been aware of some of these entries but have remained blind to their apparent meaning: the Corpus Christi play of Lincoln was performed indoors, in the chamber of a prominent official. This is precisely reminiscent of what we found at York.

The Account Books of the cathedral are complete from 1480 to 1495. During this time the canons saw the Corpus Christi play three times and the Pater Noster play twice. In the last of these years they spent 54s 9d when they saw the play *cum aliis nobilibus multis:* together with

many other men of high estate.[61] The performance was clearly for a
select audience rather than for the public at large.

In the very same accounts occur payments to chaplains for the *visus*
or *ostencione* of the Coronation of the Blessed Virgin. It might be
suggested that all the plays and pageants listed in these accounts were
of the same nature and that if the Pater Noster and Corpus Christi
plays were dramatic, then the Assumption pageant must have been
dramatic also. But the fact that the various payments occur in the same
lists means little: the expenses are found under "Allocationes" or
"Curialitates," both of which cover miscellaneous items. Moreover,
payments for the Assumption are always to the individual who was
in charge, while payments for the two plays are always for a meal. In
general the pageant and the two plays alternate with one another, but
in 1482/3 and 1489/90 the Assumption and the Pater Noster play occur
in the same account.[62]

The statement of 1495 to the effect that the canons saw the play *cum
aliis nobilibus multis* explains the interest shown in the play by both
ecclesiastical and civic officials. A play performed in the hall of some
resident of the cathedral close would provide suitable entertainment at
a banquet of Lincoln worthies on Corpus Christi day. But no circumstances of production could possibly have been more unsuitable than
these for the N-Town cycle, which was clearly performed out of doors in
a large arena.[63] Since the Lincoln Corpus Christi play was not
processional, or even designed for outdoor performance, it seems likely
that the 1554 order means that the procession on St. Anne's day was
mounted as usual in the morning, while the play of Corpus Christi was
given in the afternoon, probably at a banquet for town and church
officials. But apart from 1554, the Corpus Christi play is always
connected with Corpus Christi day, never with St. Anne's day.

THE CORPUS CHRISTI PROCESSION AT LINCOLN

It might be worth asking why it was that St. Anne's day took the
place of Corpus Christi day as the occasion for the great civic
procession of Lincoln. The town of Lincoln had several guilds dedicated
to Corpus Christi. Three of these were craft guilds: the Tilers, the
Sailors, and the Tailors. The last two of these, and probably the first as
well, made annual processions to the cathedral. The non-craft Corpus
Christi guild, also called the Guild of St. Michael-on-the-hill, was a
religious fraternity. This guild was founded in 1350, six years after the
guild of St. Anne. The 1389 guild return in which this information is

recorded specifically mentions that the guild celebrated with a procession from the beginning. Before the procession began, the guild members assembled and received "garlands of one pattern." A great torch was carried in the procession, and when the marchers entered the cathedral each member offered a farthing at the high altar.[64]

Evidently the Lincoln Corpus Christi procession never became the occasion for civic ostentation as in other English cities. This distinction seems to have been reserved for St. Anne's procession. In fact, the Lincoln Corpus Christi guild was founded practically as a party of opposition against the members of the ruling ranks:

> And whereas this gild [of Corpus Christi] was founded by folks of common and middling rank, it is ordained that no one of the rank of mayor and bailiff shall become a brother of the gild, unless he is found of humble, good, and honest conversation, and is admitted by the choice and common assent of the bretheren and sisteren of the gild. And none such shall meddle in any matter, unless specially summoned; nor shall such a one take on himself any office in the gild. He shall, on his admission, be sworn before the bretheren and sisteren, to maintain and to keep the ordinances of the gild. And no one shall have any claim to office in this gild on account of the honor and dignity of his personal rank.[65]

Certainly some other guild, like St. Anne's, would more appropriately serve the will of the common council. Consequently, some other holiday, like St. Anne's day, would more logically become the occasion of civic ostentation.

Of course the procession on Corpus Christi day was partly under the governance of the church and went whether or not it had also become an officially recognized civic activity. The register of Bishop Repingdon thus contains an order from 1419 for "attendance at 'the customary procession' on Corpus Christi Day," and on the following Sunday as well.[66] Such a repeated march (on the day and on a subsequent day also) was common practice on liturgical holidays, and implies nothing concerning a Corpus Christi play.[67] We are reminded of a civic order of 1539 for a procession on the Sunday after St. Anne's day, together with a "perambulacyon the Tewysdey next after sent anedey after the olde custom and maner."[68] The Corpus Christi procession does not rise prominently to view in the century following 1419. No doubt the procession was mounted every year, but any suggestion that it rivaled St. Anne's day for the prominence of its pageants can scarcely be justified. As far as we can tell, it never had any pageants.

The original exclusiveness of Corpus Christi guild may have persisted through the fifteenth century, but this was changed in the sixteenth. We have noted that in 1521 every citizen of Lincoln was ordered to join the guild of St. Anne. A similar order was issued in 1530 concerning the Corpus Christi guild:

> Also it is agreid that euery person shalbe contributorye to the bryngyng fourthe of Corpus Xpi gild and nott to deny the payment that they shalbe sessed to pai by sutch as shalbe assigned to sesse euery crafte and other that shalhaue proffytt of the sam.[69]

Crafts are mentioned in this order not as they have obligations to sponsor pageants, but as they have "profitt" from "Corpus Xpi gild." Even without pageants, the Corpus Christi procession was likely to draw a large holiday crowd, to the benefit of many crafts.

THE STANDING PLAY OF TOBIAS

1555 marks the last year in which payments for St. Anne's day procession are recorded. Nothing is heard of the event again. On 1 March 1569 the Lincoln council agreed "that all the geares of saynt anne guyld remanyng in the seid tenement [next to St. Benedict's churchyard] shall be laid and keipt in the lower chambre in the guyldhall and the same chambre shalbe repayred and amendyd fore the same with spede."[70] But these "geares" were probably the jewels, plate, and copes, rather than stage equipment.

In the interval between 1555 and 1569, Lincoln did mount a play which is of some interest to us. On 4 March 1564 the council issued the following order:

> Item agreid that a standyng play of some storye of the bibell shall be played ij days this somer tyme and that mr mayor shall appoynt mr fulbeck [and five others] to gather what euery person wyll gyve to the same play and the seid mr fulbeckes advise counsell and aide first to be taiken for the same.[71]

An entry in the minute book for July of the same year gives an extraordinarily detailed inventory of the equipment used in the production:

> A note of the pertic[ulars of] the properties of the staige . . . played in the moneth of July anno sexto reg[ni] Regine Elizabeth etc in the tyme of the maraltye of Richard Carter which play was then played in brodgaite in the seid cyty and it was of the storye of Tobias in the old testament

first hell mouthe with a neither chap) lying at mr Mortons
Item a prison with a couveryng } house in the tenure of
Item Sara chambre) William Smart
Item a greate Idoll with a clubb
Item a tombe with a coueryng   remanyng
Item the citie of Jerusalem with towers and pynacles   in Saynt
Item the citie of Raiges with towers and pynacles   Swythunes
Item the citie of nynyvye   churche
Item the Kynges palace of nynyvye
Item old Tobyes house
Item the Isralytes house and the neighbures house
Item the Kynges palace at Laches
Item a fyrmament with a fierye clowde and a duble clowde in the
custodye of Thomas Fulbeck alderman.[72]

This production was evidently outdoors, in Broadgate. The July
performance date argues a conscious but suppressed connection with
the defunct and prohibited St. Anne's day celebration. Two years later,
according to an entry of 26 January 1566, the play was moved to
another occasion:

> Item it is agreid that the staige play of the storye of Tobye schall
> go forward and be played in Whytson holye days next and the
> commen chambre to beare iiij[l] towardes the charges therof and
> orderers of the same to be appoynted by mr mayor and his
> brethern.[73]

We have noted before that the Whitsun holidays offered a safe
temporary refuge for plays suspected of too close an association with
ancient Catholic holidays. Once again, on 24 November 1566, the play
was scheduled to be produced at this time in the church year:

> Item it is agreid that the staige play of the storye of old Tobye con-
> teyned in the old testament shalbe played at the feast of penticost
> next cummyng and that the citie shall beare towardes the charges
> therof vj[l] xiijs iiijd.[74]

If the Lincoln play of Tobias was another example of new wine in an old
bottle, then my argument that the Lincoln Corpus Christi play was an
indoor event must be revised. The few existing references to the Tobias
play allow us to reconstruct it in some detail. The many references to
the Corpus Christi play, on the contrary, are brief and cryptic. About
the only things we can learn of it for certain are that it was mounted at
least six times, that it was for an audience of nobles, and that on three
occasions out of six it was mounted at the house of John Sharp within
the cathedral close.

7
Norwich

St. Luke's Procession on Whitmonday

For the whole of this century the Corpus Christi play from Norwich, one of the largest cities in England during the late Middle Ages, has masqueraded under the title of the Norwich *Whitsun* play.[1] But it seems certain that the play was never acted at Whitsun before the reign of Elizabeth, and it is doubtful that it was staged more than once during her reign. The document primarily responsible for the confusion is a petition offered by the Norwich guild of St. Luke, dated St. Matthew's day (21 September), 1527. It reads in part as follows:

> wher of long tyme paste the said Guylde of Saynt Luke yerly till nowe hath ben vsed to be kept and holden within the citie aforeseid [Norwich] vpon the Mundaye in pentecost weke at which daye and the daye next ensuyng many and diuers disgisinges and pageauntes as well of the lieffes and marterdams of diuers and many hooly Sayntes as also many other light and feyned figures and pictures of other persones and bestes the sight of which disgisinges and pageauntes aswell yerly on the seid Mondaye in Pentecost weke in the tyme of procession than goyng aboute a grette circuite of the forsaid citie as yerly the tuysday in the same weke in (the tyme of procession) suyng of the Lord named the Lord of Misrule at Tumlond withyn the same citie hath ben and yet is sore coveted specially by the people of the countre; biforse wherof yerly at that tyme more than any other tymes in the yeer the people of the countre have vsed abundantly for to resort to the said citie . . .[2]

Reprinted in revised form from "On Recovering the Lost Norwich Corpus Christi Cycle," *Comparative Drama* 4 (1970/1): 241-52, by permission of the editors and publisher. Copyright 1971, by the Editors of *Comparative Drama*.

This document has universally been taken as a true account of the Norwich Corpus Christi play in 1527, and "of long tyme paste."³ Such an interpretation cannot be correct. The production sponsored by St. Luke's guild consisted not of scenes from sacred history but of disguisings and pageants of the lives and martyrdoms of saints; and also of fanciful figures and pictures of people and animals. On Whitmonday these went in procession through the city of Norwich. On the next day the Lord of Misrule played master of ceremonies for revels which complemented the Monday procession. These revels took place at Tombland, an open area just outside and west of the cathedral close. The occasion was unquestionably the Pentecost Tombland fair.⁴

St. Luke's guild is not named in the returns of 1389, and may not have been founded until the fifteenth century. In 1469 the guild hired out a chair (probably used as a throne) for the reception of Queen Elizabeth Woodville.⁵ St. Luke's guild was composed of six mysteries (minor crafts), and was the only craft guild commonly known by the name of its patron saint. In a 1543 schedule recorded in the Liber Albus it is called "saynt lukes Gilde viz. Pewtrers brasers belle founders plomers glasers and peynters."⁶ The crafts which made up the guild, particularly the Glaziers and Painters, were well suited to the task of preparing scenes for a pageant show.⁷

Having described in their petition of 1527 the pageants which were a traditional part of their procession, St. Luke's guild went on to claim financial impoverishment. The guild requested that other guilds of the city make a contribution to the procession, in particular, "that euery occupacion withyn the said citie maye yerly at the said procession vpon the mondaye in Pentecost weke sette forth one Pageaunt by your discrete wysdoms to be assigned and appoynted." The civic authority hearing the petition regarded it with favor: "It is by auctorities aforeseid agreed and enacted that euery occupacion within the seid citie shall yerly from thensforth fende [support] and sette forth in the (seid) procession one such pagean as shalbe assigned and appoynted by Master Maier and his brethern aldermen as more playnly appereth in a boke thereof made."⁸

The pageants to be sustained in the future by the various craft guilds are not listed as part of the petition but were recorded in some other book. Therefore we do not know precisely what was anticipated by St. Luke's guild or by the council. But we can say this: either the craft guilds were expected to take over pageants which had traditionally been presented in the Whitmonday procession; or they were expected to add new pageants to the procession. If the former, then the procession remained substantially unchanged. If, however, new pageants were to be added, then we may ask where these pageants were to come from. We may surmise that the craft guilds were required to mount their Corpus Christi pageants in the Whitmonday procession, and in fact we know that the Grocers did so in the 1530s. But this does not necessarily mean that the pageant wagons of the crafts ceased to be used for the Corpus Christi festivities, or that the Corpus Christi cycle play was moved to Whitsun. At most it means that the wagons were used twice rather than once each year in processions.

SOME SPECTACULAR PROCESSIONS IN MEDIEVAL NORWICH

Processional pageantry was virtually a way of life in medieval Norwich. Among the guild returns of 1389 occurs the testimony of the "Peltyers," founded in 1376. The Pelterers held their guild services at the cathedral. Each year on the first Sunday after SS. Peter and Paul (29 June), the guildsmen offered two "floured [flower-covered] candelys a forn seynt Willyams toumbe in the mynstre of the trinyte . . . Also a knaue chyld innocent beren a candel that day the wygth of to pound led be twyxen to gode men tokenynge of the gloryous marter."[9]

St. George Riding

The guild of St. George is also mentioned among the returns of 1389, where its foundation date is given as 1385.[10] Unlike St. Luke's guild, which was founded as a fraternity of mysteries or minor crafts, St. George's guild was a quasi-religious fellowship which attracted the most powerful citizens of the town. A dispute concerning the common council of Norwich was in fact settled in 1452 when the presiding judge ordered that the mayor was to become alderman of the guild, while all members of the common council were to join the fellowship. The agreement included the stipulation that no non-citizen could become a member "but yf he be a knyght or a squyer, or ellys notably knowen for a gentylman of byrth, or ellys that he be a person of greet worschepe." Among the members of the guild were the earl of Suffolk, the bishop of Norwich, Sir John Fastolf, and (in 1496) Sir John Paston.[11] The procession of St. George became the most visible expression of the power of this important group of men.

Pageantry is not mentioned in either the 1389 guild return or the guild's royal charter of 1417, but an early account roll of the guild, certainly earlier than 1420, lists 8d spent "For trendeles for the George," and an equal amount "For digthyng of the George." In an inventory on the reverse side of this roll are listed many processional items, including "a garnement steyned for . . . the George at the riding"; "a sword covered with velvett with gilt harneys for the

George"; various banners and pieces of armor; "Item 4 baneres tartaryn bete with gold and silver for minstrales"; and "a dragon." A new dragon was constructed in 1420/1:

> For a dragon new made, 9s 4d.
> To John Diggard for pleyng in the dragon, 4d. . . .
> For the hire of horses for the George, 2s.

Evidently St. George and his companions rode the horses. In an inventory of 1422 four sets of harness are recorded: this was reduced to three sets by 1469.[12]

The dragon was a fabricated figure with a man inside to give it motion. The famous "Snap" dragon now in the Norwich Castle museum is probably a descendant of the fifteenth-century pageant figure.[13] When Roose Steyner rebuilt the dragon in 1534/5, he charged the guild 8d "for canvas for his nekke and for a new staffe."[14] This answers precisely to the movable canvas neck of Snap, and to the pole hidden within the neck, used to make the head move about. A guild entry for 1471 describes the actions of the pageant figures: "the George shall goo [in] procession and make a conflicte with the dragon and kepe his astate bothe dayes etc."[15]

St. George's companions can be described from extant records. In an ordinance which was probably drawn up during the reign of Henry V (1413–22), but after the granting of the charter in 1417, the aldermen are ordered to "chesen her George and a man to bere his swerd and be his keruer to for him and a man to bere the baner of Seynt George and tweye men to bere the wax or do beren with honest persones and to go with hem."[16] These men are evidently the "heynsemen" or henchmen of the George, mentioned in guild records for 1469 and 1471.[17] The concern of the entries is over the henchmen's "jakettes." By 1534/5 a female character also went in procession: "Payed for rebonds for the Marget and for the Georges horse and the dragon, xd." "Georg and Margaret" are mentioned once again in 1537, and in 1543 the guild "agreed that the Georg shalhaue xs and the berer of the dragon ijs this yeer for ther feez."[18] In 1553 the Norwich assembly decided "(for divers good causes weighed and considered) there shall be neither George nor Margaret, but for pastime, the Dragon to come and shew himself as in other years."[19] The dragon's activity survived into the nineteenth century, when the procession was finally abandoned.

The "Bachery" Pageant of 1443

One of the most curious of the Norwich pageant processions might

have escaped detection entirely if it had not ended in a riot. In the year
1443 John Gladman of Norwich, a member of a fraternity called the
"Bachery guild," was accused of inciting a civic insurrection (subsequently named in his honor) and an attack on the cathedral priory.
Gladman rode to the priory "as a King with a crown and sceptre and
sword carried before him by 3 men unknown."[20] A fair copy of a legal
declaration states that the event began as a pageant in which Gladman:

> mad a disport with his neyghbours havyng his hors trappyd with
> tynefoyle and other nyse disgisyn things corouned as kyng of crist-
> messe in tokyn that all mirthis that seson xuld end with the twelue
> monthes of the yere afore hym yche moneth disguysyd after the
> seson requiryd and lenton clad in whyte and redheryngs skynnys
> and his hors trapped with oyster shell after him in tokyn that
> sadnese shuld folowe and an holy tyme and so rod in diuerse stretis
> of the cite with other peple with hym disguysyd makyng myrth and
> disportes and plays.[21]

Another document, perhaps an original draft, states that he rode "with
smale bledders puddyngs and lynks."[22] In the context, the "plays"
made by Gladman and his fellows could hardly have been dramatic:
probably they were "merry tricks."

After the ensuing insurrection was suppressed, the crown held an
inquest on the entire affair. The crown charged that the mayor and
commonalty used the Bachery guild as a cover for inciting riots. The
city replied that they kept up the fraternity, which held its assemblies in
the Chapel in the Fields, from a sense of pure devotion.[23] Whatever the
truth, the pageant of the King of Christmas may recall to our minds the
Yule and Yule's Wife of York, which was also accused of fostering
civic unrest.

Pageants on Civic Occasions

In 1469 Elizabeth Woodville, wife of Edward IV, was received into
Norwich by its citizenry. An Ipswich resident named Parnell was hired
to help prepare the royal entry pageants. At Westwyck gate a stage was
decorated with coats of arms and two giants. The pageant represented
the Annunciation and the Salutation. After witnessing this the queen
heard a boy choir directed by one "Fakke."[24] Further shows were
prevented by a great shower of rain, which so soaked the performers
that dry clothes had to be rushed to them. It is recorded that great
damage was done to costumes for patriarchs, apostles, and virgins, and
thus it is clear that the pageants were essentially biblical in subject.[25]

In 1537 Norwich mounted a great civic triumph for the birth of
Prince Edward. Most of the expenses recorded in the chamberlains'
accounts are for the firing of cannons,[26] but certain craft guilds
contributed their pageants. The Grocers' pageant "went that yere in
October at the procession for the byrthe of Prince Edward,"[27] and the
chamberlains paid a sum "to men beryng the Taillou[r]spageont vnto
the paleys [perhaps the bishop's palace at the priory]."[28] The craft
pageants might thus easily be used for occasions other than the Corpus
Christi procession.

Three years later, in 1540, "Thomas Nicholas of his gode mynde
[gave] to the commonaltie his pageant called the moremayd, the
xxiiij^{tie} daye of Maye."[29] Robert Withington has suggested that this
" 'mermaid' is, perhaps, one of the inhabitants of the Red Sea."[30] This
is patently absurd, even though Nicholas was, as Withington points out,
a Cordwainer, and thus a member of the company which sponsored the
Moses pageant in the Corpus Christi procession. Perhaps the mermaid
was one of the "light and feyned figurs" of the St. Luke's procession:
the twenty-fourth of May in 1540 fell one week after Whitmonday.

The 1540s were mercurial for the Norwich citizens. In the Chamberlains' Account for 1543/4 occur two successive references to civic
triumphs. First the assembly paid for bonfires at a triumph "made for
the victorye had at Edynburgh and litthe." At this time they paid 16d
"to the iiij waytes ⌈playeng⌉ at the crosse in the tyme of procession and
at Tombland." This is reminiscent of the procession sponsored by St.
Luke's guild, which also involved both a procession and a spectacle at
Tombland. Later, in celebration of "the opteyneng of Boleyn," the
assembly spent a similar amount in "like expences of fyres in the
market and at Tombland made in tyme of procession solemly had at
the tryumphe."[31]

In 1544 England's involvement in foreign wars intruded into the
city's affairs and brought the pageants to a halt:

> This daye [17 May] vpon many consideracions declared aswell for
> many charges leyde vpon the commonaltie (to) and for the charges
> of xl ablemen for Warres to be sent to the Kynges maiestie and
> also for the charges of the Knyghtes mete ["Payment of the
> Burgesses in Parliament"], and other vrgent causez apparant and
> for ease of pore people it is agreed that the Pageantes shalbe
> spared and left for this yeer.[32]

It is not clear from the context which pageants were meant. However,
by 17 May St. George's day was already past; and in 1546 the Grocers
paid a large sum "For charges of Corpus X^i daye etc. for 3 yeres etc."[33]

This evidently means that the Corpus Christi pageants were shown in 1544. Hence it was probably the Whitmonday pageants which were suppressed.

The fortunes of the city and of the nation changed the next year, when a civic triumph was mounted "for a pece concluded bitwen englond and fraunce." Partly by chance, partly by design, the triumph coincided with two major ecclesiastical festivals. The triumph proper, with the shooting of cannon and with two bonfires in the market place and another in Tombland, was made "on Trynytie Sondaye"; but the chamberlains also paid William Walby "for his labour Rydyng to yermouth with master mayers letter to have home our gonnes ageynst corpus X^i day." They subsequently paid Thomas Warlow "for shoteng them iiij seuerall tymes."[34] This must have been on the same day as the Corpus Christi procession and play.

In 1547 the city of Norwich mounted a triumph for the coronation of Edward VI (Sunday, 20 February). The pageants included Thomas Nicholas's mermaid:

> Item to Robert Nycholles for his horses caryeng a pageant of Kyng salamon about processyon, xijd.
> Item to iij men that toke payn aboute the forsayd pageant and to ij men that bare the moremayde, xxd; for sope, nayles, lyne, poyntes, and other thynges for the pageant, xd.
> Item for mete and drynke for iiij persons with chargis of havyng the pageant out and Inne, xiiijd.

The triumph was held at Tombland, and cannons were fired and bonfires built, as befitted a civic triumph.[35] This combination of sacred and secular pageants at Tombland under civic sponsorship corresponds closely to St. Luke's procession. Later the same year, on 12 May, the assembly "agreed that the pageantes shall not be sette forthe this yeere vpon diuers and many vrgent causes and consideracions declared for and in the same."[36] Once again this must refer to the Whitmonday procession, for in the same year the Grocers spent 3d (in conjunction with other payments for Corpus Christi) for "perfumes for the gryffyn."[37]

Again, on 11 May 1548, the assembly decided that "settyng forth pageantes this yeere" would be "differryd vpon diuers consideracions."[38] This time the decision seems to have been fully effective, for nothing more is heard of the Corpus Christi pageants until the reign of Mary. The city mounted another triumph in 1549/50, however, "for the pece concludyd Betwyxt the kynges mageste the frenche kyng and the quene of Scottes."[39]

Another spectacle of unusual scope was mounted for the installation of the mayor in 1556. This took the form of a royal entry and included a "paggeante" which was "a Skaffoolld made at Sancte Peters of howndegate Church-Styelle, rowunde like a pavillioun Richele adorned, full of targetts with a morien [Moor] on the toppe staunding naked, with a targett and a greate Darte in his haunde; within the which stood an auncyente personage who represented Tyme."[40] In 1563 the Grocers "preparyd their Paradise pageant ageynst the daye of Mr Davy his takynge of his charge of the Mayralltye," and the surveyors agreed to "furnysh the same and prepare a devyce agaynst the day."[41]

It seems, then, that Norwich was inclined to take its pageants seriously and used the guild pageants on many occasions other than Corpus Christi. In view of this propensity, it should come as no surprise to discover that in certain years the city ordered the guild pageants to go on Whitmonday as well as on Corpus Christi day.

Civic Ridings and the Wrestling Place

The ridings of Norwich officials were numerous and for the most part highly disciplined. Thus the ordinances of 1449 command:

that all and singuler craftis shall be redy aswell craftis vned with mysteris as craftis allone, in theire lyuere to go with the mair shirreves and aldermen vnto the Cathedrall chirch of the Trinite in the said Cite or to any other place and at all tymes wher as the mair will assigne and at soche hour as the mair will assigne vppon these iij festiuall dayes that is to wite halowemesseday [1 November] Cristemesseday and tweltheday and other dayes whan the mair will assigne.

The same ordinances also specify the manner in which the order of march was determined:

Also it is ordeyned and graunted to the worshipp of the said craftis that from hens forth that that crafte in which the mayr of the cite for the tyme beyng is inrolled shall ryde and walke nexte afore the mayr at the tyme of his ridyng, and at all other rydynges and walkynges to the worshipp of the said crafte durynge the tyme of hese mairalte.[42]

As Hudson notes, "the position of honour [was] the rear of the procession. . . . it is noteworthy that those [guilds] nearest the Mayor are just those from which the earlier Mayors were chosen, almost in the same chronological order in which they became entitled to that honourable privilege."[43]

Many of the ridings were annual events. Others were occasional in nature. In 1456, for example, the "Mayor, Sheriffs, Aldermen, Common Council, the 24 constables of the city and 2 masters of craft of the 24 honorable crafts" mounted a special riding "for keeping the day of the obit and commemoration of the benefactors of the Community in the College of the blessed Mary in the Fields." This riding was on 30 September.[44]

The sheriffs and aldermen of Norwich also held a "Watche in Harnes" on the feast of St. Mary Magdalene, 22 July. But though it had been mounted "all the tyme wherof the remembraunce of man is not had to the contrarye," in 1532 the assembly lamented that it had lately been discontinued. The assembly decided that the aldermen and sheriffs should "awayte vpon the seid Mayre redy at h[is] gate atte the houre of oone after the myddes of the daye of the fest of sa[ynt] Marye Magdalene and from thens to procede to the fayer aforesaid." The site is specified as a "fay[er] stede nere adioyneng to the citie callid magdalen fayre." The officials were to ride to the fair on horseback, and upon arriving they were to do "ther devocion within the chapell of Saynt Marye Magdalen ther; And after that in passyng of the tyme in the wrestlyng place atte the coste and charge of the seyd mayer. . . . And that don to retorne agen to the seyd citie accordyngly."[45]

In 1539 the assembly decided that "for asmoche as the feste of Marye Magdalen is nowe abrogate and not halowed therfor itte is nowe ordened and enacted that yerely from hensforth shalbe had the tuysday in Pentecosteweke a like wetche withyn the seid citie."[46] This order constitutes an early example of the transfer of a civic activity from a disapproved holiday to the safer Whitsun days.

Both before and after this transfer the assembly paid for a "bothe at maudelyn feyer."[47] In 1541/2 they also took responsibility for "diuers expensses about the wrastlyng place." The following year the assembly spent a great deal on the wrestling place, paying a carpenter "for vj dayes worke preparyng tymber worke," and six laborers for two days each "castyng doun an olde butte and makyng a new butte and preparyng the bankes and grounde mete for the peple." These preparations suggest that the wrestling place was a large arena intended for public displays of military skill. This interpretation fits in well with the nature of the riding, which was an annual display of armor and an opportunity for the city to assess its defensive strength. The assembly also paid a carpenter for two days "setting vp the bothe," and paid watchmen "for kepyng the bothe ij nyghts." The booth was probably an enclosure like the castles of Beverley, a temporary stand from which the civic officials watched the events. The entire wrestling place was a demountable structure: the assembly paid for the hire of eight "teltes," or tents, and they "paid to a carpenter and ij laborers for oone dayes worke takyng doun the wrestlyngplace and for caryeng the tymber Inne and oute."[48]

What makes the wrestling place of such interest to us is that that the mayor and citizens of Norwich who sat there witnessed not only displays of military prowess but fabricated pageant figures as well. In these very same accounts occur expenditures "for makyng of a Tevell [Devil]"; "paper and lyne for the same"; "sedge for strowyng"; "for newe peyntyng of the gorgyn"; "for canwas and peyntynge of ij apryns for ij giantes"; and "for iij men beryng them." The pageant figures were probably carried in the procession, and then shown in the center of this theaterlike wrestling place. The effort of "preparyng the bankes and grounde mete for the people" suggests the kind of preparation which would have been necessary for a theater-in-the-round production of the *Castle of Perseverance,* or of the N-Town cycle.[49]

THE CORPUS CHRISTI PROCESSION

The procession of Corpus Christi is mentioned in the 1389 returns of two Norwich guilds. Both guilds were associated with the Collegiate Church of St. Mary, the very "community in the College of the blessed Mary in the Fields" honored by a civic procession in 1456. The guild of the Annunciation kept two processions, one on the fourth Sunday after Easter and another on Corpus Christi. This guild had existed from "time without memory" and may have been nearly as old as the chapel itself, which was founded as part of a hospital prior to 1250. The second guild is not assigned a name in the returns. It was founded in 1278 "by the devotion of the chaplains, in honor of Corpus Christi, and to increase divine worship."[50] The foundation date coincides exactly with the year the founder of the Chapel in the Fields, John le Brun of Norwich, changed his title from Master to Dean: that is to say, when the hospital became a college.[51] We may conclude from a memorandum of 1458 that this guild was known by the name of Corpus Christi.[52] In 1557, twelve years after its disestablishment, it was referred to as "the prestes gylde."[53]

In the fifteenth century the procession on Corpus Christi day included not only religious fraternities but civic officials. In the Old Free Book occurs an order, undated but in a mid to late fifteenth-century hand, for "The procession on the feast of Corpus Christi to the Chapel in the Fields of Norwich."[54] The Chapel of the Blessed Mary in the Fields was thus itself the destination of the procession. This chapel, mentioned frequently in civic documents, served for a time as the Norwich town hall. The original Norwich guildhall was evidently little more than a toll booth. After the city had been granted a charter by Henry IV, the assembly commissioned a new and proper guildhall. Work began in 1407, and the building was virtually completed in 1453. In the meantime civic assemblies, beginning at least as early as 1402, were held in the Chapel in the Fields. In 1406 the citizens even claimed four-and-a-half acres of land belonging to the chapel. The college easily established its title to the property, but the dispute suggests that the distinction between civic property and the chapel's was not always clearly drawn. Part of the civic records were kept in the chapel and were brought to the new hall only in 1440.[55] In making their procession to the Chapel in the Fields, therefore, the mayor, aldermen, sheriffs, and craftsmen simply marched to their assembly hall; and when their new guildhall was built, they were content to maintain the old tradition.

At the head of the procession on Corpus Christi marched "the light-bearers around the body of Christ [*Corpus Xti*]." Then followed "each craft with a banner," thirty-one crafts in all. These were followed by "The procession; The Shreves clethyng [men in livery]; Maistere Shreves; The Maires clethyng; Maister Mayere; Maistere Aldermen with bokes or bedes in ther handes."[56]

"The Procession," which went between the Mercers and the sheriffs' livery, probably consisted of the twelve pageants which are listed in a later hand (ca. 1530) on the same page of the Old Free Book. These pageants include eight scenes from the Old Testament and four from the New Testament. The order of march in the Norwich Corpus Christi procession was thus much the same as in the procession of York: first the Host, accompanied by priests; then the crafts with their banners; then the pageants; and finally the civic officials. Once again it is impossible that a cycle of lengthy dramatic plays could have been presented in such a procession. Shorter presentations, however, may have been delivered in the course of the march. This is suggested by a 1534 payment by the Grocers "to sir Stephyn Prowet for makyng of a new balled."[57] This ballad may have been a short speech, perhaps along the lines of the Prolocutor's speeches in the extant Grocers' play. Music was certainly performed. On Corpus Christi day of 1546 the Grocers paid ld "to the 4 waights," and they paid similar amounts in 1547 and 1558.[58] These expenditures are comparable to payments made in 1420/1 by the St. George guild, which at that time seems to have had a hand in the celebrations of Corpus Christi: "To the minstrels for the Mayors riding and Corpus Christi with their expenses, 13s."[59]

The early sixteenth-century pageant list is written alongside the older order of march for Corpus Christi. This fact in itself suggests that the pageants were primarily associated with Corpus Christi rather than Whitsun, which is not mentioned anywhere on the relevant page of the Old Free Book. The pageant list ascribes the pageants to the various craft guilds of the town. Not only does it say nothing of St. Luke's guild, but the crafts making up St. Luke's guild are divided between "Helle Carte" and "The Birth of Crist with Shepherdes and iij Kynges of Colen." The conclusion once more is that St. Luke's guild as such had nothing to do with the Corpus Christi pageants before 1527.

John Kirkpatrick, whose early eighteenth-century transcripts of guild records have only recently been rediscovered, made the following note from the Worsted Weavers' books: "In the 21 yeare of H. 8. [1529/30] the Pagent of the Holy Ghost was made Robert Leche headman of the Craft. . . . The fellowship of the worsted weavers was anciently called the Gild of the Holy Ghost."[60] The Worsted Weavers are also assigned the pageant of "The Holy Gost" in the Old Free Book. Likewise, the Grocers, whose sponsorship of the Paradise pageant is abundantly documented in their books for 1533–70, are assigned the pageant of Paradise in the Old Free Book. These documents help to confirm the accuracy of the list of pageant assignments.

The numerous entries which Kirkpatrick transcribed from the Norwich Grocers' Book include many references to Corpus Christi, but name Whitsun only once, for the year 1537: "Item thys yere the Pageant went not at Wytsontyde, howbeyt ther went out in costes in makyng therof redy and also yt went that yere in Octobyr at the Processyon for the byrthe of Prynce Edward."[61] In any year after 1527 the pageant wagon would normally have been readied for the Whitsun procession, and so it was this year, though for some reason it was not actually used then, or at Corpus Christi. In other years the major festival day for the Grocers' pageant remained Corpus Christi. Payments on Corpus Christi for the pageant are recorded nearly every year from 1533 to 1547, and also in 1556, 1557, and 1558.

Norman Davis, who supports Harrod's claim that the pageants (and dramatic plays) were mounted on Whitmonday, argues that "Though the costs of the Pageant and of Corpus Christi Day are usually mentioned together [in the Grocers' records], this certainly does not mean that the play was performed on that day—rather the reverse."[62] Davis is right to point to ambiguities in the earlier entries: but the entry for 1557 can leave little doubt that the pageants were mounted on Corpus Christi: "Payde upon Corpus X^i daye for settyng furth the Prosession: Paid for the hyer of an Angells cote and for 2 Crowyns and hearis to bearis to beare the arms, 8d . . . for theyr brekfasts that daye, 8d." Davis argues that the expenses were incurred on Whitmonday, and that the payments were made ten days later, on Corpus Christi. But "that daye" can only refer to "Corpus Christi daye," since no other day is mentioned in the account. Moreover, pageant expenses were normally paid on the day of the pageant. The business meeting of the guild, at which outstanding accounts might be settled, was held not on Corpus Christi day, but on the following Sunday. Thus in 1547 the Grocers "Paid on Corpus X i day" for "perfumes for the gryffyn, 3d." But the annual expenses for "sir Kemp prest of the Common Halle" and for "Howse ferme of the Pageant" were paid "sonday next after Corpus X i."[63] We must conclude that Corpus Christi remained the principal occasion for the Corpus Christi pageants.

Sometime during the 1530s the destination of the procession on Corpus Christi was changed from the Chapel in the Fields to the Blackfriars' church, a large building now known as St. Andrew's Hall and used to this day for civic events.[64] Thus the new ordinances of 1543 include an "order of the procession of occupacions on Corpus X i daye from the comon hall [St. Andrew's Hall] by cutlerrowe aboute the market by holter [now Dove Street] and so directly to the seid hall."[65] The marchers simply made a circuit through the city, beginning and ending at the Common Hall.

Evidence of the Corpus Christi Dramatic Play

The earliest probable reference to dramatic plays in Norwich appears in a letter from J. Whetley to John Paston II, dated on Corpus Christi eve, 1478. In this letter Whetley compares the Lord of Suffolk to Herod in the play, remarking that "ther was never no man that playd Herrod in Corpus Crysty play better and more agreable to hys pageaunt then he dud."[66] From this we may infer that the Norwich plays were called by the name of their proper festival in the fifteenth century and were thus traditionally performed on Corpus Christi.

The Norwich dramatic plays clearly bore some significant relationship to the twelve pageants presented in the Corpus Christi procession, for the Grocers, who had the pageant called "Paradyse," are the guild which provided the play of Adam and Eve. Two versions of this play survive, and no other dramatic play is extant.[67] We can surmise from the Paston letter, however, that one of the plays included a raging Herod. This must have been "The Birth of Crist with Sheperdes and iij Kynges of Colen," sponsored by the "Dyers, Calaundrers, Gold-smythes, Goldbeters, and Sadelers, Pewtrers, Brasiers." No doubt all twelve of the pageants which went in the procession were performed dramatically in the cycle.

Kolve observes that the Norwich list of pageants includes no Passion or Doomsday, and he suggests that "if we must limit ourselves to this list, we had best recognize it as the record of a civic authority that never rose to the Corpus Christi occasion with the sustained intelligence characteristic of the six or seven other English towns whose records survive in greater detail."[68] On the one hand, however, we need not necessarily limit ourselves to this list, which refers in the first instance to processional wagons rather than to dramatic plays. The dramatic cycle may easily have included episodes not presented on the wagons. Thus the Dyers' pageant embraced many episodes, including the Nativity, the Shepherds, and the Magi. Possibly the seventeen guilds, many of them important, which sponsored "The Baptysme of Criste" produced a dramatic play which encompassed the whole life of Christ, including the Passion. If this were the case, the Norwich cycle would correspond to the structure of the N-Town cycle. More to the point, the Norwich cycle should not be dismissed as unintelligent merely because it does not conform to a hypothetical protocycle.

Itemized accounts directly testifying to the Grocers' sponsorship of a dramatic play occur only for the year 1533, when the total expenditure was something over 20s.[69] In subsequent years the payments were all lumped together in one sum. Entries or assessments approximating 20s are recorded almost every year from 1535 to 1543, and also for three years in 1546. The levy for 1536 was reduced significantly "bycause the Pageant went not forth that yere." In 1537 the charge was only 14s 4d, apparently because "the Pageant went not at Wytsontyde." The year 1546 is the last time expenses even approaching 20s were recorded and may have been the last time that the dramatic cycle was performed until the reign of Elizabeth.

New itemized pageant entries occur in 1556–58 (probably for 1555–57), but total payments remain under 10s. In 1556 the Grocers spent 3s 4d out of a total of 9s 3d "for payntynge and gyldinge the Gryffon." Gone are payments to any persons except to one angel and to bearers of banners and pennants.

These expenses for the Marian period are all associated with Corpus Christi. It seems certain therefore that the procession was not suppressed on its proper festival day until after the accession of Elizabeth. In 1559 there was "no solemnite." In 1563 the pageant went, but was "preparyd ageynst the daye of Mr. Davy his takynge of his charge of the Mayralltye." Two years later, on 13 April 1565, the Norwich assembly "agreyd that souche Pageauntes that wer wont to go in this cittie in the tyme of Whitsonholydayes shalbe sett furth by occupacions as in tymes past haue been vsyd."[70] Since the occupations were to mount the pageants, we may assume that the assembly was referring to the biblical pageants.

The B text of the Grocers' Paradise play begins with the statement that the play was "newly renuid and accordynge vnto the Skripture, begon this yere Anno 1565. Anno 7 Elizabeth." That this revised version was actually performed in 1565 is indicated by the Grocers' inventory of that year, which lists costumes for the chief characters of the play, including "a cote and hosen with a bagg and capp for dolor stayned." Dolor is one of two allegorical characters who appear only in the late version of the play.[71]

The two separate prologues of the revised B text were intended to be used for two different circumstances of production.[72] The first prologue is introduced by the rubric: "Item yt ys to be notyd that when the Grocers Pageant is played with owte eny other goenge befor yt then doth the Prolocutor say in this wise." The first prologue follows. The second prologue is introduced by these words: "Note that yf ther goeth eny other Pageants before yt the Prolocutor sayeth as is on the other syde and leaueth owte this." The second prologue follows. In the original manuscript, now lost, it evidently was written on the verso side of the leaf.

The second prologue, which fits the traditional circumstances of production, is evidently older than the first[73] and makes no mention of either Corpus Christi or Whitsun. The first prologue, which is for an independent production of the Grocers' play, may represent part of the Elizabethan revision. It is only this late prologue which makes reference to Whitsun:

> Lyke as yt chancyd, befor this season
> owte of Godes scripture reuealid in playes
> was dyvers stories sett furth by reason
> of Pageantes apparellyd in Wittson dayes.
> and lately be falen into decayes.
> which stories dependyd in theyr orders sett
> by seuerall devices much knowledge to gett.

If we trust this prologue, then at some time prior to its composition (in 1565) the plays were mounted as pageants during Whitsuntide. But they had been allowed to lapse. Now they were to be revived.

Our reconstruction of the events of the 1550s and 1560s fits in well

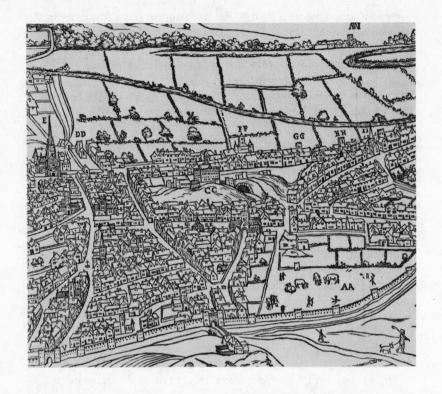

Fig. 5. Detail from map of Norwich, 1558. From William Cuningham, *The Cosmographical Glasse* (London, 1559), insert following fol. 8, courtesy of The Newberry Library, Chicago. Chapel Field is at bottom right, marked AA. Norwich Cathedral is at far left, marked E.

with all the assertions in this prologue except the statement that (dramatic) plays had formerly been mounted at Whitsuntide. Perhaps the plays had been moved to Whitsun in the early 1560s. There is no evidence for this, however. More likely the poet was distorting history: the vague phrase "in Wittson dayes," like "Whitsonholydays" of the 1565 assembly order, may merely be a Reformation euphemism for "Corpus Christi."

We may conclude that the Norwich Corpus Christi procession was regularly mounted on its proper festival day, even if the wagons were used also for the St. Luke's procession after 1527, or for civic pageants in 1537 and in 1563. The pageant vehicles, suppressed along with the cycle play after 1547, were revived during the reign of Queen Mary, only to be suppressed again at the accession of Elizabeth. The pageants and plays were revived according to reformed principles in 1565, and perhaps during one or two other years in the early 1560s. But after 1565 the entire venture fell into decay. In 1570 the Grocers' pageant wagon was sold for scrap to pay off a debt of six years' standing for rental of their pageant house.[74]

THE SITE OF THE CORPUS CHRISTI DRAMATIC CYCLE

If the Corpus Christi cycle of Norwich was not performed in a moving procession, it was probably staged at some stationary site in or near the city. The most obvious possibility is that, in the early years at least, the cycle was staged in Chapel Field. This eight-acre field, which still survives as a large public park, was an open space quite separate from the collegiate buildings. The field is clearly shown in a pictorial map of ca. 1558 (fig. 5): cows are grazing in the field, and archers are practicing with longbows. The verisimilitude of the detail is entirely confirmed by an assembly order of 1579 that Chapel Field should be used for testing and practicing with "handegonnes, harquebuzes, callivers, or suche lyke."[75] Thus plenty of space was available, and we have subsequent confirmation that the field was used for civic (military) sports. An alternative site is Tombland, the site of the Pentecost fair and the Whittuesday revels. If the dramatic plays were mounted out of doors, the pageant wagons may have been used as stages. A pageant like "Helle Carte," for example, could have been used several times during the course of the cycle.

We cannot entirely overlook the possibility that the plays were mounted indoors. We have seen that the Chapel in the Fields was frequently used as a civic assembly hall during the fifteenth century. We have also seen that in the 1530s the Corpus Christi procession, which formerly terminated at the Chapel in the Fields, now ended at the new Common Hall, formerly Blackfriars. Within this hall was a chapel of St. John, and there mass was celebrated at the end of the procession: thus in 1546 the Grocers spent 4d "on Corpus X ^{i} day for the offryng at the Common Halle." Similar expenses were recorded in 1547 and 1558.[76]

By the early 1540s Common Hall had become the usual site for dramatic plays in Norwich. In 1534/5 the chamberlains had paid 6s 8d "to the Kynges pleyers at Saynt Olaves gild."[77] This may be a reference to an indoor play in a guildhall. In 1541/2 the circumstances of a production in Common Hall were recorded in much greater detail:

> Item payd for sedge to strowe the halle ther whan the prynces players playd an enterlude ther, ijd; drinke for the players, ijd; to ij laborers that fechyd barrelles and tymbyr and made a scaffold for them, ijd.[78]

Similar items are recorded for the next year, and from the accounts of 1543/4 it is possible to learn how the stage was constructed:

> Item paid on the sonday after Twelth day to vj laborers that caryed xij long popill plankes from the comon Inne to the comon halle to make a scaffold for an Interlud to be playd ther by my lord of sussex men.[79]

Entries from 1546/7 are even more detailed, and include the name of a lost play:

> In primis gaf in reward to the qwenys players who playd an Interlud at the comon halle on the tewysday in the vj th weke after Myhelmes whose matter was the market of myscheffe, xs; of the whyche was gatherd amonges the pepyll ther, vjs iiijd; and so was payd by the accomptant, iijs viijd.
>
> Item paid for fechyng of tymbyr and makyng the scaffold at the ovyr end of the halle, ijd; . . . Item gaf in reward to Mr byrde scolemaster of the Gramer scole for his scolers playeng an Interlud in the chappell of the comon halle the sonday after Twelth Day, xs; . . . Item gaf in reward on the sonday beyng sent Jamys Evyn [24 July] to certen spanyerdes and italyans who dawnsyd antycks and played dyuerse proper bayne feetes at the Comon Halle before Mr mayer and the Cominalitie, xiijs iiijd; . . . Item to dyuers men that removyd the tabylles trustylles and fourymes and set them ageyn whan all thynges was don, iiijd.[80]

The final item in particular is reminiscent of the materials used in "hangyng" the chamber near Common Hall gates at York.

These are only samples of numerous entries showing that sums of this sort were paid out every year from 1541/2 to 1548/9.[81] For the record I add an entry from the Court Books for 1548:

> Item it is orderd that the Kynges players shall make an interlude at the hall late the Blak freres at the charges of the citie and they to haue for the same xxs of the comon goodes.[82]

In 1549/50 the king's players were given xs for not playing, "by reason of the late comocion."[83] This commotion was probably Kett's rebellion, an uprising which occurred at "the assembling of such members of people as resorted [to Wymondham, a village outside Norwich] to see that plaie, to enter further into their wicked enterprizes."[84] We do not know where the Wymondham play was performed, but we do know that even an indoor play could be the occasion of civic unrest. Evidence for indoor plays in sixteenth-century Norwich is clear. Whether the Corpus Christi plays were ever performed indoors must, however, remain unknown for lack of evidence.

8
Coventry

THE RENOWN OF THE COVENTRY CORPUS CHRISTI PLAY

The Corpus Christi play of Coventry surpassed all others in popular renown. In *The Playe Called the Foure PP* by John Heywood (a courtier associated with London rather than the provinces), the Pardoner boasts:

> Thys deuyll and I were of olde acqueyntaunce,
> For oft in the play of Corpus Cristi
> He hath played the deuyll at Couentry.[1]

In *A C Mery Talys* (*A Hundred Merry Tales*) occurs the story "Of the curat that prechyd the artycles of the Crede." It concerns a priest from a Warwickshire village who was "no gret clark nor graduat of the vnyuersyte, yet he prechyd to his paryshons vpon a sonday, declaryng to them the .xii. artycles of the Crede." The twelve articles are recited. Then the clerk "sayd to his paryshons further that these artycles ye be bounde to beleue for they be trew and of auctoryte. And yf you beleue not me, then for a more suerte and suffycyent auctoryte, go your way to couentre, and there ye shall se them all playd in corpus cristi playe."[2]

A C Mery Talys was published in 1526 by John Rastell, father-in-law of John Heywood.[3] Both works were addressed to wide audiences, and both assume an acquaintance, even if only second hand, with the Coventry dramatic cycle. Certainly both suggest that the plays must have been available to popular audiences. We have no similar allusions to the plays of York or other English cities.

The popularity of the Coventry plays is attested in a description published by William Dugdale in 1656:

138

Before the suppression of the Monasteries, this City [Coventry] was very famous for the *Pageants* that were play'd therein, upon *Corpus-Christi*-day; which occasioning very great confluence of people thither from far and near, was of no small benefit thereto; which *Pageants* being acted with mighty state and reverence by the Friers of this House, had Theaters for the severall Scenes, very large and high, placed upon wheels, and drawn to all the eminent parts of the City, for the better advantage of Spectators: And contain'd the story of the New-Testament, composed into old English Rithme, as appeareth by an antient *MS.* intituled *Ludus Corporis Christi,* or *Ludus Coventriae.*

I have been told by some old people, who in their younger years were eye-witnesses of these *Pageants* so acted, that the yearly confluence of people to see that shew was extraordinary great, and yeilded no small advantage to this City.[4]

William Dugdale was born in 1605. His study was published about eighty years after the last production of the plays, and the people he consulted as eyewitnesses were old and had not seen the plays since their youth.[5] These considerations should make us wary of accepting all that Dugdale says here as fact. We must try, insofar as possible, to check his account against other historical records.

Collections of records from medieval Coventry suffered two disasters during the past hundred years: in 1879 the Public Library of Birmingham was destroyed by fire; and on 14 and 15 November 1940, the Coventry Free Public Library was destroyed in an air raid. Few original records survive.[6] We are therefore deeply indebted to Thomas Sharp, the early nineteenth-century scholar who published hundreds of individual records concerning the Coventry Corpus Christi plays and related festivals, and to Hardin Craig, who transcribed other civic and guild records in his *Two Coventry Corpus Christi Plays.*[7]

Some parts of Dugdale's account are supported by the evidence preserved by Sharp and Craig. The Coventry plays were applauded not only by commoners, but by the nobility. Royal visits to the plays were all but habitual.[8] In 1492, for example, "the King and Queen came to Kenilworth; from thence they came to Coventry to see our plays at Corpus Christitide and gave them great commendation."[9] Kings and queens visited Corpus Christi plays and pageants in other English cities in other years, but no play was as popular with royalty as the Coventry cycle. The visit of the king (Henry VII) and queen in 1492 is recorded also in MS Harley 6388: "The King and Queen came to see the playes at the greyfriers and much commended them."[10]

In this last entry Grey Friars' Church is named as the site of the plays.

Dugdale claims that the friars themselves acted the parts. We know, however, that the plays were mounted by the guilds and acted by laymen. Dugdale may have misinterpreted a note, subsequently published by Sharp, "(not older than the *beginning* of Cha. I's reign) of Henry VIIth's visit to the City in 1492, 'to see the Plays acted by the Grey Friers.'"[11] If Dugdale saw this note, he may have taken the ambiguous preposition "by" to signify agency rather than propinquity.[12]

The play manuscript known to Dugdale was not the true Coventry cycle but the Cottonian manuscript Vespasian D. 9. viii. Nothing in this manuscript points to Coventry, but Sir Robert Cotton's librarian Richard James explained that the book was popularly called *Ludus Coventriae* or *ludus corporis Christi*, and we have suffered with this misnomer ever since.[13] The Cottonian manuscript is best called the "N-Town cycle."

The N-Town cycle contains both Old and New Testament episodes. The subject matter of the true Coventry plays, most of which have been lost, can be determined only in part, but we have no evidence that Old Testament plays were ever part of the cycle. It is curious to note that although Dugdale was wrong about the manuscript, he was apparently right about the nature of the Coventry cycle, to which he ascribed only plays of the New Testament. His eighteenth-century editor "corrected" him on this point, and printed "[Old and] New-Testament," where Dugdale had written only "New-Testament."[14]

PROCESSIONS IN MEDIEVAL COVENTRY

The Coventry Corpus Christi play probably had its origin in an earlier Corpus Christi procession. The Corpus Christi guild at Coventry, founded in 1348, was assigned the responsibility for carrying torches, banners, a cross, and a spear about the Host.[15] Records of the procession continue until at least 1554.[16] In all likelihood the procession continued into the early years of Elizabeth.

The role of the craft guilds in Coventry processions is defined by an act of the Coventry Leet from 1445, stipulating the order of march for the craft guilds. The list is entitled, "Pur le ridyng on Corpus xpi day and for watche on midsomer even."[17] The fact that the event is called a "ridyng" indicates that it was a moving procession and not an occasion for dramatic plays.

In this act the craft guilds are required to ride or march in both the Corpus Christi "ridyng" and the watch on Midsummer eve, and to maintain the same order on both days. Both processions were the occasion for certain entertainments. In 1536 the Weavers paid 2s "to the mynstrell for Corpus Christy day and myssomer nyȝght."[18] Earlier, in 1452, the Carpenters recorded an "Exspens on Corpus Xpi tyde midsomer nyȝt and seynt peter nyȝt in bred ale torcheberers to the menstrells and all other things, vs vd ob."[19] St. Peter's eve was thus the third occasion for a procession in fifteenth-century Coventry.[20] (It is not clear whether St. Peter's day here is St. Peter ad Vincula [1 August], or SS. Peter and Paul [29 June].) Each of these three processions had its own focus of interest. The Corpus Christi procession was held in honor of the Host, and was an ecclesiastical festivity joined by lay guilds. Midsummer watch was a riding of the mayor. The procession on St. Peter's eve was a riding of the sheriffs.[21]

The chief spectacle offered for the delectation of Midsummer merrymakers was a huge wicker giant and his gigantic wife.[22] The figures which the Corpus Christi guild mounted for the Corpus Christi procession, on the other hand, were distinctly religious in subject matter:

[1501] payd for a Crown of sylver and gyld for the mare [Mary] on Corpus xpi day, xliijs ixd.
[1539] Corpus Xpi euen and the day. . . .
peny bred for the appostells, vjd. . . .
beiff for the appostles, viijd.
to the marie for hir gloves and wages, ijs.
for beryng the Crosse and candelsticks the even and the day, viijd. . . .
the marie to offer, jd.
Kateryne and margaret, iiijd.
viij virgyns, viijd.
to gabriell for beryng the lilly, iiijd.
to James and Thomas of Inde, viijd.
to x other apostells, xxd.
iiij burgesses for beryng the Canape over the Sacrament, xvjd.
[1540] for makyng the lilly, iijs iiijd.
[1541] to gabryel for beryng the light, iiijd.
xij torches of wax for the apostles . . .
[1544] a new coat and a peir of hoes for Gabriell, iijs iiijd.[23]

The unusual choice of processional figures suggests that we have to do here with more or less randomly selected marching figures rather than with connected processional pageants as at York. These accounts are all from the early sixteenth century, but the distinctive character of the procession may be traced to the fifteenth century: in 1476 the Smiths paid 3d "for hors hyre to Herod," and in 1489 the same guild paid 20d "for Arroddes garment peynttyng that he went a prossasyon in."[24]

In civic and guild records after the middle of the fifteenth century a persistent distinction is maintained between the Corpus Christi pageants and the Corpus Christi procession. In an order of Leet from 1474, "Hit is ordened . . . that every crafte with-in this cite com with their pageaunts accordyng as hit haith byn of olde tyme, and to com with their processions and ridyngs also, when the byn required by the meir for the worship of this cite."[25] Similar instructions occur in a directive to the journeymen of the Smiths, dated 1498:

> Also that they wate upon the hede mayster upon Corpus Xpi daye to goo upon prossession also to wate upon the maysters and attende upon the pageaunt to the worsshipe of this cite, and the crafte in like wyse to wate upon the maisters of the crafte and so likewise to goo upon wache on myssomer ny3ght and santte peter ny3ght.[26]

In 1531 the Barbers paid the Girdlers a sum "toward ther charges of the pagyant [singular] and processions [plural],"[27] and in 1534 the Drapers recorded an ancient order that the masters shall "se the prossecyon kept on Corpus Cristy daye, the pageond and play well broughte forth with harnessyng of men and the watche kept at Mydsomer on Seynt Peters nyght with oder and good custumes usyd in old tyme."[28] The Corpus Christi liturgical procession, as we have seen, was a morning riding with costumed figures. The pageants, at least from the latter half of the fifteenth century, were a separate phenomenon, presented after the conclusion of the liturgical procession.

THE CORPUS CHRISTI PAGEANTS AND PLAYS
Pageant Vehicles

The earliest record of a pageant at Coventry appears in a document from 1392/3, where a house in Little Park Street is described as being located "inter tenementum priorum et conventus ex parte una et domum pro le pagent pannarum Coventre ex altera."[29] From this we may conclude that in 1392 the Drapers of Coventry had a pageant wagon and a pageant house. But a wagon is not necessarily a dramatic play. From 1406/7 comes a record of "one pageant-house [*uno Pagenthous*] in Hull Street occupied by the Masters of 'Whittawerescraft.'"[30] In 1414 the "pynners and nedelers" agreed "to bear the charges and reparations of 'her pagent callyd the takyng down of God fro the cros for evermore amongs hem,' and to eschew faults and mischiefs of false men of the same craft, they agree that they shall be clothed in one livery against Corpus Christi day, from year to year, and ride on that day with the mayor and bailiffs, 'all in asute in worshep of the citee.' "[31] The order permits us to date the marching of the guilds in the procession from at least 1414. Whether their pageants went in the procession is unclear; in none of the early fifteenth-century records are the pageants called plays.

Evidence for the Dramatic Production of the Corpus Christi Play

In 1441 occurs the first use of the verb, "to play": "Ordinatum est quod Robertus Eme et omnes alii qui ludunt in festo Corporis Xpisti bene et suficienter ludant, ita quod nulla impedicio fiat in aliquo ioco."[32] Perhaps this is a reference to genuine acting. Certainly it implies a procession of pageants, either mute, or presentational, or dramatic. In 1443/4 the city council informed the "cardemakers, sadelers, masons, and peyntours of the cite of Coventre" that "ther shall no man of the said iiij craftes play in no pagent on Corpus Xpi. day save onely in the pagent of his own crafte, without he have lycens of the maior that shalbe for the yer."[33] This probably refers to roles assigned for a dramatic cycle. In 1450 fines were issued to "Crystover Dale playing Jhu," and to "Hew Heyns pleynge Anne."[34] Evidence for full dramatic production of guild pageants by this year, though not unequivocal, seems beyond reasonable doubt.

By the 1450s the dramatic productions on Corpus Christi day were evidently in full bloom. This is suggested by references to players and to an "original" in a contract drawn in 1453 between the Smiths and Thomas Colclow:

> . . . Thomas Colclow skynner fro this day forth shull have the Rewle of the pajaunt unto the end of xij yers next folowing he for to find the pleyers and all that longeth therto all the seide terme save the keper of the craft shall let bring forth the pajant and find Clothys that gon abowte the pajant and find Russhes thereto and every wytson-weke who that be kepers of the crafte shall dyne with Colclow and every master ley down iiijd and Colclow shall have ȝerely for his labor, xlvjs viijd and he to bring in to the master on sonday next after corpus xpi day the originall and fech his vij nobulleȝ and Colclow must bring in at the later end of the termeȝ all the garments that longen to the pajant as good as they wer delyvered to hym.[35]

Colclow had the responsibility for paying players and for keeping their costumes, but the keepers of the craft retained financial responsibility for the pageant wagon.

The total lack of evidence for true Corpus Christi drama prior to 1440 contrasts strongly with the numerous records from the fifth and sixth decades of the fifteenth century. This cannot be attributed to a paucity of early records: the Coventry Leet Book, which contains many ordinances governing the plays from 1441 and after, also contains numerous entries from the fourteenth and early fifteenth centuries. But with the exception of the pageant notices already mentioned, it is silent about plays.

In the absence of a specific memorandum, it is difficult to trace the cycle play back to its moment of origin. But a document from 7 July 1442 suggests that some significant expansion of the festivities on Corpus Christi was occurring about that time:

> Inspeximus and Confirmation of Henry the Second's charter to the Burgesses of Coventre: with further grant by Henry VI. to the Mayor bailiffs and community of licence to hold yearly a fair for eight days, beginning on the Friday next following the Feast of Corpus Christi, as freely as they have hitherto from ancient time held a yearly fair for one day, on the morrow of the Feast of Corpus Christi.[36]

Prior to 1442 the fair was held on Friday after Corpus Christi, but in this year it was expanded to encompass the entire week after. The expansion of the fair may have been a consequence of the expansion of the procession into a cycle play; or the recent popularity of the play may have given grounds for enlarging the fair to the greater advantage of the city.

The historical relationship of the pageants to the Corpus Christi procession is partly illuminated by the guild lists of 1445 and 1449. The two lists are similar in most respects but are in inverse order. The 1445 list, for the Corpus Christi procession and Midsummer watch, begins with the "fysshers and cokes" and ends with the Drapers and Mercers.[37] The 1449 list, appearing in a document which has nothing to do with processions or plays, begins with the Mercers and Drapers, and ends with the Cooks.[38] Presumably the first list is in reverse order because in a procession the last often come first, the first, last. The Mercers and Drapers, the most venerable of the guilds, maintained their priority by bringing up the rear.

The Drapers were first in priority after the Mercers, and the last in the procession. It seems likely that the Drapers were therefore assigned the Last Judgment when the guilds marching in procession first took on their pageant episodes. Not all pageant assignments conform to the inverse order of priority, however. Certain guilds probably selected particular pageants for thematic reasons: the Shearmen presented the play of the Shepherds, the Mercers were the guild of the Assumption, and so forth.[39] But where no thematic considerations forced a displacement, marching order evidently prevailed. It is at least possible, then, that the Coventry pageants originated in the liturgical procession but were severed from the procession when they became too elaborate or too lengthy to present in that context.

If each major guild in the 1445 list contributed a pageant, the total number would have been seventeen.[40] We do not know how many plays or pageants made up the cycle. The number ten has been suggested, but is partly conjectural.[41] We do know that the Shearmen and Tailors had the Journey to Bethlehem through the Slaughter of the Innocents, while the Weavers presented the Purification and Christ with the Doctors.[42] The Smiths had a play on the Trial and Crucifixion of Christ, the Pinners and Needlers (in 1414) a pageant on the Taking of Christ from the Cross, the Cappers a play on the Harrowing of Hell through the Appearance of Christ to the Marys, and the Drapers a play of the Last Judgment. Hardin Craig argues that the Merchants must have had the Assumption.[43] From *A C Mery Talys* we may be fairly certain that the cycle contained a play on Pentecost, for this was the occasion when the apostles first recited the twelve articles of the Creed. This makes seven guilds and eight groups of plays, covering the greater part of the New Testament.

Coventry had other major guilds which may have presented pageants and plays. But we are under no compulsion to seek a total of seventeen pageants, or a sufficient number to make up a "generically complete" cycle.[44] If seventeen pageants existed in 1445, many of these may have been combined into longer pageants by the sixteenth century. This would explain the "bunching" which occurs in the two extant plays, where each pageant covers many episodes.

Stations for the Corpus Christi Play

Dugdale's claim that the wheeled pageant wagons for the plays were "drawn to all the eminent parts of the City" once led Hardin Craig to speculate that the cycle, which may have consisted of ten plays, was also performed at ten stations.[45] Craig all but renounced this theory in a later publication, however, admitting that "for the playing of these long plays all in one day ten stations seem too many."[46]

Coventry civic records make it clear that pageant vehicles were used on many different occasions, including royal entries. An investigation into the stations for these pageants will provide grounds for conjecture concerning the Corpus Christi play. In 1456, when Queen Margaret came to Coventry from the west at the feast of the Holy Cross, she saw spectacular presentations at Bablake gate; within the gate at the east end of St. John's Church; at the Conduit in Smithford Street; at the cross in Cross Cheaping; between the cross and the next conduit; and finally at the conduit in Cross Cheaping (see fig. 6). One pageant vehicle was stationed at St. John's Church, and nine more at the penultimate station.[47] (This is regarded by Craig as evidence that the cycle consisted of ten pageants.)[48]

In 1474 Edward IV, coming out of Wales, beheld spectacular presentations at a "stacion" set up "at Babulake yate"; at the "Condite" (in Smithford Street); at "Brodeyate" ("a pagiont"); at the "Crosse in the Croschepyng"; at "Croschepyng afore the Panyer" ("a pagent and iij Kyngs of Colen"); and at the "Condite in the Croschepyng."[49]

In 1498 Prince Arthur saw presentations at "Sponstrete yayte" (Bablake gate); at the "turnyng into the Crosschepyng" ("barkers paiant"); at the "Crosse in the Croschepyng"; and at the "Cundyt."[50] In 1526 "The Princess Mary came to Coventry and was presented with an 100 marks and a kercher, and [saw] the mercers pageant play being finely drest in the Cross Cheeping and lay at the Priory."[51] In 1567, for the reception of Queen Elizabeth, the Tanners' pageant stood at St. John's Church (Bablake); the Drapers' pageant at the cross (in Cross Cheaping?); the Smiths' pageant at Little Park Street End; and the Weavers' pageant at Much Park Street End.[52]

In all these cases the route of the royal entry was eastward from Bablake into Smithford Street and then further east or, more commonly, north into Cross Cheaping. A record concerning the 1460 reception of Edward IV makes no specification of place: the Smiths paid a sum "for the havyng owght of the pagent when the pryns came yn brede and ale and to Samson wythe hys iij knyghtys, and to an harper."[53] In 1510/11, apparently entering from the east, "King Henry [VIII] and the Queen came to Coventry. . . . Then were 3 pageants set forth, one at Jordan Well with 9 orders of Angells, another at Broad gate with divers beautifull damsells, another at the Cross Cheeping with a goodly stage play."[54] Broadgate station was probably along the high street at the intersection of Broadgate ("the turnyng into the Croschepyng"), where Grey Friars' Lane also meets that street. Of the three spectacles, all called "pageants," only one is designated as a "stage play."

In most of these instances the pageants were displayed as nonmimetic

Fig. 6. Detail from Samuel Bradford's survey of Coventry, 1748/9.
Reprinted from *Two Coventry Corpus Christi Plays,* ed. Hardin Craig,
EETS, e.s. 87 (London, 1902, rpt. 1957), by permission of the Early
English Text Society. St. John's Church and Bablake gate are further
west along the extension of Smithford Street.

tableaux vivants. Exceptions are noted ("another . . . with a goodly stage play"). The presentational speeches delivered in many of the pageants are extant: these are universally short, and would not have added much time to the processional royal entries.

When Queen Margaret visited Coventry in 1457 she came for the explicit purpose of seeing the Corpus Christi play:

> On Corpus Xpisti yeven at nyght then next suyng came the quene from Kelyngworth to Coventre; at which tyme she wold not be met, but came prively to se the play there on the morowe; and she sygh then alle the pagentes pleyde save domes-day, which myght not be pleyde for lak of day. And she was loged at Richard Wodes the grocer, where Ric. Sharp some-tyme dwelled; and there all the pleys were furst pleyde.[55]

Richard Woods's house was on Earl Street at Little Park Street End.[56]

It could not have been normal practice to forgo Doomsday at the first station, or indeed at any of the stations where the play was performed. Even if the presence of the queen was itself the cause of the delay, this record confirms our belief that the cycle was long even at a single station and that the cycle could not therefore have been played at many stations. Indeed, if the two extant plays are fairly representative of the putative ten original plays, a full true-processional production at ten stations would have taken nearly twenty-four hours.[57]

The 1457 document is almost certainly a description of a true-processional production. We are compelled therefore to ask at how many stations the cycle was performed. A record from 1453 offers evidence of a general nature:

> Also it is ordenyd that the jorneymen of the seyd crafte [the Weavers] schall haue yerely vjs viijd and for that they schall have owte the paggent and on Corpus Christi day to dryve it from place to place ther as it schal be pleyd and then for to brynge it ageyn into the paggent howse without ony hurte nyther defawte and they for to put the master to no more coste.[58]

Specific information concerning time and place is lacking here. Indeed, though this is probably an account of a true-processional event, the wording is similar to an order governing the conduct of the non-dramatic Chester Midsummer Show.[59]

Several items from the craft accounts confirm the true-processional character of the Coventry cycle play, without at the same time suggesting a limit to the number of stations. Thus from 1494 comes an entry: "Item in expences on the pleares for makyng them to drynke and hete at every reste, xijd."[60] In 1553 John Careless, according to Foxe, was "let out [of prison] to play in the pageant about the city."[61] And in 1557 the Drapers "payd to the plears when the fyrste paggen was pleyd to drynke, ijs."[62]

Many records suggest a limit of two stations. In 1567 the Cappers paid a sum "to the players at the second stage." An identical entry occurs in 1568 and 1571.[63] No third stage is ever mentioned. In 1535 the Weavers "spend between the plays, vjd."[64] An undated record of the Cappers reads: "Drink to the players between the play times, 13d," and "Paid Pilate, the Bishops and Knights, to drink between the 'stages,' 9d." Similar Cappers' entries come from 1562 and 1565: "Item payde to the players betwene the stages, viijd" and (undated) "Paid for drynking for the playars betwen the play tymes, xiiijd."[65] The use of the definite article in most of these entries suggests two stations or stages, and not more.

A final piece of evidence comes from the Drapers' records, in the years 1556 and 1558. In 1556 the Drapers paid 2s "to Crowe for makyng of iij worldys," and in 1558 they "payd for iij worldys" and "payd for settyng the world of fyer."[66] If each performance of the Drapers' play required the destruction of a world, there could be no more than three full mimetic performances in a year.[67]

In 1457 the plays were given first before the queen at Little Park Street End. Another acting place, as we have already seen, may have been the Grey Friars' Church. The performance here was probably exceptional, however, for this church is located at a distance from the traditional processional route through Coventry. Grey Friars' Lane, on the other hand, which intersects High Street, would have been quite suitable as a station for a procession: this is "the turnyng into the Crosschepyng."

A fourth possible station lay still further west along the high street. In 1486 "The King [Henry VII] came to Coventry to see our plays, and lodged at Rob. Onely's house in Smithford Street before the conduit."[68] This conduit lies about as far beyond Grey Friars' Lane as that street lies from Little Park Street End. It is not stated, however, that the king saw the plays at this place.

These four are the only stations which can be inferred from the records concerning the Corpus Christi plays. It is certainly true, however, that Coventry had many other places which might have served: for example, any of the stations named for the royal entries. Some of these lie along the east-west high street, and some correspond to those mentioned in connection with the cycle. Not all of the four which may have been used for the play were necessarily used in any given year: the performance of the plays before the house of a private individual may have been exceptional, determined by the convenience of the king or queen and for the honor of the host. The plays, then, were probably given at two stations along the east-west high street (Much Park Street End and Little Park Street End), and perhaps at a third station farther west, or north in Cross Cheaping. If the first station was Little Park Street End, as in 1457, then the dramatic pageants may have followed the stational route of Henry VIII in 1510/11: Jordan Well (intersects with Little Park Street); Broadgate (at the intersection with High Street and Grey Friars' Lane); and the cross in Cross Cheaping. Even three stations may seem too many, however: each additional station would have added about an hour and a quarter to the total length of the production.[69]

Gosford Street, the east end of the high street, is mentioned several times in the records, but only as an assembly area for the pageants. An order of Leet from 1460 declares that "every craft that hath a pagant to pley in, that the pagant be made redy and brought furth to pley."[70] In 1450 the Smiths spent 5d "to bryng the pagent in to Gosford-stret."[71] An almost identical entry occurs in 1462 and another in 1471.[72] In 1494 the city council "ordeyned . . . at the request of the inhabitaunts dwellyng in Gosseford strete, that the pageants yerely frohensfurth be sette and stande at the place there of olde tyme used lymyt and appoynted."[73] An earlier practice, now to be restored, was apparently disrupted by the severe disputes which strained good fellowship among the guilds in the 1490s.[74] There is no evidence that plays were ever performed in Gosford Street, only that the pageants should be "sette and stande" there. In 1480 the Smiths paid for "havyng furth the pagent on the Wedonsday,"[75] no doubt to be parked in Gosford Street in preparation for the production the next day.

CIVIC PLAYS IN THE REIGN OF ELIZABETH

The pageant vehicles quite certainly antedated the Corpus Christi drama at Coventry. They also survived it and were adapted for secular plays performed on Coventry's other major summer festivals. Thus on 19 May 1591:

It is agreed by the whole consent of this house that the destruction of Jerusalem, the Conquest of the Danes, or the historie of K[ing] E[dward] the X., at the request of the Comons of this Cittie shalbe plaied on the pagens on Midsomer daye and St. Peters daye next in this Cittie and non other playes. And that all the mey poles that nowe are standing in this Cittie shalbe taken downe before whit-sonday next and non hereafter to be sett up in this Cittie.[76]

The Destruction of Jerusalem, written in 1584, replaced the Corpus

Christi cycle and simulated some of its production methods.[77] The Conquest of the Danes, apparently also known as the History of King Edward X, was a "Hox-Tuesday" pageant-play that had been shown before Queen Elizabeth at Kenilworth in 1575.[78] (Hock Tuesday is the second Tuesday after Easter.)

Coventry, like many other English cities, moved its major annual theatrical event from Corpus Christi to the more secular holidays in order to escape Reformation censure. The Conquest of the Danes, while it roused the ire of Protestant preachers, had received Elizabeth's tacit approval, and the Destruction of Jerusalem, commissioned in 1584, was no doubt consciously designed to skirt the controversies aroused by the suppressed Corpus Christi play.[79] These two plays were a new phenomenon for Midsummer and St. Peter's days. Midsummer, it is true, had long known processional figures. But neither of these festivals had ever before witnessed dramatic plays.

WHEELED PAGEANTS AND THE CORPUS CHRISTI CYCLE TEXT

Records of wheeled pageants for the Destruction of Jerusalem are abundant, and Glynne Wickham has found evidence that special scaffolds were used to supplement the acting area provided by the pageant wagons proper. Wickham argues that a "pageant" is a wagon with scenery, while a "scaffold" is an identical wagon with no scenery. He suggests that the empty scaffold was drawn up alongside the pageant, constituting a portable forestage.[80]

Wickham is, I think, correct in a general sense but wrong about details. In the first place, two or more scaffolds seem to have accompanied some individual pageants.[81] More important, the scaffolds must have been quite unlike the pageant wagons proper. A conventional medieval wagon had a bed which was narrower than its wheelbase. Placed side by side, the beds of two wagons would be separated by the wheels protruding from each wagon. For the platform to be wider than the wheelbase, a superstructure would first have to be built upon the wagon bed or wagon frame, sufficiently high to clear the top of the wheels. Then a platform could be built of any convenient width. Such a pageant would be top-heavy, however, and would be particularly liable to tipping during a turn. To build a "house" upon this elevated superstructure would be to court disaster.

Some late sixteenth-century pageants may have been built in this manner,[82] but it is difficult to believe that guilds would have stood the expense of two or more additional wagons, similar to the pageant in design but empty and suitable to no other use. In fact, the Coventry "scaffolds" were probably on the order of large pushcarts with two large wheels and one or two "trundyl" or caster wheels.[83] These could have supplied either empty playing spaces or additional *loca* (stage houses) according to need. The scaffolds were certainly smaller than the pageant wagons they were intended to supplement, as indicated by their more primitive undercarriage.

The use of these scaffold-pageant complexes can be inferred from the surviving texts of the Coventry plays.[84] Much of the action in the cycle plays apparently took place on the street level. Not only did Herod rage "in the pagond and in the strete also," but the shepherds went "forthe of the place," and "the iij kyngis speykyth in the strete." The Magi enter and depart on horseback, and Herod, having commanded his men to "Saddull my palfrey," tears out after them at the end of the play.

In the Weavers' pageant Simeon and his clerks "gothe *vp* to the tempull." (Italics here and in the following quotations are mine.) When Simeon and Anna go forth to meet the Holy Family, they descend to street level: "Here the cum *downe* with pressession to mete them." But the pageant itself also has two levels. After Simeon gives the Child his blessing, "There Mare and Josoff departis *owt of the upper parte of the pagand.*" This is probably not a two-storied stage, but a normal pageant with an adjoining area only slightly lower: the Holy Family first "all goo *vp* to the auter," and then "*There the goo done into the for pagond* and Iesus steylyth awey." The pageant is evidently the primary stage vehicle, decorated as a church with an altar, while the "for pagond" is a special scaffold stage, drawn up alongside the main pageant, and perhaps lower by a step.

Leaving Jesus behind in the temple, Joseph and Mary go "whomwarde" to another platform or scaffold. Once at home, they realize that their son is missing, and Joseph suggests that they "serche well yondur sytte." Having decided to go "Bake agane," "Here Mare and Josoff *goth downe* into the tempull-warde," that is to say, down from the raised platform which represents their home. Their journey is covered by the long debate between Christ and the Doctors. Finally arriving before the temple, Mary exclaims: "See, husebond, where he syttyth *aloft* / Amonge yondur masturs soo moche off myght."

Coventry's Corpus Christi plays, the most famous in all England, were also, on the evidence presented here, relatively complex in their technique of production. Each play required a main pageant vehicle, a forepageant scaffold, and perhaps other scaffolds for distant *loca.* Each play, moreover, was staged at each of several stations along the principal streets of the city. The various pageants and scaffolds had to be moved from station to station with a minimum of fuss or loss of time. In sum, Coventry adopted the technique of true-processional production, but the number of stations was limited to two or three.

9
Chester

THE CORPUS CHRISTI PROCESSION, PAGEANT,
AND PLAY IN THE FIFTEENTH CENTURY

According to late sixteenth-century Chester antiquarians, the Chester "whitson playes" were "first made" about 1327.[1] F. M. Salter, however, has shown that this dating is not reliable, and that related claims for Randle Higden as the author of the Chester cycle, or for mayor John Arnway as its first champion, are equally untenable.[2] But Salter's claim that the plays were founded about 1375 by Sir Henry Francis is also based on fragile evidence and is open to doubt.[3]

The Chester antiquarians probably had some basis for their conjecture: perhaps they mistook an early reference to the Corpus Christi procession as signifying the cycle plays. By 1399 the city craftsmen marched in the Corpus Christi procession with their torches. This date is recorded because the procession gave rise to a horrifying fracas between the masters and journeymen of the Weavers and Fullers. The battle took place in front of St. Peter's church at the intersection of the four major streets of the city.[4] This was also the site of the Pentice, the civic offices where the mayor usually sat to watch the processions.[5]

By the year 1422 the Chester crafts also mounted pageants and plays on Corpus Christi day. The evidence is contained in an agreement, now in the hands of the Coopers' guild, which mentions both pageants and the "originale."[6] It is certain that the pageants and play were always mounted on Corpus Christi at least until near the end of the fifteenth century. In 1430 the Weavers, Walkers, Chaloners, and Shearmen agreed to pay the "expenses del lumeir de nostre dame sainte marie & de corpus xpi & al Iwe [Jeu] de Corpus xpi"; in 1462 the Bakers sponsored a "play and light on Corpus Christi"; in 1468 the Coopers agreed "to pay for the sustenacion and fortheraunce of the light of Corpus xpi; And other charges that shall to the playe of Corpus xpi"; and in 1471 the Saddlers were responsible for a "pagine luminis et ludi corporis xpi."[7]

An entry in the Mayor's Book, dated 1475, records an agreement between the Bowyers and Fletchers and the Coopers "for beryng and goyng in procession with thair lightes on the said day." The mayor ordered that the Coopers were to "bere thair lightes yerely iij lightez on that on side the pauement and iij on that other from seint marie kirke vpon the hill of the cety aforesaid vnto the colage of Seint Johns next before the lightes of the saides fletchers and bowers."[8] As at Norwich, therefore, the procession bore lights (and the Host) to a collegiate establishment on the outskirts of the city (St. Johns was situated outside the walls not far from Eastgate—see fig. 7). But the lengthy plays of the Chester cycle as we know it could not conceivably have been mounted in the course of this liturgical procession. They must therefore have been given after the conclusion of the mass celebrated at St. John's church.

Since city and craft records are silent on the matter of early play performances, we are forced to turn to the difficult and doubtful evidence of the Early Banns. These banns are almost certainly fifteenth-century in origin but were revised to an undeterminable extent to fit new circumstances in the sixteenth century.[9] The "unrevised" stanzas devoted to individual pageants sometimes indicate that an action of some scope was to be performed on the pageants. These may have been brief presentations, but they may also have been episodes in a true-processional play.[10]

In 1471, as we have seen, the Bakers had a pageant, light, and play on Corpus Christi. But fifty years later, in 1521, the Smiths, Founderers, and Pewterers entered into an agreement "to berre and drawe to whitson playe and Corpus xpi light."[11] Corpus Christi light is of course the ecclesiastical procession still celebrated on its proper liturgical day. The play, however, had now been moved to Whitsun, where it remained through the penultimate performance of 1572.

The pre-Reformation removal of the plays from Corpus Christi to Whitsun is unique to Chester and is not explained by surviving documents. It is possible that Chester ran into the same difficulties as York and that to provide more time for both the procession and the cycle play the city council shifted the play from one festival time to another. An alternative explanation is suggested by a close examination of the calendar. According to a credible antiquarian tradition, the

Chester Midsummer watch was inaugurated in 1497 or 1498.[12] At the turn of the century, therefore, Chester evidently had both a Corpus Christi play and a Midsummer watch. On rare occasions these two festivals coincide. They did so once between 1471 and 1521, in the year 1519. In anticipation of this coincidence of major festivals, the Chester council may have advanced the plays to Whitsuntide, the beginning of the previous week. Such a move would insure that the plays would never interfere with the activities of the Midsummer watch. In 1523 the Cappers complained that they had recently been "onerated" with a play which they were unable to support.[13] Their complaint suggests a recent change in play assignments, and is consistent with the suggestion that 1519 was the year the shift occurred.

THE CORPUS CHRISTI PROCESSION AFTER 1521

Though the Corpus Christi procession and the craft pageant and play were substantially independent of one another after 1521, they are both announced in the Early Banns. The account of the Corpus Christi procession is particularly intriguing:

> Also maister Maire of this Citie
> with all his bretheryn accordingly
> A Solempne procession ordent hath he
> to be done to the best
> Appon the day of corpus xpi
> The blessed sacrament caried shalbe
> And A play sett forth by the clergye
> In honor of the fest
> Many torches there may you see
> Marchaunty and craftys of this Citie
> By order passing in theire degree
> A goodly sight that day
> They came from saynt maries on the hill
> the churche of saynt Iohns vntill
> And there the sacrament leve they will
> The sauth as I you say.[14]

As usual, the Corpus Christi procession was partly under the jurisdiction of the mayor and civic officials. The Host was borne in the procession, and the various crafts carried torches. The route, from St. Mary's on the Hill to St. John's, was the same as in the fifteenth century.

An unusual element of this procession was the play set forth by the clergy. The play is mentioned a second time in the same register: "On corpus xpi day the collegis and prestys bryng forth A play at the

Fig. 7. Detail from map of Chester, originally drawn ca. 1577. From
Georg Braun and Francis Hohenberg, *Civitates Orbis Terrarum*
(Cologne, 1612–17), 3, following fol. 3, courtesy of The Newberry
Library, Chicago.

Assentement of the Maire."[15] This clerical "play" may have been a
pageant presented to the mayor during the procession, or a dramatic
performance offered in advance of the procession or after it was over.
Since the verses in the banns which concern the play are sandwiched
between others which concern the procession, it seems more likely that
the play was a pageant-like part of the march.

The Chester Corpus Christi procession continued, perhaps with an
occasional lapse, through the reign of Mary. During these last years the
Smiths still paid "on Corpus Christi day for caringe lights, vjd; to
seuerall mynstrell[s] [blank]; to William luter minstrell and Randle
Crane [another minstrel], xd."[16]

THE WHITSUN PAGEANTS AND CYCLE PLAYS AFTER 1521

The sixteenth-century cycle plays of Chester were unusual among
plays of their kind in being presented over a span of three successive
days. The cycle may have expanded between 1471 and 1521, and the
expansion may have been either a cause or a consequence of the
removal of the plays from the cramped circumstances of Corpus Christi
day to the wider vistas of Whitweek.

The Early Banns (as revised) suggest that the Chester cycle plays were
mounted in the true-processional manner for some part of the sixteenth
century.[17] The Late Banns advertise a true-processional play even more
explicitly.[18] In addition we have David Rogers's late and well-known
account of how the pageants were mounted:

> And they first beganne at the Abbay gates and when the
> firste pagiente was played at the Abbaye gates then it was
> wheeled from thence to the pentice at the highe crosse be-
> fore the mayor, and before yt was donne the seconde came,
> and the firste wente into the watergate streete and from thence
> vnto the Bridgestreete, and soe all one after an other tell all
> the pagiantes weare played appoynted for the firste daye,
> and so likewise for the seconde and the thirde daye: . . . And when
> they had done with one cariage in one place they wheeled the same
> from one streete to an other, first from the Abbaye gate to the
> pentise then to the watergate street, then to the bridge streete
> throughe the lanes and so to the ⌐lanes⌐ estgate streete. And thus
> they came from one streete to an other keapeinge a direct order in
> euery streete, for before the first cariage was gone the seconde
> came, and so the thirde, and so orderly till the laste was done all in
> order without any stayeinge in any place, for worde beinge
> broughte how euery place was neere done they came and made no
> place to tarye tell the last was played.[19]

This account cannot be an entirely accurate picture of a true-processional production of the Chester cycle, for the irregularity in length among the various plays would have required considerable "stayeinge" on the part of the individual pageant wagons. On the other hand, the use of couriers is consistent with a form of modified free advances.

THE SITE OF THE WHITSUN PLAYS
DURING THE EARLY REIGN OF ELIZABETH

Chester, like its distant neighbor Coventry, seems to have mounted its cycle plays for some length of time on pageant wagons. In Chester this practice prevailed in the first half of the sixteenth century, and probably earlier. In the 1560s the pageant wagons continued to be shown in the streets, but the dramatic plays were given indoors. An entry in the Chester Mayor's Book, dated 5 June 1568, twelve days before Whitsun, bears witness:

Memorandum that whereas varyaunce presently dependeth betwene John whitmore esquier vpon thon partie and Anne webster wedow tenaunt to Georg Ireland esquier vpon thother partie for and concerning the claime right and title of a mansyon rowme or place for the whydson plaies in the Brudg gate strete within the Cyty of Chester which varyaunce hath ben here wayed and considered by Richard dutton esquier maior of the cyty of chester (and William gerrard esquer recorder of the said cyty) by whom it is now ordered that forasmuche as the said mistres webster and other the tenantes of the said Mr Ireland have had their places and mansyons in the said place now in varyaunce in quiet sort for ij tymes past whan the said plaies were plaied, That the said Anne webster in quiet sort for this presente tyme of whydsontide during all the tyme of the said plaies shall enioy and haue her mansyon place and the said place and Rome now in varyaunce. Provided alwaies that the having of the (said) possessyon of the said Rowme place or mansyon shall not be hurtfull nor preiudice to nether of the said parties in whom the right of the said premisses is or hereafter shalbe found or proved to be; And also yt was then further ordered by the said maior that after the feast of pentecost next coming at some convenient tyme and [sic] Indifferent enquest shalbe charged and sworne for the triall of the right of the said Rowme or place now in varyaunce; And that in case yt be found by such enquest that the said Mr whytmore hath a (better) right to the said premisses than the said Mr Ioreland and his tenantes: yt is ordered that then the said Mistress webster shall content and pay vnto the said Mr whytmore so much money for the

said Rowme and place as hath ben accustomed for this one yere to
be payed (heretofore) within the said cyty of chester.
                              (Signed) Richard Dutton
                                      William Gerrard[20]

It might be argued that the parties to the disagreement were dis-
puting the right to erect stands for viewing the processional play. But
Rogers's words for the viewing stands are "scafoldes and stages,"[21]
whereas the subject of the dispute is clearly "a mansyon rowme or place
for the whydson playes." In a legal context these words signify a room
in an enclosed building or tenement.[22]

Of the three principals to the Chester dispute, only John Whitmore,
the complainant, can be identified further. He was a member of an
established Chester family, a descendant of the John de Whytmore's,
father and son, mayors of Chester in 1370/1–1373/4, 1399, and 1412/3–
1413/4. A William Whitmore was mayor in 1450/1 and in 1473/4.[23] At
some time between 1385 and 1410, a John de Whytemore was a customary tenant paying an annual rent of 16d. He had one gable rent in
Bridge Street, and another in Northgate Street.[24] In 1542 his descendant was listed twice in a similar legal context:

Brudge Strete:
Johannes whitmore armiger pro messuagio modo in tenure Rogeri
orton de citie predicta sherman. . . .
                        Northgate Strete:
Johannes whitmore armiger pro messuagio modo in tenure Johannis yenun de citie predicta wyuer.[25]

By the sixteenth century the Whitmores had moved from Chester to
the neighboring Thurstanton: from their burgher status of the fifteenth
century, they had become a substantial, landed family.[26] The John
Whitmore who owned the Chester properties in 1542 died on 30 September 1553. The official inquisition post mortem includes the following among the financial statements which he recorded in his will:
"sex solidos de et in vno messuagio in Cestrienso predicto vocato le
Blackhall in le brigge strete iam in tenura Johane ledstham Vidue."
The same document names as Whitmore's heir his brother, also called
John Whitmore, just over fourteen years of age at the time of the
inquisition.[27]

Le Blackhall, possibly the old family residence, was clearly the subject of the 1568 dispute. John Whitmore the younger was the owner of
the hall, George Ireland his tenant in 1568, and Anne Webster, widow,

a subtenant. Mistress Webster had used the building for plays during the last two times the Whitsun plays were performed and was now granted the right to do so once more in 1568. The seventeenth-century transcription of the Smiths' Black Book of Accounts shows that Chester mounted the Whitsun cycle once during the reign of Mary, in 1554, and three times during the 1560s, that is, in 1561, 1567, and 1568.[28] The "ij tymes past whan the said plaies were plaied" were thus 1561 and 1567. Evidently the plays were moved indoors when they were first played after the death of Mary and remained there at least through the production of 1568.

David Rogers's transcription of the Late Banns ends with the injunction:

> But of common and contrye playeres take yow the storye
> And if any disdaine then open is the doore
> That lett him in to heare, packe away at his pleasure
> Oure playeinge is not to gett fame or treasure.[29]

The literal import of these lines is that the plays were performed indoors. Scholars who have taken note of the lines have suggested that they are late and egregious. Certainly they are late, in the sense that they are post-Reformation. They are also tacked on to the end of the banns in a most disconnected manner. Salter suggests that they were written by David Rogers himself, for an anticipated late revival of the plays. As evidence he notes that the initials D. R. appear at the end of the banns.[30]

It is impossible, however, that David Rogers, a self-confessed enemy of the plays, could have had a hand in reviving the plays, or in composing an apology for them. In fact the Late Banns must antedate the 1575 production of the plays, for the Banns announce the plays for Whitsuntide, while in 1575 the production was moved to Midsummer. The self-righteous Reformation aura of the Late Banns suggests that they were written either during the reign of Edward VI or during the early reign of Elizabeth, when towns all over England were reviving their plays in a clear understanding that the plays needed all the apology that could be given them. The original version of the Late Banns must have been written when the dramatic plays were still mounted on the processional carriages. The final injunction was evidently written during the 1560s, when the plays had been moved indoors. The air of Protestant bigotry cast over the cycle by the Late Banns and by some restructuring of the pageants may have been responsible for John Whitmore's opposition to the plays in

1568: Whitmore was a stout Roman Catholic who later in the reign of Elizabeth was persecuted for recusancy.[31]

The evidence for an indoor production helps make sense of the term "generall rehearse," which first appears in the Smiths' records of 1561.[32] The earliest list of expenses for pageants and plays in the Smiths' account, from 1554, makes no mention of rehearsals, though we may be certain that rehearsals were held. Individual rehearsals would logically be required of pageants destined for production on separate pageant wagons in a true-processional play. But what would be the point of a general rehearsal unless all the plays were to be mounted on the same stage in the form of a single long play (or three long plays, one on each day)?

If this argument carries weight, then the dramatic plays were performed indoors on each of the five times during the reign of Elizabeth when they were mounted: the term "generall rehearse" occurs in the Smiths' accounts not only in the 1560s, but in 1572 and in 1575 as well.[33] The term also occurs in the Painters' accounts for 1572, and may be inferred for 1567 and for 1575.[34] The Smiths' play was performed indoors on at least one occasion after the lapse of the cycle in 1575. In 1576 the Smiths gathered money "for the please," and then paid 16d "an ouer plas at Alderman Mounforts on midsomer eve."[35]

THE LAST YEARS OF THE CHESTER PAGEANTS AND PLAY

According to all accounts the Whitsun plays were mounted twice in the 1570s. However the penultimate performance is variously dated 1571 or 1572, while the last performance is dated 1574 or 1575. The dates 1571 and 1574 are erroneous and in every instance occur through confusions promoted by earlier antiquarians or more recent scholars.[36] In their last year, 1575, the plays were mounted not in Whitweek, but at Midsummertide.

MS Harley 1046 notes for the year 1575 that "Sir Iohn Sauage [mayor of Chester] caused the popish plaies of Chester to bee played the Sunday Munday Tuesday and Wensday after Midsummer day."[37] Henry Hardware, mayor in 1575/6, gave a somewhat different account for the same year: "Sir John Savage did cause the saide pagions and plays to be sett furth and playde as is aforesaide which did begyn the xxvi[th] of June laste paste in the afternone of the same day and there contynued vntill the Wednesday at eveninge then nexte folowinge."[38]

A look at the calendar will show that both statements are problematic. In 1575 Midsummer day (24 June) fell on a Monday. If the first statement is correct, the plays began the following Sunday, 30 June, and finished on Wednesday, 3 July. If the second statement is correct, the plays began on Wednesday, 26 June, and finished on Wednesday, 3 July, eight days later.

By a fortunate coincidence, Midsummer eve in 1575 fell on a Sunday. In all likelihood the plays were given on Monday, Tuesday, and Wednesday, 24–26 June. They probably ended rather than began on 26 June; and they were probably not given on Sunday, Midsummer eve, the traditional day of the Show. If this interpretation is correct, the errors in the accounts are slight, and the plays were performed on the weekdays traditional since the early part of the century.

MS Harley 2057 notes of the production of 1572: "This yeare the playes were plaid, but an inhibition came from the Archbishop of Yorke, to stay them, but came not in time." For 1575: "the plaies likewise this yeare (whitson plays) plaied at Midsomer; and then but some of them leauing others vnplayed which the Maior was ioyned (by the Archbupp of Yorke) not to proceed there withall."[39] This last account is verified by a recorded decision of the Chester council, taken on 30 May, to present the plays "in such orderly maner and sorte as the same haue ben accostomed with such correction and amendement as shalbe thaught convenient by the said maior." Amendment included suppressing plays which "might not have been iustified, for the supersticions in them."[40]

The 1575 production, despite cutting and despite its removal to Midsummer, caused many difficulties. On 25 October the council lodged a complaint against one Andrew Tailer of the Company of the Dyers because he had refused to cooperate when the company was taxed and assessed "for the charges in the setting furth of their parte and pagent of the plaies sett furth and plaied in this citie at midsomer laste past comonly called whytson plaies."[41]

Tailer's refusal was part of a growing and ultimately victorious opposition to the plays. News of the 1575 production reached London, where representatives of the crown charged Sir John Savage with having "sett furthe and caused to be plaide the accostomed pageons and plays called the whitson plays in the tyme of his maioraltie at midsomer laste of him sellf to satisfy his owne will and pleasure and contrary to his othe and dutie without the assente or consente of the reste of his bretherne and of the commen counsell of the same."[42] This charge was quoted by the Chester assembly as it rallied to the defense of Savage and also of John Hankey, who was accused of having committed a similar crime in 1572. The assembly, in a statement of complicity, replied that the mayors had not acted on their own but rather "that the saide plays set

furthe in their seuerall maioralties was seuerally don by thassent
consente good will and agreamente of the aldermen sheriffes sheriffes
peeres and comen counsell of the saide citie and so determyned by
seuerall orders agried vpon in open assemblie acordinge to the auncyent and lawdable custom of the saide citie."[43] It is interesting to note
that the council came to the defense of Hankey and Savage under the
mayoralty of Henry Hardware, who in 1600 "would not suffer any
Playes."[44] In 1575 Hardware apparently put loyalty to a fellow mayor
above partisan objections to the plays.

MS Harley 2125 notes under the mayoralty of John Savage: "The
whitson playes played in pageantes in this cittye." The entry is extended
by another hand: "at midsomer to the great dislike of many because the
playe was in on part of the Citty."[45] This last entry might be understood
to mean that in previous years the cycle play was performed in a
true-processional fashion, whereas in 1575 the play was performed on
pageants at a single site in the city. This of course would contradict our
interpretation of the 1568 memorandum. But the interpolated reference to plays in one part of the city is capable of another and more
probable interpretation.

Our chief evidence for the processional route of the pageant carriages
through the city is Rogers's Breviary. Rogers traces the procession from
its start at the Abbey gates to the Pentice at the High Cross, then to
Watergate Street, Bridgestreet, and "throughe the lanes and so to the
ꞁlanesꞁ estgate street." MS Harley 1948, also by Rogers, specifies the
Abbey gates, "the highe Crosse before the mayor, and so to euery
streete," meaning perhaps the four principal streets.[46]

In 1572 the Coopers spent 2s "at the brengeng vp of [the caryge] to
the menster gatte."[47] This confirms the starting point of the route.
From there the pageants evidently proceeded to the Pentice, then west
into the Watergate Street, south along two smaller streets to the castle
and St. Mary's on the Hill, and north into Bridgestreet. Evidently the
pageants then returned to the Pentice, and turned east into Eastgate
Street. If they followed the route of the Corpus Christi procession, as is
reasonable to suppose, they continued through Eastgate, and then to
St. John's. (Salter claims that the pageants were performed at four
stations: the Abbey gates, the Pentice, the castle, and the Roodee, a
patch of low-lying grassland northwest of the city bounded by the river
Dee. As far as I know, however, this is pure speculation.)[48]

The Midsummer Show, Chester's other spectacular procession, took
an entirely different route. It began at the Barrs, outside Eastgate, and
proceeded into the city.[49] Although we have no further information
concerning the route of the Show, it probably went into Eastgate Street,

then into Northgate Street, ending at the Abbey gates, the site of the Midsummer fair.

In 1575 the pageants were shown at Midsummer rather than at Whitsun, and the procession evidently followed the route of the Midsummer Show: the Smiths paid "for the banes and dring at the bares, xijd at medsamar yven," and "at the banes for glowffes, and to the plears and Aldermen at bringinge of our pagen forth, 3s 2d."[50] Thus the 1575 complaint that "the playe was in on part of the Citty" was evidently directed against the processional pageants, which were seen only in Eastgate and Northgate Streets, and not in Watergate or Bridgegate Streets.

MIDSUMMER SHOW

Midsummer Show was a processional spectacle mounted annually during much of the sixteenth century and lasting far into the seventeenth. About 1609 David Rogers wrote of the Show:

> Heare we maye note that the showe or watche, on midsomer eaue, called midsomer showe, yearely now vsed within the Citti of Chester was vsed in the tyme of those whitson playes and before so farr as I canne vnderstande, for when the whitson playes weare played, then the showe at midsomer went not: And when the whitson playes weare not played then the midsomer showe wente only: as many now liueinge canne make theire owne knowledge proffe sufficient.[51]

Rogers is clearly wrong in his insistence that the two events alternated with one another over the course of the years: we have seen that they were produced together in 1575, and in the two decades prior to this year expenses for the Whitsun play and the Midsummer Show frequently occur together in the records of the Smiths, Painters, and Coopers.

The spectacle of the Midsummer Show was supported by the city and by the crafts. An agreement between the city and two painters, Thomas Poole and Robert Halwood, on 21 April 1564, reveals that the city's part of the pageant included "foure Jeans [giants], won unicorne, won drambandarye, won Luce, won Camell, won Asse, won dragon, sixe hobby horses and sixtene naked boyes."[52] In later years many other pageant figures were added. Since this was a "Show," it also included men marching in armor.[53]

The craft guilds which marched in the Show are named by MS Harley 2150, in a list with the heading, "There is in the Citty 26 companyes viz as the goe at Midsomar and their ould names."[54] An extraordinarily high correlation obtains between this list and the twenty-odd guilds which presented pageants in the Whitsun play, both as to the names of the guilds and as to the order in which they are named. An original close relationship between the two processions is suggested, not only by this coincidence of marching order, but even more by the fact that the marching guilds presented in the Show the very biblical characters for which they were responsible in the Whitsun play. The Butchers, who displayed "the divill in his fethers" in the Show, had the play of the Temptation in the Whitsun cycle, including "the deuill in his featheres all ragged and rente" named in the Late Banns.[55] "A man in womans apparell with a divill waytinge on his horse called cuppes and cans" in the Show corresponds to the Cooks' Descent into Hell, with its Alewife who laments:

> of cannes I kepte no trewe mesuer
> my cuppes I soulde at my pleasuer
> deceavinge manye a creature
> tho my ale were naughte . . .
> therfore I maye my handes wringe
> shake my cannes and cuppes ringe . . .

(In MSS B and D, the last line reads "cupes and canes.")[56] The Bricklayers, who presented "balaam and Balaams Asse" in the Show after 1602, had recently amalgamated with the Cappers, who presented the same play in the cycle. The Barbers and Barber-surgeons provided "one to Ride Abraham and a yonge stripelinge boy to Ride Isaacke" in the Show and had the same play in the cycle.[57]

The records of the Smiths, Painters, and Coopers show that the custom of presenting biblical characters in the Midsummer Show long antedated the coincidental production of play and Show in 1575. The Painters, who had the play of the Nativity, paid 10d in 1567, a year of the play, "to tow shepperttes for goyng vppon mydsomer euen." In 1572 they spent 12d "for pentynge the houke [ox] and ass the styltes and the stare." This may have been in part for the play, but the stilts were certainly for the Show: in 1576 the Painters gave 20d "to the ij shepertes for going vppon the styltes." The previous year they paid 10d "to my alderman halwod for the makinge the pye and pentenge the styltes."[58] The nature of the "pye" remains a mystery. Alderman Halwood was the very painter who held the contract for the civic pageants in 1564 and after.

The Coopers, who had the play of the Flagellation, spent 16d in 1568 "for the hyre of too copes and men to were them and pennes and for the wrytyngs and for drenke whan the were in driseng and vndreseng on medsomer euen."[59] Perhaps the Coopers presented Annas and Caiaphas, the two high priests, in the Midsummer Show. The Smiths, whose cycle play combined the Presentation and Christ among the Doctors, presented Simeon in the Show on at least one occasion, evidently in 1554; but their practice in the 1560s was to present two doctors and "little God" on horseback.[60]

It would be useful to know exactly when this practice was introduced. We have noted the antiquarian histories which assert that "the wach on midsomer Eve was first sett out and begun" in 1497 or 1498.[61] The earliest Treasurer's Account Roll from the sixteenth century, for 1447/8, lists wages for a swordbearer and a macebearer but makes no mention of Midsummer Show. The next extant roll, for 1554/5, includes a payment of 28s 6d "for mydsomer wache for the Caredge of the pagions and paynters."[62] The pageants were thus established in the Show by 1554.

The half-dozen or so accounts of the Smiths transcribed from years prior to 1554 are in a state of great chaos and are not of any great help in establishing precise historical antecedents. Two different accounts are marked 1547, one of them referring to "the kinges dyrrige." This entry seems to support the ascription of the account to 1547, but it is possible that the scribe mistook a reference to the death of Edward VI for a reference to the death of his father. On this argument the account could also be for 1552/3. However this may be, the account lists a payment of 13d "at (Mr) Thomas Aldersey Tavarne on midsomar eve." Similar payments occur in other years during the 1550s and after. But no reference is made to characters in the procession prior to 1554, or between that year and 1561.[63]

On this doubtful evidence we may surmise that characters from the Whitsun plays were introduced into the Midsummer Show in 1554, a year of the cycle play. The history of the characters in later years can be told with a greater certainty. The tendency over the years was to replace the costumed biblical figures with young boys who were also mounted on horseback but who no longer represented historical characters. This change had already begun before 1575. The Smiths, who presented the two doctors and "little god" with a gilded face in the 1560s spent 7d ca. 1570 "for things that went to dresse our child," and 16d "for our syne." Several years later they secured "gere for the child that ridd on midsomer even," and again paid "for our signe." Gone are all references to the gilding of the child's face, or to the two doctors. The extent of the change may be gauged from a series of entries for 1576: "for horsebred when I went to borow gere for the child to ride before vs,

4d; for lace pynns and thred to stych the Juells, 4d; for dressinge our signe, ijs vjd; for hose and showes for child, xiiijd; for gloves for child and footman, vd."[64]

The Painters, who sponsored two stilt-walking shepherds through 1576, spent 3d in 1578 "for dressyng the boye," and the same amount "for horse bread for the boyes horsse." In 1582 they once more paid a man (Edward Doby) "for goinge vppon the styltes," but usually, and until at least 1623, they spent money "at dressing the child" on Midsummer eve.[65] The other guild whose records antedate 1575, the Coopers, introduced their boy in 1572: "Item a perre of gloues to the chylde that caryede the armes and a quarte of wyne to hys mother and for makynge of his cloke, xjd." This follows an expenditure of 12d "for the armes one medsomer euen."[66]

Changes in taste, fostered no doubt by changes in religious sentiment, hastened the replacement of biblical characters by boys in civilian dress. Thus in 1599/1600 Mayor Henry Hardware "put down the divell Ryding for buchers and caused a boy to ride as other companies."[67] The costumes became more and more elaborate and the expense accounts grew to include dozens of entries and endless yards of cloth. In 1606 the Mercers and Ironmongers sponsored "some comely striplinge or boye, to Ride before the same companye, and also . . . some other child, to Ride as a gentlewoman or ladye in respecte that the saide companyes of mercers and Iremongers are vnited and made one companye and fellowshipp."[68]

INDOOR PLAYS IN ELIZABETHAN AND JACOBEAN CHESTER

In Chester it was apparently Reformation pressure rather than ancient tradition which accounts for the cycle plays being performed indoors. Later, indoor performances were evidently the rule. In 1577 the earl of Derby and his son were present when "the scollers of the frescole . . . playd a comedy before them at Mr maiors howse."[69] In 1583 ecclesiastical officials apparently rejected a bid to allow an indoor performance: "Payd the xiij[th] of Maye unto Mr. Rogers whiche he gave to the Earle of Essex Players, when they woulde have played in Mr. Deanes house, ijs."[70] This was Archdeacon Robert Rogers, father of David Rogers. The players were probably paid for *not* playing.

By the seventeenth century the Common Hall (St. Nicholas Chapel in Northgate Street)[71] became the usual place for performing plays in Chester. In 1615 the council, disturbed by "the Comon Brute and Scandell which this citie hath of late incurred and sustained by admittinge of Stage Plaiers to Acte their obscene and vnlawfull Plaies or tragedies in the Comon Hall of this citie," ordered that:

from hensforth noe Stage Plaiers vpon anie pretence or color what soever shalbe admitted or licenced to set vp anye Stage in the said Comon Hall or to acte anie tragedie or Commedie or anie other Plaie by what name soever they shall terme it, in the said Hall or in anie other Place within this Citie or the Liberties thereof in the night time or after vj ^{e} of the Clocke in the eveninge.[72]

This order constitutes an absolute prohibition against plays in the Common Hall, and a qualified restriction against plays elsewhere. Salter suggests that the qualification was meaningless,[73] but it need not have been made at all. Evidently plays were tolerated elsewhere during the daylight hours.

10
London

EARLY PLAYS AT CLERKENWELL

A well-known description of London by William Fitz-Stephen bears witness to the production of miracle plays in the twelfth century: these plays were of a more spiritual bent than others, "representations of miracles which the holy confessors had performed, or representations of the passions by which the steadfastness of the martyrs was made known."[1] Miracles remained a popular form of entertainment into the fourteenth century. "Miracles" and "wrestlings" (*miracles* and *luctas*) gave rise about 1301 to complaints by the prioress of Clerkenwell against citizens of London, who "came in great numbers, both on horse and on foot [*tam equites quam pedites in magna multitudine*]," to the detriment of the hedges, ditches, and crops of the priory.[2]

Clerkenwell, or Skinners Well, remained the principal site of London's civic plays for more than a century after these complaints were issued. The chronicler Malvern records for 1384: "On the 29th day of August the clerks of London made near Skinners Well a certain exceedingly sumptuous play [*quendam ludum valde sumptuosum*], and it lasted for five days."[3] The performance was evidently given Monday through Friday of the week after St. Bartholomew day (24 August). On 12 August 1385 the same plays were forbidden because of Richard II's military expedition to Scotland.[4] For 11 July 1391 the Issue Roll of the Exchequer includes a payment "to the clerks of the parish churches, and to divers other clerks of the City of London. In money paid to them in discharge of 10[1] which the Lord King commanded to be paid them of his gift, on account of the play of the Passion of our Lord and the Creation of the World [*causa ludi de Passione domini & creacione*

170

mundi] by them performed at Skynnerwell after the feast of Saint Bartholomew [24 August] last past."[5] The payment suggests that Richard II was in the audience. Judging from the dates, this performance occurred in 1390, a bare month before the renowned Michaelmas tournament at Smithfield. This tournament, one of the most famous of the late Middle Ages, is recorded in glowing colors in the *Chronicles* of Jean Froissart.[6] In 1391, again at Skinners Well, but this time beginning on 18 July and performing over four days, the London clerks put on a play (*Ludum satis curiosum*) "in which the Old and also the New Testament were displayed to the view in the manner of playing [*oculariter ludendo monstrabant*]."[7] In 1393 "the pley of seynt Katerine" was performed, perhaps also at Skinners Well.[8]

Records are silent for many years after 1393, but MS Harley 565 notes for 1409: "this yere was the pley at Skynners Welle whiche endured Wednesday Thorsday Fryday and on Soneday it was ended."[9] *Gregory's Chronicle* also testifies to the "grette playe at Skynners Welle," and MS Cotton Julius B. 1. to "a grete plaie at Clerken Well" this yere.[10] The *Chronicle of the Grey Friars of London,* which assigns the play erroneously to 1411, gives a more comprehensive view of the event: "And this yere beganne a gret pley from the begynnyng of the worlde at the skynners welle that lastyd vij dayes contynually; and there ware the most parte of the lordes and gentylles of Ynglond."[11] Once again, as the 1409 Wardrobe Accounts make clear, the Clerkenwell (Skinners Well) play was an entertainment preliminary to great jousts in Smithfield:

> Scaffold of timber at Clerkenwell for our lord King [Henry IV], the lord Prince [the future Henry V], earls, barons, knights, and ladies for a great play showing how God created Heaven and Earth out of nothing and how he created Adam and on to the Day of Judgment.
>
> Another scaffold beside the Hospital in St. Bartholomew in Smithfield for feats of arms in an open area [*loco spacioso*] called *ludus hastiludi.*[12]

The two events, in other respects so dissimilar, evidently had the same audience and the same essentially social purpose.

It can hardly be doubted that the London history-of-the-world plays were known to Chaucer. We may discount the Wife of Bath's visits to plays, since *The Romance of the Rose,* Chaucer's source, mentions weddings, processions, festivals, plays, and carolings. But the Miller's Tale, which was certainly written after 1384, seems to have been directly influenced by the London plays at Skinners Well. London was evidently the only English city in which parish clerks were the producers of this drama; and Absolon, who played Herod "upon a Scaffold hie," was by occupation one of these. The venerable carpenter had learned of Noah's tormenting wife from an Old Testament play. And the Miller was given to crying out "in pilates voys."[13]

It is indeed possible that Chaucer himself was responsible for erecting the timber scaffolds for the 1390 Clerkenwell play. We have seen that in 1409 the scaffolds for the Smithfield jousts were recorded together with the scaffolds for the plays in the Wardrobe Accounts. This suggests that the two structures were erected under the same auspices. We also have abundant evidence that in 1390 Chaucer, as clerk of the king's works, supervised expenditures for the erection of scaffolds in Smithfield for the jousts of both May and October.[14] Although no records survive to connect Chaucer directly with the plays performed in late August of that year, we do know that he was in the London area about this time: it was early in September, in the immediate vicinity of London, that Chaucer was relieved several times of his money, his goods, and his horse.[15]

It would seem natural to interpret the various London records as signifying a play similar in many respects to the later Corpus Christi dramatic cycles. Indeed, though the Corpus Christi processional plays developed from nondramatic antecedents, the London play may have given the impetus for the further development of the early pageants into drama. It may even have been the literary source and example for some of the cycle play texts. Most scholars, however, have insisted that any identity between the London play and the provincial cycles is to be discounted. Their reasons are several: (1) the London play was stationary rather than processional; (2) it was given for the benefit of noblemen, perhaps even to the exclusion of commoners; (3) it was not given on Corpus Christi day; (4) it lasted more than a single day; and (5) the London play was an example of the southern "Passion play," whereas (6) the Corpus Christi play was a northern institution.[16]

We have already disposed of most of these objections. The Corpus Christi dramatic plays were normally stationary and many were given primarily or at least incidentally for the benefit of persons of high station. Plays of the history of the world were by no means confined to Corpus Christi, and some history-of-the-world plays, as in sixteenth-century Chester, were given over several days.

As for the London play being a "Passion" play, only one of the documents even mentions the Passion; and while the Passion was doubtless played, the chroniclers are at great pains to emphasize the comprehensiveness of the plays, naming incidents from the Creation to the Last Judgment, from the Old as well as the New Testament. Nor must we necessarily believe that the London play was significantly more comprehensive than the known cycle plays: if the York cycle were played over five days, it would make five plays each one of which would still be of a very respectable length.

The proposition that the Corpus Christi play was an exclusively northern institution is belied, as we shall see, by the example of Canterbury. The proposition that the kind of play represented by the extant cycles is a northern institution is belied by Weever's statement in his *Ancient Funerall Monuments*:

> This *Marlow* was Lord Maior in the yeare 1409, in whose Maioral-tie there was a play at Skinners Hall, which lasted eight days (saith *Stow*) to heare which, most of the greatest Estates of England were present. The subject of the play was the Sacred Scriptures, from the creation of the world: They call this *Corpus Christi* Play in my country, which I haue seene acted at Preston, and Lancaster, and last of all at Kendall, in the beginning of the raigne of King *Iames*: for which the Townesmen were sore troubled: and vpon good reasons the play finally supprest, not onely there, but in all other Townes of the Kingdome.[17]

Hardin Craig, in a nodding mood, says of this excerpt: "Weever was born in Lancashire in 1576. He wrote about 1631, and he seems to recognize that the Corpus Christi play was a northern rather than a southern institution."[18] On the contrary, Weever seems to recognize that the play had no regional bounds. He merely knew the play by a particular name, drawn from the feast on which the play as he experienced it happened to have been performed.

The Corpus Christi Procession

London Corpus Christi festivities date back to at least 1327, when a procession was established by a Skinners' guild of Corpus Christi.[19] Unfortunately, little more can be discovered from civic documents concerning the nature of the early march. This gap in our knowledge may be partly filled by the "ordenaunce of a precessyoun of the feste of corpus cristi made in london . by daun John Lydegate."[20] This poem, which we have already discussed at length, was conceived as a sequence of speeches addressed to a real audience. These speeches, as shown by the last stanza, describe pageants in a moving procession:

With theos figures shewed in youre presence,
By diuers liknesses you to doo pleasaunce,
Resceiuethe hem with devoute reverence,
This bred of lyfe yee kepe in Remembraunce
Oute of this Egipte of worldely grevaunce,
Youre restoratyff celestyal manna,
Of which God graunt eternal suffysaunce
Where aungels sing everlasting Osanna.

The first two lines testify to the substantial nature of the thirty-six
images shown in the procession. The last lines of the stanza recapitulate
the persistent emphasis of the procession and poem upon the Corpus
Christi. This emphasis was clearly grasped by a reader of the manuscript who glossed "bred of lyfe" as "eucaristia."

The Lydgate cycle did not, so far as we know, constitute a major or
durable variant of the English Corpus Christi pageant plays during the
fifteenth or sixteenth centuries. Moreover, the celebration of Corpus
Christi may have been more diffuse in London than in other cities. As
in earlier days, the major civic procession was conducted under the
auspices of the Skinners' company, the fraternity of Corpus Christi.
According to John Stow:

> This fraternitie had also once euery yere on *Corpus Christi* day
> after noone a Procession, passed through the principall streetes of
> the Citie, wherein was borne more then one hundred Torches of
> waxe (costly garnished) burning light, and aboue two hundred
> Clearkes and Priests in Surplesses and Coapes, singing. After the
> which were the shiriffes seruants, the Clarkes of the Counters,
> Chaplains for the Shirriffes, the Maiors Sargeants, the counsell of
> the Citie, and Maior and Aldermen in scarlet, and then the
> Skinners in their best Liueryes.[21]

Thus the chief London procession was much like those of the provincial
cities, except that one craft guild only, the Skinners, took part in the
march. This may explain why the procession failed to develop the
long-lived sequences of craft pageants which characterized the processions of other English towns and cities. Extant records of the Skinners
begin in 1492, and each year contain expenses for the Corpus Christi
processsion. In 1505 the Skinners disbursed sums for the repair of
angels' wings and for the gilding of sunbeams.[22] Thus the procession
did include images, even if it did not always involve full-scale pageants.

In addition to the Skinners' procession, London had minor Corpus
Christi processions in the several parishes. One such event is recorded
in the returns of 1389.[23] Other records, beginning in 1447, demonstrate

that the parishes marched with garlands of roses and woodruff, and
with canopies, flags, torches, cressets, banners, and bells.[24] The London
processions were suppressed in 1548: "This same yere was put downe
alle goyng abrode of processyons, . . . and the Skynners' processyon on
Corpus Christi day."[25] But they were revived again in the reign of
Queen Mary, as Henry Machyn notes for the year 1554:

> The xxiiij day of May was Corpus Christi day, and . . . ther wher
> mony goodly pr[oss]essyons in mony parryches. . . . mony had long
> torchys garnyshyd [in the] old fassyouns, and stayffe torchys
> bornyng, and mony [canopies] borne a-bowt the strett.[26]

MIDSUMMER WATCH AND LORD MAYOR'S SHOW

The Corpus Christi procession was probably London's most important annual riding in the fourteenth and fifteenth centuries. In the early
sixteenth century the chief London procession was the Midsummer
watch, held on 23 and 28 June. The watch apparently dated from the
early part of the fifteenth century. By 1504 civic guilds mounted
pageants in the watch along with the traditional armed men, torches,
and other elements of processional spectacle. In contrast to practices in
York and elsewhere, the London pageants were provided only by the
companies from whose ranks the mayor and two sheriffs for the year
had been selected. These pageants were frequently on biblical subjects.
The pageant of Our Lady and Elizabeth was presented in 1519; Jesse in
1521 and 1529; Christ and the Doctors in 1541; and the Assumption of
the Virgin in 1512, 1521, 1522, 1529, 1536, and 1541. In 1535 the
Skinners mounted a pageant of Corpus Christi, precise subject unknown. Other pageants were based on the lives of saints, and some few
were mythological.[27]

The pageants constituted only a part of the London Midsummer
Show. Stow prints a list of about twenty different military ranks or
specialties among the men in armor:

> there were also diuers Pageants, Morris dancers, Constables, the
> one halfe which was 120. on S. *Iohns* Eue, the other halfe on S.
> *Peters* Eue . . . the Waytes of the City, the Mayors Officers, . . . the
> Mayor himselfe well mounted on horseback . . . The Sheriffes
> watches came one after the other in like order, but not so large in
> number as the Mayors, for where the Mayors had besides his
> Giant, three Pageants, each of the Sheriffes had besides their
> Giantes but two Pageants, ech their Morris Dance . . .[28]

The London pageants were prepared at Leadenhall. Stow explains:

> The vse of Leaden hall in my youth was thus: In a part of the North
> quadrant on the East side of the North gate, was the common
> beames for weighing of the wooll, and other wares, as had beene
> accustomed: on the west side the gate was the scales to way meale:
> the other three sides were reserued for the most part to the making
> and resting of the pageants shewed at Midsommer in the watch:
> . . . the lofts aboue were partly vsed by the painters in working for
> the decking of pageants and other deuises, for beautifying of the
> watch and watchmen.[29]

This scene is probably typical of the activities surrounding pageant
processions wherever they were mounted. The early London pageants
were carried by porters, usually from eight to sixteen per pageant.[30]
Speeches evidently had no place in the London Midsummer Show.
Children were paid for singing, however, and perhaps for performing
on musical instruments.[31]

In 1519 the Skinners rented one pageant (St. Thomas Becket) from
St. Giles, and another (Our Lady and St. Elizabeth) from Barking.[32]
This was probably exceptional, for Stow's account suggests that
pageants were constructed and maintained explicitly for the Midsummer Show. The exception is instructive, however, for it suggests that the
London parishes maintained pageants for their private use.

The London Midsummer pageants ceased, apparently for good, in
1545. The Midsummer watch was revived in 1548, and again in 1567,
1568, and 1571, but evidently without pageants.[33] Processional pageants remained an integral part of civic ceremony but were mounted on
29 October, the day after SS. Simeon and Jude, for the investiture of the
new mayor. This "Lord Mayor's Show" was inaugurated in 1535 when
the Mercers bore a pageant before Sir John Allen, one of their number
who had attained to the high office. From this modest beginning, the
Lord Mayor's Show gradually developed into the sumptuous pageant
spectacle of the seventeenth century.[34] The Show survives, of course, to
this day, and continues to exemplify the natural affinity between an
ostentatious display of civic power, and spectacular pageants of every
kind.[35]

Guild and Civic Plays in the Fifteenth and Sixteenth Centuries

In 1511 the London Skinners celebrated Christmas with "an enterlude done at Mr Shryffes."[36] Such indoor plays on special guild
occasions were common in late medieval London. In the fifteenth and
sixteenth centuries, for example, the Assumption guild of St. Margaret's, Westminster, sponsored a triennial banquet for which they
disbursed sums "to the players for a pley," and to "mynystrelles."[37]

The London Drapers made annual payments for "mynstrelles pleyers and Russhis" beginning as early as 1485.[38] No doubt these payments were also for an indoor entertainment at a guild banquet. So frequent had indoor guild plays become by 1542 that the lord mayor commanded the aldermen to forbid "any commen playes or enterludes in any wise to be had or played at ony tyme Herafter within the commen Halles of ony the mysteries companyes or fellowships of this Citee." When the earl of Hertford's players came to London in 1545 they were forbidden to play, "excepte it be in the howses of the lorde mayer, Shreves, aldermen or other substancyall comminers."[39] Henry Machyn describes a performance of 1562:

> The x day of August was Barbur-surgyons' fest, and they captd ther communion at sant Alphes at Crepull-gatt, and master Recherdsun dyd pryche, the Skott; ther was good syngyng; and after to ther halle to dener, and after dener a play.[40]

Thus London experienced many indoor plays on guild occasions. Some of these followed closely upon guild processions, much in the manner of the provincial Corpus Christi plays.

John Stow was of the opinion that the "Comedies, Tragedies, Enterludes, and Histories, both true and fayned" of his time (the Elizabethan age) were a direct outgrowth of the dramatic activity at Clerkenwell in 1391 and 1409.[41] This seems doubtful. The London religious drama was probably not sufficiently active over a long enough span of time to have had that kind of influence. The church of St. Margaret, Southwark, it is true, supported dramatic plays around the middle of the fifteenth century.[42] In 1508 a play or "spectacula" of St. John was deemed worthy of being recorded by Henry VII's annalists.[43] More significantly, on 7 June 1557 during the Marian reaction, "a stage play . . . of the Passyon of Cryst" was begun "at the Grey freers."[44] The seventh of June was Whitmonday: the play may have been attached to the ecclesiastical holiday in the manner of the provincial Corpus Christi plays. In the same year on 29 July (St. Olave's day) "was the church holiday [of St. Olave's church], in Silver street; and eight of the clock at night began a stage play of a goodly matter, that continued until xij at mydnyght, and then they mad an end with a good song."[45] This was probably an indoor performance. But the subject matter is not specified, and four hours seems too short a time for the history of the world.

Whether any of these plays, particularly the 1557 "Passyon of Cryst," was a history-of-the-world play like the London play of 1409, or like the provincial Corpus Christi plays, we may never know. The old London play at Clerkenwell was also called a Passion play, even though it contained Old Testament episodes and a Last Judgment; it too lasted for several days. But the silence of the intervening years seems overpowering. Even if the old play was revived in 1557 to demonstrate English loyalty to its Catholic past, London seems to have had no unbroken dramatic heritage from its early religious plays.

11
Miscellaneous
Towns and Cities

PAGEANT PROCESSIONS, CONTINENTAL AND INSULAR

Most of the foregoing chapters have been devoted to cities and towns where a procession of pageants on Corpus Christi day depicted the sacred history of the world, and where this procession was followed by a full-length cycle play on the same topic. Hardin Craig indeed has argued that the cycle play was the *sine qua non* of the processional pageant, and that historical figures in a procession therefore ineluctably bear witness to an antecedent theatrical tradition:

> Various late descriptions, or lists, of actors from Corpus Christi pageants and of the pageants themselves in the Corpus Christi procession have been taken as indications of dumb show, but such things are merely continuations of the old custom of putting actors and pageant wagons in the procession. It is taken for granted, but without proper warrant, that the plays at Dundee, Dublin, and Hereford were already defunct at the time the descriptions of Corpus Christi processions with figures and floats from Corpus Christi plays were recorded. Sometimes these processions are described by modern writers as "mimetic." There is no evidence, and it is most unlikely. These records do indicate that there once had been and probably still were Corpus Christi plays played at these places.[1]

Craig realizes that pageants displayed in the liturgical processions could not themselves have been mimetic. But he insists that the pageants must have derived from preexisting dramatic cycles. His certitude applies not only to England but to the Continent: "Creizenach [supported by D'Ancona] argues on insufficient grounds that the great

179

processions of Vicenza (1379), Milan (1336), Florence (1454), and
elsewhere, some of which reveal the presence of the full scope of the
Corpus Christi play, were not accompanied by acted drama."[2] Craig
makes this assertion to save his (circular) argument that processional
pageants were the consequence rather than the source of the dramatic
plays. But it is an assertion made in the teeth of the evidence.
Processional pageants were the rule, acted drama the exception.
Nondramatic pageants are a natural adjunct of a civic procession: this
was as true in the Middle Ages as in the Renaissance or in our own day.

Barnabe Googe's translation, *The Popish Kingdome, or reigne of
Antichrist,* of a composition in Latin by the German Protestant
Thomas Naogeorgus (Kirchmayer), includes a lengthy but valuable
description of the Corpus Christi procession as it was often celebrated
on the Continent:

Then doth ensue the solemne feast of Corpus Christi day,
Who then can shewe their wicked vse, and fonde and foolish play:
The hallowed bread with worship great, in siluer Pix they beare
About the Church, or in the Citie passing here and theare.
His armes that beares the same, two of the welthiest men do holde,
And ouer him a Canopey of silke and cloth of golde
Foure others vse to beare aloufe, least that some filthie thing
Should fall from hie, or some mad birde hir doung thereon should fling.
Christes passion here derided is, with sundrie maskes and playes,
Faire Ursley with hir maydens all, doth passe amid the wayes:
And valiant George with speare thou killest the dreadfull dragon here,
The deuils house is drawne about, wherein there doth appere
A wondrous sort of damned sprites, with foule and fearefull looke,
Great Christopher doth wade and passe with Christ amid the brooke:
Sebastian full of feathred shaftes, the dint of dart doth feele,
There walketh Kathren with hir sworde in hande, and cruell wheele:
The Challis and the singing Cake, with Barbara is led,
And sundrie other Pageants playde in worship of this bred,
That please the foolish people well, what should I stande vpon,
Their Banners, Crosses, Candlestickes, and reliques many on,
Their Cuppes and carued Images, that Preistes with countnance hie,
Or rude and common people beare about full solemlie:
Saint John before the bread doth go, and poynting towardes him,
Doth shew the same to be the Lambe that takes away our sinne:
On whome two clad in Angels shape do sundrie flowres fling,
A number great of sacring Belles, with pleasant sounde doe ring.
The common wayes with bowes are strawde, and euery streete beside,
And to the walles and windowes all, are boughes and braunches tide.
The Monkes in euery place do roame, the Nonnes abrode are sent,

The Priestes and schoolemen lowde do rore, some vse the instrument.
The straunger passing through the streete, vpon his knees do fall:
And earnestly vpon this bread, as on his God doth call.
For why, they count it for their Lorde, and that he doth not take
The forme of flesh, but nature now of breade that we do bake.
A number great of armed men here all this while doe stande,
To looke that no disorder be, nor any filching hande:
For all the Church goodes out are brought, which certainly would bee
A bootie good, if euery man might haue his libertee. . . .[3]

"Christes passion," presented as one of many "sundrie maskes and plays," must have been a tableau pageant like the remainder of the spectacle.

Processions of this sort were not limited to Corpus Christi. In 1520 Albrecht Dürer witnessed the great *Ommeganck* of the Cathedral of Notre Dame at Antwerp, held the Sunday after the Assumption of the Virgin. The procession included all the craftsmen of the city, a troupe of armed men, monks, members of a sisterhood, and the clergy of the city, in whose midst was carried an image of the Virgin and Child. Dürer continues:

> In the course of this *Ommeganck* there were many amusing devices introduced, all very ingeniously constructed. These were mounted on numerous cars or waggons, exhibiting sports and pastimes upon ships and other great bulky carriages. There were also the prophets of the Old Testament, in number and succession, followed by those of the New, the Annunciation of the Virgin, the three Magi mounted upon huge camels, and surrounded by other wonderful rarities, very ingeniously arranged; such as the flight of the Virgin into Egypt, and many other things which I must forbear mentioning. Towards the last came a great dragon, which St. Margaret and her maidens, who were very handsome young ladies, led by a girdle, followed by St. George, with his esquire, a very comely cavalier, armed cap-à-pie. Among this host of personages were introduced, whenever they were necessary, a number of youths and maidens, in elegant and appropriate costumes, representing the necessary number of saints, &c. The time the *Ommeganck* took to pass by our residence, from beginning to end, was more than two hours; for there were so many things that I should never be able to write them in a book, so I shall leave it alone.[4]

Illustrations of the Antwerp procession survive from the middle of the sixteenth century: by this time the pageants had become less biblical and more classical in theme. The beautifully illustrated *Ommegang* of

Brussels, 1615, on the other hand, retained pageants of the Annunciation and of the Nativity. The illustrated Louvain pageant of 1594,
records of which go back more than a century before that date,
contained nearly a dozen biblical pageants in something like a connected sequence.[5]

Most of the English processions we have examined so far boasted
pageants which, like the Louvain pageants, were unified in a connected
sequence of subject matter. But the Coventry Corpus Christi liturgical
procession, the Lincoln St. Anne's day procession, the Norwich St.
Luke's procession, and the London Midsummer Show and Lord
Mayor's Show, all contained pageants on more or less random biblical
and nonbiblical themes. As we shall now see, many insular Corpus
Christi processions apart from those we have already discussed also
contained pageants, some with connected, some with more randomly
chosen subject matter.

Towns with Corpus Christi Pageant
Processions but without Related Dramatic Plays
Hereford

Hereford may be taken as the chief example of an English town
whose processional pageants on Corpus Christi never developed into
dramatic plays. In some undetermined year of the early sixteenth
century the journeymen of the Corvisers confessed in a petition that
they were "bound to bryng furth certen torches in the procession on the
day of Corpus Xpi yerlye." But they complained that "the wardens of
the sayd occupacion, and certen other frowarde persons . . . of theyre
perverse mynd dyd dystribute and geve away the torches of the sayd
occupacion at theyre plesure."[6] As elsewhere, therefore, the crafts
played a major role in the procession.

The Hereford crafts were also responsible for mounting processional
pageants. Thus a memorandum from early in the reign of Edward VI
recalls:

> there was before thys tyme dyuers corporacions of artiffycers,
> craftes, and occupacions in the sayd cytey, who were bound by the
> grauntes of their corporacions yerely to bring forthe and set for-
> ward dyuers pageaunttes of ancyentt historyes in the processyons
> in the sayd cytey upon the day and feast of Corpus Xpi, which
> now ys and are omitted and surceased.[7]

The pageants are described as historical in subject matter and regarded
as civic in nature.

A list of guilds and their pageants survives from 1503. It is entitled

"The paiants for the procession of Corpus Xpi," and includes some twenty-seven entries constituting a near normal "protocycle" of pageants. Unusual pageants include "Jesse," "The castell of Is-rael," and at the end of the list, "knyghtes in harnes," and "seynt Keterina with tres (?) tormentors."[8] No Doomsday is included, nor indeed any biblical episode after the Resurrection. There is no reason to regard this procession of pageants as anything but a dumb show. A 1440 reference to a book of plays (*unius libri de lusionibus*)[9] is not enough evidence upon which to construct a dramatic cycle.

Bungay (Suffolk)

Bungay had a Corpus Christi procession with five pageants. A Bill of Riot filed by Bungay citizens in 1514 against Richard Warton, town bailiff, complained:

> That the seyd Richard Warton Thomas Wodcok and John Wod-cok and dyuers other euyl aduisyd persons arreyed as Riottors and in riottous maner at Bungey aforseyd at xj of the clok on the frydaye at nyght nex after Corpus Xpi day in the sixthe yere of the most noble reyngn of Kyng Henry that now is; And at that tyme the sayd Richard Warton Thomas and John, brake and threw down fyve pagents of your seyd inhabitaunts that is to sey hevyn pagent, the pagent of all the world, Paradys pagent, Bethelem pagent, and helle pagent the whyche wer euer wont tofore to be caryed abowt the seyd Town vpon the seyd daye in the honor of the blissyd Sacrement.[10]

The primary use of these pageants was for the Corpus Christi proces-sion. It is interesting to note that the five pageants take their names from sacred geography rather than sacred history. This vaguely suggests that they may have been used as *loca* in a stationary dramatic play. Nothing in the evidence, however, substantiates this possibility.

Walsingham, Lanark (Scotland)

In 1541 the Little Walsingham guild of the Annunciation awarded 4d "To the berar of the dragon at Corpus Christmes and this Gild time." The Annunciation guild had recently amalgamated with St. George guild, and this may have been the source of the dragon.[11] Lanark, Scotland, also mounted a Corpus Christi procession, first noted in 1488. The dragon is mentioned in 1490, and in 1503 and after, the dragon was one of several pageants displayed on Corpus Christi day. Others included a St. George, a chapel, "Cristis cors" or "Cristis pascione," ladies with crowns ("gold fulyie [to the] ladis crownis"), and some unnamed "padyen." Another pageant, "the Kingis of Cullane," was associated either with this procession or with Martinmas.[12] There is nothing to suggest that Lanark had a dramatic play of any kind, much less a dramatic cycle.

Worcester

Worcester sponsored a pageant procession which, according to the ordinances of 1467, was to consist of "v pagentes amonge the craftes, to be holden yerly."[13] No festival day is specified in this document, or in the new ordinances of 1559:

> Also, it ys ordeynd by this present yeld, that alle maner of Craftys withyn the seid cite, that haue pageants, goynge to the worshippe of god and profite and encrese of the seid cite, and also alle the craftis that ben contributory to the same, and to the light3 of torches and tapers amonge the seid crafts, vsyd in the seid cite, haue and enyoie ther good, feithfull, and trew approved customes and vsages, in susteynynge ther pageants, lightes, and other necessaries to their craftys . . .[14]

The Worcester pageants may very well have gone in procession along with the torches of the crafts, but nothing points to a dramatic play.

The new Worcester ordinances of 1559 also required that "euery crafte havynge the name of pageant, shullen fynde oon cresset yerly brennynge, to be born biforn the Baillies of the seid cite, in the Vigille of the natiuite of Seynt John Baptiste, at the comyn Wacche of the seid cite";[15] but the pageants did not go on this occasion. A cathedral inventory of 1576 records certain items of "players gere," but these do not by any means imply a cycle. A lease of 1584 which mentions the "vacant place where the pagantes do stand" may allude to the five processional pageants.[16]

Haddington (Scotland)

Haddington may have had a tradition of presenting pageants on Corpus Christi, for in 1534 the crafts agreed "to play thair pagis on corpus cristis day." In subsequent years the pageants were evidently moved to Midsummer day. Thus in 1537 the governors ordered "the craftis to play thair pagenis quhill midsomir day." This is complemented by an order naming certain crafts which "sall playe thair pagenis 3eirly and this 3eir on midsomerday." In 1541 "the baillies chargit the dekynnis of the craftis of haidynton personly present to play thar piad3anis this 3eir as thai did afoir."[17] We cannot tell whether this refers to a production on Corpus Christi or Midsummer.

The zealous preacher Wishart inveighed against a Haddington play in 1546: "I have heard of thee, Hadingtoun, that in thee wold have bein at ane vane Clerk play two or three thowsand people."[18] The size of the audience suggests a stationary outdoor play. But we have no evidence to connect this play to the processional pageants.

Dundee

A single document survives from Dundee on the matter of Corpus Christi. This is an inventory which probably derives from the mid-fifteenth century:

> the grayth [ornaments] of the prossession of corpus xpi deliuerit sir thomas barbour to kepyng
>
> In primis iii[xx] [60] of crownis, vj pair of angel veynis, iij myteris, cristis cott of lethyr with the hoss and glufis, cristis hed, xxxj suerdis, thre lang corsis of tre, sanc thomas sper, a cors til sanc blasis, sanc johnis coit, a credil and thre barnis maid of clath, xx hedis of hayr, the four evangellistis, sanc katerins quheil, sanc androwis cros, a saw, a ax, a rassour, a guly knyff, a worm of tre, the haly lam of tre, sanc barbill castel, abraamis hat, and thre hedis of hayr.[19]

Clearly these items, reminiscent of Kirchmayer's poem, are all for a spectacular procession on Corpus Christi. Perhaps some of the saints were impersonated by men in costume, but many of the figures were fabricated. These include "cristis hed," "thre barnis maid of clath," "the four evangellistis," and "a worm of tre."

SOME TOWNS WITH PAGEANT PROCESSIONS AND NON-CORPUS CHRISTI PLAYS
Dublin

Dublin mounted a full but rather mixed procession of pageants on Corpus Christi day. A 1498 list from the Dublin Chain Book, entitled "Corpus Christi day a pagentis," begins with a brief historical notice: "The pagentis of Corpus Christi day, made by an olde law and confermed by a semble befor Thomas Collier, Maire."[20] In many respects the list recalls the standard cycle. Certain descriptions, however, show that the pageants were for a procession rather than for a play: "Adam and Eve, with an angill followyng berryng a swerde"; "The three Kynges of Collynn, ridyng worshupfully, with the offerance, with a sterr afor them"; "The Nine Worthies ridyng worshupfully, with ther followers accordyng." This last item is one of several nonscriptural pageants which follow after the Passion. Others include "Arthure, with knightes," and St. George and the dragon.

The pageants on scriptural incidents betray an irregular character. Thus the pageant of the Skinners, House-Carpenters, Tanners, and Embroiderers is described as follows in the first and second lists respectively:

> for the body of the camell, and Oure Lady and hir childe well aperelid, with Joseph to lede the camell, and Moyses with the children of Israell, and the Portors to berr the camell.

> The body of the camel. Steynors and Peyntors for to peint the camel. The camell, with the children of Israell; is hede, skenns, and tanns [thongs], to mayntene the hellyng [drawing] of the camel with Oure Lady. The Porters to ber the camel.

What are we to make of all this? We know that the preceding pageant was "Pharo, with his hoste." It would make sense, therefore, for this pageant to include Moses with the children of Israel, followed by Joseph and by the Virgin holding her son (the Flight into Egypt). But it is doubtful that the two scenes were presented in correct historical sequence. The chief spectacular element in this pageant was evidently the camel, a fabricated beast borne by porters. It may be that the organizational principle of the pageant was thematic rather than historical: that the camel, a symbol of Egypt, simply attracted to itself two other episodes associated with Egypt. The two pageants which follow are the Magi and the Shepherds (in reverse order), both of which should have preceded the Flight into Egypt if the procession had been organized historically.

It is difficult to believe that any connected dramatic cycle was associated with the Dublin pageant procession as a whole. Nor was the St. George pageant, which was also entered in the Chain Book,[21] in any obvious sense dramatic. However, some noncycle plays may have been distantly associated with the pageants. The 1528 Christmas festivities included dramatic plays of Adam and Eve, Joseph and Mary, the Passion of Our Savior, and the martyrdoms of several saints. These were presented on a stage erected upon Hoggin Green and were sustained by guilds and perhaps also by clerics. More than a decade later, in 1541, the city witnessed a play of the Nine Worthies.[22] The procession itself continued into the reign of Elizabeth but was moved to a different time of year: a directive of 1569 required the crafts to keep the same order in their Shrove Tuesday riding "as they are appointed to go with their pageants on Corpus Christi daye by the Chayne Boke."[23]

Shrewsbury

The town of Shrewsbury had a normal Corpus Christi procession, first indicated in 1461. Certain crafts submitted to an order for the procession, including an agreement concerning their banner, wax (lights), and aldermen.[24] The procession is mentioned again in 1478 and in 1480.[25] In 1517/8 it is listed along with a festival interlude:

> In vino expendito super tres reges Colonie equitantibus in interludio pro solacio ville Salop in festo Pentecost, iiijd.

> Et in vino dato abbati Salop et famulis suis ad generalem processionem in festo Corporis Christi pro honestate ville Salop, xviijd ob.[26]

The reference to riding shows that the Pentecost "interlude" was at least in part a mounted procession.

The association of the costumed figures and the interlude with the Whitsun rather than the Corpus Christi procession suggests that Shrewsbury, like sixteenth-century Chester, regularly presented its civic plays and pageants on the earlier festival day. In 1495 the Shrewsbury corporation spent money for wine "dato domino Principi [Arthur] ad ludum in quarell." This quarry where Prince Arthur saw the play is mentioned again in 1516 when the abbot and his entourage came for a "ludum et demonstrationem martiriorum Felicianae et Sabinae." It is not clear when these plays were mounted, but the splendidly full accounts for 1533 are for a production at Pentecost. Sums were spent for the construction of a covered platform of two "stages" (*pro factura unius mansionis de duobus stagiis*). This structure, perhaps two stories high, was built for the convenience of the bishop of Exeter and for the town bailiffs. Certain ornaments were prepared by the players, and food and drink were purchased for audience and actors alike. In 1542 an interlude was presented "in cimitirio sancti Cedde," but evidently the quarry remained the usual site for the plays: in 1570 the council leased pasture "behind the walles, exceptinge the Quarrell where the plases have bine accustomyd to be usyd."[27]

A relatively elaborate spectacle known as the "Shrewsbury Show" endured into the nineteenth century. All pageants but the first, the Tailors' Adam and Eve, presented distinctly nonscriptural episodes. The Shearmen, Shoemakers, and Barbers each presented a different saint. The Skinners and Glovers presented the King of Morocco; the Smiths, Vulcan; the Painters, Rubens; the Bricklayers, Henry VIII; and the Bakers, Venus and Ceres.[28] If these pageants can claim an ancestor, it is more likely to have been the Pentecost interlude than the Corpus Christi procession.

Leicester

Several towns had both processions and plays, but the relation between them remains unclear. Leicester mounted a procession on Whitmonday and a play at some unspecified time of the year. The procession went from the churches of St. Martin and St. Mary to the church of St. Margaret, with pageant figures of the twelve apostles in the march.[29] The play may have been mounted on Corpus Christi, but such a date is suggested only by the fact that the Leicester corporation was closely associated with the Corpus Christi guild: thus a breach of official confidentiality was to be met with a fine "levied by the mayor and the two masters of Corpus Xti gild."[30]

The Passion play is mentioned together with "pachents" in a civic entry dated 26 March 1477:

> The pleyers the which pleed the passion play the yere next afore brought yne a byll the whiche was of serten devties of mony and wheder the passion shulbe put to crafts to be bounden or nay. And at that tyme the seid pleyers gaff to the pachents ther mony which that thei had getten yn playng of the seid play euer fore to that day and all ther Rayments with al other maner of stuff that they had at that tyme. And at the same Common Halle be the advyse of all the Comons was chosen thies persones after named for to have the gydyng and Rule of the said play. [19 persons with two "bedalls" named.][31]

It is not clear, however, whether the "pachents" were wagons, or merely dramatic episodes. In 1495 six overseers were chosen to look after "seche guds as ys yn a store hows in the Setterday marcat that ys to say wodde tymber and vdyr playyng germands yf ther be ony."[32] It is not inconceivable that the matter in question was a dramatic play on Corpus Christi. There is no evidence for this, however, and it might just as well have been a pageant or play mounted at another time altogether.

Reading (Berkshire)

Reading town records bear witness to a Corpus Christi procession in 1509, 1512, and 1539. A play of Adam and Eve performed on "the Sonday afore Bartylmastyde" during some unspecified year was given "in the Forbury" and required a "schapfold" and "pagentts." Whether these were processional pageants is not, however, clear. In the same year the town paid for a "resurrecyon pley." In 1499 the churchwardens of St. Lawrence made "a gaderyng of a stage-play." In 1499 and 1539 the play was the "Kings of Cologne"; in 1512, a "play of Kayme"; and in 1515 "Caymes pageaunt" was given in the market place. A "pageaunt of the Passion on Easter Monday" occurred in 1508; and further payments were made in 1533 to 1535 to "Mr Laborne" "for reforming the Resurreccion pley" and "for a boke" of it.[33] Here the evidence is perhaps less than ambiguous: we have no warrant for drawing these fragments together into a connected cycle.

TOWNS WITH NONCYCLE PLAYS ON CORPUS CHRISTI

Lincoln has been our chief example of a town with a Corpus Christi play whose subject is unknown and which cannot be related to a known cycle of pageants or surviving texts. Many other cities and towns had plays on Corpus Christi, and many of these were probably also noncyclic in form and subject.

Cambridge, Salisbury, Glasgow

When William de Lenne and his wife Isabel joined the Cambridge Corpus Christi guild in 1350, they spent half a mark "in ludo Filiorum Israelis."[34] This may have been a Moses play, or a play of the Slaughter of the Innocents, but we cannot tell whether it was a pageant or a dramatic play, or even whether it was mounted on Corpus Christi. In the 1461 Salisbury churchwardens' account appears an entry "for all apparel and furniture of players at the Corpus Christi." Our knowledge of a Corpus Christi procession in Salisbury around 1445 does nothing to clarify the nature of the players or their play.[35] In the very late year of 1599, a Glasgow ordinance commanded the citizenry to come to "the playe and pastyme on Thurisdaye nixt," that is, on Corpus Christi day.[36] It seems quite unlikely that this was the occasion of a full cycle play, since by this time such plays were generally prohibited.

Bury St. Edmunds

The guild returns of 1389 include reports of two Corpus Christi guilds from Bury St. Edmunds. One guild consisted of a master and twelve priests, and also laymen and women, and was evidently the clerical fraternity which supervised the procession. The members were closely associated with the St. Nicholas guild, also founded by priests. The second Corpus Christi guild, from a different church, had existed from "time without memory." The brothers and sisters of the guild were to provide lights in the church and on Corpus Christi day were to wear suits of one color, and were to have an "interlude [*interludum*] of Corpus Christi," at which they were to "maintain and support a certain interlude."[37] Since this interlude was the responsibility of a single guild, it was probably not a dramatic cycle but rather a single play. We do not know its subject matter.

Processional pageants are first recorded ninety years later, in 1477, when one half of a certain fine was awarded to "the sustenacion and mayntenaunce of the payent of the Assencion of our lord god and of the yiftys of the holy gost as yt hath be customed of olde tyme owte of mynde yeerly to be had to the wurshepe of god amongge other payenttes of the procession in the feste of Corpus Xpi."[38] This pageant of the Ascension of Christ and Descent of the Holy Spirit would fit into a Corpus Christi procession of the familiar pattern. We have no idea, however, how many pageants were shown, whether the others were also biblical in subject matter, or whether they were related in any way to the fourteenth-century interlude of Corpus Christi.

King's Lynn

Like Bury St. Edmunds, King's Lynn witnessed a Corpus Christi interlude in the fourteenth century. In 1385 the Lynn chamberlains paid 3s 4d "to certain players, playing an interlude on Corpus Christi day." In the same year they paid the same amount, probably on a different occasion, "by the Mayor's gift, to persons playing the interlude of St. Thomas the Martyr."[39] The nature of the play and the manner of payment suggest that the players were a professional company rather than guildsmen.

The chamberlains paid minstrels and players in many prior and subsequent years but normally recorded the information in less complete detail.[40] An exception of unusual significance occurs in the Chamberlains' Roll for 1462, which contains a payment of 2s "for two flagons of red wine, spent in the house of Arnulph Tixonye by the Mayor and the most of his bretheren, being there to see a certain play at the Feast of Corpus Christi."[41] The location of the play in the house of an important official answers almost precisely to the contemporary situation we have discovered at Lincoln. As at Lincoln, however, we have no evidence concerning the matter of the play.

The Lynn Corpus Christi guild was founded in response to the plague of 1349.[42] In 1400 Thomas Ploket and Thomas Trussebut, treasurers of the guild, presented their accounts. Payments included 15s 5d for making thirty-five torches from a large piece of wax, and 11s "to divers minstrels making their performances" at the feast of Corpus Christi. The torches were probably for the procession. The minstrels may have marched with the procession but probably also provided entertainment for a guild feast which cost 103s 2d.[43] Here we have yet one more example of a formal banquet with entertainment for the feast of Corpus Christi.

A Lynn Tailors' ordinance of 1449 provides for certain fines, the proceeds of which were assigned "to the sustentacioun of the procession upon Corpus Christi day."[44] And in the Corpus Christi guild accounts of 1462, a payment of 20s is entered, "given by way of reward to the Skinners of the town for their labour about the procession at the Feast of Corpus Christi, this year."[45] Evidently the civic officials of Lynn devoted the morning of Corpus Christi to an ecclesiastical procession, and later in the day retired to a feast in the home of a private citizen. In various years they were diverted by minstrels, or by players, or both.

King's Lynn was thus the center of much dramatic and nondramatic entertainment. In 1409/10 Lady de Beaufort came to the city to see a play. In 1444 the town corporation gave a play with Mary and Gabriel before Lord Scales. This play was presented at Middleton, however, rather than Lynn.[46]

Yarmouth

Dramatic plays were given indoors at Yarmouth as well. L. G. Bolingbroke has detected a play on Corpus Christi day in the church of St. Nicholas in 1473 and 1486; at Bartholomew-tide in 1489; and a "game" played on Christmas day in 1493.[47] We have no way of telling whether the play on Corpus Christi presented subjects from the sacred history of the world or bore any relation to the Society of Corpus Christi which is recorded in the guild returns of 1389.[48]

In 1538 a "Game House" was constructed at Yarmouth. The contract for this structure included the provision that Robert Copping, who was the manager, should "permitt and suffre all such players and ther audiens to have the pleasure and ese of the said hous and gameplace, att all suche tyme and tymes as eny interludes or playes ther shal be ministered or played at eny tyme withought eny profight thereof by hym or his assigns to be taken."[49] Perhaps Copping planned to derive his profit from nondramatic entertainments such as wrestling or bearbaiting. In any case this represents an early example of a building constructed explicitly for plays and other forms of diversion. We have seen, however, that Yarmouth did have a tradition of indoor plays. This tradition continued to the end of the sixteenth century, for up until 1595 certain players were "licensed to play in the Guildhall."[50]

Aberdeen

The Aberdeen Burgh Records mention a play as early as 1440. Richard Kintor, abbot of Bonaccord, was granted certain privileges in return for expenses incurred "in quodam ludo de ly haliblude ludendo apud ly Wyndmylhill." The same privilege was offered to Thomas

Lawson in 1445.[51] These entries, together with other records, have been taken as evidence of an early Corpus Christi play. But while "hali-blude" suggests both the Passion and the Sacrament of the Altar, it is by no means synonymous with Corpus Christi. During the fifteenth century the Precious Blood was the subject of an important theological controversy concerning its value relative to the Body of Christ.[52] Perhaps the play had something to do with this controversy. There is nothing to tie the Aberdeen Holy Blood play to the festival of Corpus Christi.

In 1449 Nicholas Benning was accorded civic privileges in return for the 5s which he gave to "waltero balcancole pro scriptura ludi in festo corporis xpi." Nicholas Benning was a notary public: whether this concerned an original play, a transcription, or signs for pageants, cannot be determined. In 1471 Thomas Watson won privileges for his expenses "circa ludum de bellyale." It is conceivable that this was one play of a cycle, but it may just as well have been one of a number of different plays performed on different occasions in various years. A "play to be plait in the fest of corpus xpi nixt tocum" is recorded in 1479. Since this was to be subsidized from "the common gude," it was probably not a craft play.[53]

The Aberdeen crafts sponsored pageants or pageant figures from 1442, but these are always associated with Candlemas rather than Corpus Christi until the fourth decade of the sixteenth century. The pageants do not conform to the protocycle list and can scarcely be thought of as a biblical sequence. In 1442 the pageants included "the emprioure and twa doctourez"; "the three kingis of Culane"; "oure lady, Sancte bride [Bridget], Sancte helene, Ioseph"; "twa bischopes, foure angelez"; "Symion and his disciplez"; "the messyngeare and moyses"; "twa or foure wodmen"; "the knyghtez in harnace"; and "the menstralis." In each case the figures were accompanied by "alsmony honeste squiarez as thai may."[54] This item suggests that the entire spectacle consisted of marching figures from random subjects, as in the Coventry Corpus Christi procession. No mention is ever made of pageant wagons.

A later list, from 1505/6, is practically identical to the list of 1442, thus pointing to an impressive consistency in the processional pageant over a period of sixty years. Orders regulating the procession and pageants at Candlemas are numerous. In 1503/4 and in subsequent years the word "play" occurs frequently in these orders.[55] Anna J. Mill argues convincingly that the word "play" is ambiguous and cannot be interpreted as necessarily signifying a dramatic performance. She suggests that the "offerand" which followed the procession may have involved a dramatic play, but her only evidence is the unconvincing analogy of the Beverley guild of St. Mary.[56]

The Aberdeen Corpus Christi procession is first mentioned early in 1512/3, when the council ordered "that euery craft within this townne sall haue a pair of Torcheis . . . to decoir and worschip the sacrament one corpus xpi day and at the fest of pasche at the resurrexioun at ʒoule and at all vthir tymes quhene neid is."[57] Candlemas may be implied in the mention of Yule but is not specifically named. Nor are pageants prescribed for any of the processions.

In 1530 Corpus Christi fell on 16 June. On 17 June the council ordered "the craftismen of this burght to keip thair pagganis in the processioun on sonday nyxt cumis." The Sunday was 19 June, neither Corpus Christi nor Midsummer, but halfway between. On 22 May 1531 an "Ordour of corpus xpi processioun" was devised. This order reaffirms "the auld lovabill consuetudis and ryte of this burgh," in particular that "The craftismen of this burgh in thair best array keipe and decore the processioun on corpus cristi dais and candilmes day als honorabillye as thai can Euery craft with thair awin baner with the Armez of thair craft thairin." A list of guilds follows. Then occurs an order that "euery ane of the said craftis in the candilmes processioun Sall furnis thair pageane conforme to the auld Statut." From this document we can infer that Corpus Christi traditionally involved a marching or a riding of the guilds, but that the pageants were displayed at Candlemas. By this time the pageants had undergone a change of character. In a list of pageants appended to the order (written in a different ink, but apparently contemporary with the original order), nearly all the biblical characters have been replaced by saints.

In 1532 Corpus Christi fell on 30 May. On 31 May the Baxters were called before the civic authorities "for the wanting of thair pagane in corpus xpi processioun tha vsit afore." Pageants were thus mounted on Corpus Christi in 1532 and perhaps in some earlier years. Nothing points to this as a practice of long standing. In subsequent years the pageants were often limited to Corpus Christi. In 1546, however, certain craftsmen were ordered "to haue thair banar and pagane as wther craftis of the said burght hes ilk ʒeir on corpus xpi day and candilmes dayis processionis." Records from the next ten years indicate that the pageants were moved to Corpus Christi, to the exclusion of Candlemas.

We may conclude from this survey that Aberdeen had two rather different and unrelated kinds of play. The dramatic plays sponsored by the city and performed on Windmillhill included a Holy Blood Play, a Play of Belial, and an unknown play of Corpus Christi. The pageant procession, sponsored by the crafts, was mounted on Candlemas day from 1442 until about 1532, when it was transferred to Corpus Christi. There is no convincing evidence of a connection between these two events nor of a dramatic play accompanying the pageants.

Another series of pageants, including the Salutation of the Virgin, the Adoration of the Magi, and the Expulsion from Paradise, was mounted for the entry of Queen Margaret, wife of James IV, in 1511. Chambers suggests that these pageants (described briefly by Dunbar) came from "the Nativity cycle."[58] It is doubtful, however, that there was such a cycle. Furthermore, only the Adoration of the Magi occurs in common between these royal entry pageants and the pageants in the procession at Candlemas.

Edinburgh

In Scotland, as in England, plays on Corpus Christi were occasionally presented to royalty. Court records of 1503 mention "the Kingis passing to the Corpus Christi play," and in 1504 3s 4d was "payit to James Dog, that he laid doun for girs on Corpus Christi day, at the play, to the Kingis and Quenis chamires."[59] The "girs," which was grass, or sedge, was clearly used to strew the floor of the royal chamber where the play was performed. A play was evidently performed in 1554 also, when the city of Edinburgh spent 20s, "payit for beireing of burds and trestis to the Queenis luging on Corporischristeis day [24 May]." A subsequent entry records a payment of 16s "the day of the playing of the play at the trone, with the convoy of the moris; payit for graithing [decorating] of the Quenis luging foiranent the samyn, for flours, beirks, and rocheis, and beiring of furmes and trestis thairto." This entry, reminiscent of York and Norwich, may however concern a second play performed some days later. An entry of 15 June authorizes payment of £37 16s 2d to persons who "furneist the grayth to the convoy of the moris [?Moors; ?morris] to the Abbay and of the play maid that samyn day the tent day of Junij instant."[60] From this we may perhaps infer a procession (convoy) followed by a play within the Abbey.

Elaborate pageants for royal entries, many of them on religious subjects, were erected on a number of occasions during this same period.[61] There is no evidence that any of these were dramatic in nature. Edinburgh sponsored an elaborate clerk play, however, several times, beginning in 1553.[62] In that year the city spent 26s "the xxij of Junij, gevin to George Tod for making of ane skaffalt on the hill to the clerk play, the bering of daylis and punschonis thairto, and the aill and the wyne that day thai playit, and furnessing of sax sparris thairto." Another play, very popular and recorded in detail, was given late in the summer in 1554 and later years. It was mounted on "the playfield."

According to a relatively late civic record (1531), Edinburgh's Corpus Christi procession was normally mounted on the day of the festival, and again on the octave.[63] The extensive records of the Hammermen's guild from 1494 and after reveal that the guild marched annually in the Corpus Christi procession with standards, candlesticks, and torches.[64] The guild also furnished a pageant of "errot [Herrod] and his vj knychtis." In 1496 this pageant was fitted out by the "abbot of narent," Edinburgh's Lord of Misrule (master of civic ceremonies). The Hammermen's pageant evidently changed slightly from year to year. At various times it included "werlots," "knapis," "twa doctouris," and "four wiffis." Minstrels played as the procession made its way to St. Catherine's, and indeed the day was distinguished by all manner of spectacle: men in harness, gunners, and musicians performing on a bombard (a bassoonlike instrument). In 1504 the Hammermen spent 4s for "herod and his ij doctouris hors." This implies a mounted spectacle. As Anna J. Mill has observed, "There seems, indeed, to be little to distinguish [Herrod and his companions] from the numerous torch-bearers and standard-bearers and minstrels; and there may have been nothing more dramatic than a spectacular religious riding with biblical characters."[65] Herod and his companions drop from the records in 1512–15, reappear in 1516–29, and then disappear forever. The musicians and other marchers remain into the reign of Elizabeth.

If we had records of other guilds besides the Hammermen, we might very well discover that Edinburgh had a Corpus Christi play of extensive proportions. There is nothing to suggest, however, that this was anything but a processional spectacle, or that it bore any relationship to the play mounted for the king or queen on Corpus Christi.

Louth (Lincolnshire)

The Louth Corpus Christi guild was founded in 1326. Both this guild and the guild of the Twelve Apostles, founded in 1361, mounted annual processions on Corpus Christi.[66] An inventory of 1486, drawn up by the churchwardens of St. James, the principal church of Louth, and entered into their books in 1513/4, includes a note: "also j quare in the wilke is contenyd the fest of corpus Xpi." This was not a dramatic play, but a service book for the liturgical offices on Corpus Christi.[67] The same inventory also mentions "j ferter of syluer gilted and

enameld to the said ferter."[68] This "ferter" was evidently the shrine of
the Corpus Christi procession, mentioned by name in 1544/5 when the
church paid "for watching the fertar vpon corpus christie day with in
the cherche."[69] It was also called a "hutch," as in 1527/8: "A smyth
makyng ij cais to corpus xpi huche, vjd; for watchyng kirke, iiijd"; and
in 1517/8: "John Hareson mendyng huche and for a bolte of iryn to ytt,
5d."[70] The shrine evidently contained precious treasure, and therefore
required a careful guard. In the words of Barnabe Googe, it would have
been "A bootie good, if euery man might haue his libertee."

The guild of Corpus Christi and two other guilds mentioned in the
returns of 1389—the guild of the Blessed Virgin Mary (1329) and the
guild of the Holy Trinity (1376)—were three of the five guilds which in
1527/8 were required to pay for pageants on Corpus Christi day:

> It is agreed by the hole Body of the Towne of Louth that the
> pagents yerely of Corpus Xpi Day shalbe brought forth as the
> Course is of the Costs and charges of Trinite Gild, vjs viijd; Corpus
> Xpi, vjs viijd; Saint Petur Gild, vjs viijd; Saint Michylls light, vjs
> viijd; and the Reist of our Lady Gild how muche so ever it Cost.[71]

The phrase "as the course is" implies that the pageants were traditional.

The accounts of the churchwardens of St. James include scattered
entries concerning the pageants on Corpus Christi day. In 1518/9 the
wardens spent 3s 4d "for payent of corpus xpi day at procession."[72]
This suggests that the pageants were in the first instance processional,
an observation which is borne out by an entry of the following year: "4
men beryng payents to saynte Marye Kirke, ivd."[73] Evidently the
procession with its pageants began at St. James church and ended at
the church of St. Mary.

The wardens paid William Foster 4d in 1525/6 "for part of the cost
of the pagent," and in 1527/8 they gave 4s 8d "for beryng pagentes."[74]
In 1534/5 the wardens gave 16d "for removyng the pageandes," and in
1535/6 they gave 3s 8d "to robert bayley for stuff takyn offe hym for the
pageandes agaynst corpus xpi tyde."[75] The pageants were evidently
stored in a barn in Ulpyn Lane. This barn was rethatched in 1528/9,
and at that time it was called "the pagent Lathe." In the same year
Trinity guild received 10s rent for the pageants which were stored
there.[76]

These entries demonstrate that the pageants continued as an important part of the Corpus Christi festivities: they do not, however, tell us
much about the nature of the pageants beyond the fact that they went
in procession and were the property and responsibility of religious
fraternities rather than craft guilds.

Nothing in the records we have noted suggests a dramatic play. In an inventory of 1515/6, however, the churchwardens recorded as part of the church library, the "hole regenall of corpus xpi play."[77] This entry suggests that the church may have been involved in the production of a Corpus Christi play but reveals nothing about the nature of the play. Several other entries suggest a connection between dramatic plays and Corpus Christi, but none of them is definitive. In 1527/8 the church-wardens of St. James spent 2s 8d on "The players of Gremysby whan thay spoke thaire bayn of thaire play," and listed next after this in the account, "William Foster for rynging agayn corpus xpi day to haunge clos of haros [cloth of arras] in hey qwere, viijd."[78] Any presumed connection between these two entries is, however, entirely speculative. Much later, in 1556/7, John Goodall, schoolmaster, received 13s 3d "for money laid furthe of him at the playes." In 1557/8 Goodall received 16d at the order of the mayor, "for certeyn mony laid furth for the furnishing of the play played in the markit stede on corpus xpi Day the yere before my entring."[79] This must also refer to 1556/7. But these two entries are even further removed in time and auspices from the fraternal guild pageants on Corpus Christi.

Ipswich

Much more can be said about pageants and plays in Ipswich. An Ipswich Guild Merchant that received a charter from King John in 1200 was reestablished by the priors of Holy Trinity and St. Peter in 1325 as the guild of Corpus Christi. The new guild was devoted to the Holy Trinity, to the Blessed Virgin and All Saints, and in particular to the honor of the Eucharist. The procession on Corpus Christi began at nine o'clock in the morning. The marchers assembled at the Church of the Holy Trinity in one year and at St. Peter's in the next. They proceeded with crosses and banners to the other church, and then back to the point of origin, where mass was celebrated. If the march was prevented by the weather, it was to be deferred until the next year rather than postponed to another festival.[80]

Civic records concerning the procession and plays at Corpus Christi are extant from the middle of the fifteenth century, and again from the reigns of Henry VII and Henry VIII.[81] In 1443 the "common marshe, with all the houses and grounds, for 3 yeres" was demised to four persons "to maintaine and repaire the pageants of the Guilde."[82] Much more informative records survive in a Petty Pleas Court Roll for 1445. John Causton was admitted a burgess of Ipswich on the condition that for the next seven years he would "care for all the ornaments of the pageants of the guild of Corpus Christi, and provide and supervise the repair of the pageants and furnish the stages [lez Stages] for the players, those of the city as well as those from outside the city." Together with Thomas Bysshop, common clerk, Causton was to supervise "each and every expense for the repair of the pageants as well as for transporting the decorations, vestments, and other things necessary to the said pageants." (A note at the end of this entry explains that Causton died within the term of this agreement.)[83]

Evidently, then, Ipswich had a procession of pageants and also a sequence of plays, both under the primary supervision of a single burgess, who acted on behalf of the town government and who received the proceeds of town properties for his expenses and salary. The plays were mounted on stages evidently set up in a single location and were performed by local actors and by "foreigners" (out-of-towners) as well.

Three surviving lists describe the procession of pageants in some detail (see Appendix C).[84] The first of these lists, none of which has previously been published, was drawn up during the reign of Henry VI, that is, sometime between 1422 and 1461,[85] possibly during the tenure of John Causton. The list is entitled simply "lez pagentz." The first three items in the list are "Saynt George," "Saint Ion [John]," and "Saynt Thomas." Then follow the names of twelve major crafts, then three orders of friars—the Carmelites, the Friars Preachers, and the Minorites (Franciscans)—then the *Tabernaclum* with the priors of Trinity and St. Peter, and finally the bailiff or sheriffs with the "portmen." The "tabernacle" was clearly the shrine, accompanied by the priors of those churches which, as we have seen, were the terminal points of the procession. Clearly no dramatic plays could have been performed on pageants in this context.

The next list, on the verso side of the same folio, contains the same information in greater detail. All the guilds presenting each of the pageants are named. Six guilds plus the "Generosi" presented St. George, the Taylors presented St. John, four guilds presented St. Eligius, two presented St. Thomas, and eight presented St. Luke. Nine other groups of guilds are listed, along with three pageants: "le Culle" (a fish), the Image of the Assumption of the Blessed Mary, and a ship. Then follow the three regular orders, and the *Tabernaclum*.

The final list is in a late fifteenth- or early sixteenth-century hand. It is entitled, "Howe euery occupacion or craftes men shuld order them selffes in ther goung [going] with ther pagauntes in the procession of Corpus Xpi." It is almost precisely like the second list, except that it omits the "Culle," and adds "a Dolphyn."

The pageant procession described in these lists is even more like the

Corpus Christi procession described by Kirchmayer and Googe than the processions of Lincoln, Norwich, or London. It may owe something to this Continental tradition, but it may also owe something to its fourteenth-century background, as a guild devoted to the Holy Trinity, the Blessed Virgin, All Saints, and the Eucharist.

The three lists of pageants all occur in the White Doomsday Book, a manuscript in which are written the ordinances of the town of Ipswich. This very book and its lists are mentioned in the Petty Court Book entry for 1521, where the occupations and inhabitants of Ipswich are ordered to "keep the order of the procession as it is recorded in the book of the constitutions."[86] A similar order was issued in 1504,[87] and the White Book may also have been referred to in 1493, when John Regnero was chosen burgess on the condition that he would assist "in all things for the pageant of Corpus Christi according to his skill [*Ingenium*] in making and amending the book of Corpus Christi [*libri Corporis xpi*]."[88] The pageant was not itself the dramatic play. Regnero may have been paid for writing new presentational speeches: or perhaps he was selected to recopy the list of pageants in the procession. We may suspect that the third list was written about this time, and Regnero may have been the man who wrote it.

The pageants are not mentioned every year, but neither were they ever canceled. "Le Pagent" was certainly prepared in 1520, and in 1531 William Nottyngham and Richard Humfrey were elected "masters of the pagent of *le Shippe*" and were ordered to have their pageant ready for the day of Corpus Christi.[89] This is clearly the ship named in the White Book pageant lists.

William Parnell received a financial consideration for his work on "lez pagent" in 1492, and was elected in the same year along with John Balhed to oversee "all the utencils and ornaments of Corpus Christi."[90] The ornaments, which we have noticed before, probably belonged to the pageants or play. The utensils, inventoried in 1515, consisted of "a Doseyn Sponys"; "v Masers"; "v Tabelclothes ij of crest cloth iij of iij quarters clothe"; "a Garnyshe of newe vessell excepte ij saucers"; "ij Chargers, v Platers, iiij dishes, v saucers, xiiij saultes, a panne, and ij Brasse Pottes."[91] These were for a Corpus Christi dinner, first mentioned in 1492.[92] The dinner was actually canceled this year but evidently was a long-established tradition. In subsequent years it was often canceled and often reinstated, usually accompanied by orders concerning the Corpus Christi play. Thus on 15 April 1515 the play (*ludus vocatus Corpus Cpi Pley*) and the dinner (*prandium vocatum Corpus Cristi dynner*) were both canceled.[93] On 26 September 1515 the burgesses decided to hold the dinner "according to ancient custom," but not the play.[94] But on 11 April 1516 the dinner was also canceled.[95] The dinner alone was held in 1520.[96] In 1521 the play was laid aside again, and in 1531 it was laid aside once more, forever.[97]

We have noted the references to stages and actors in the court roll for 1445. In 1505 the town granted John Stangilts 20s 8d "yerely for 12 yeres, to finde the stageing for Corpus Christi play," and John Parnell 33s 4d "to find the ornaments during such time, and collecters named of assessments for the play."[98] In this instance the ornaments seem to have belonged to the dramatic play.

In the Ipswich records the word *pageant* is always used in connection with the processional tableaux, while *play* always signifies the dramatic Corpus Christi play. The pageant procession is virtually always dealt with in an ordinance of its own. The dinner and play, on the contrary, are usually dealt with in the same ordinance. This suggests that when the play was mounted it was actually performed, as at York, for the banquet of civic officials on Corpus Christi day. In the absence of further information, it seems best to withhold judgment on the nature of the dramatic play. It must be noted, however, that if the play was indeed related to the pageants, it must have been quite unlike any of the extant Corpus Christi cycles.

The Corpus Christi liturgical procession may have continued without serious interruption after 1531, but the pageant spectacle was evidently revived only once, in 1542, when the council ordered that "Every householder, with their family, shall follow the pageants of Corpus Christi in due order." The twelve "Portmen," or aldermen, and their wives were excepted, and may very well have viewed the procession from a special station. The council also ordered that "Every Warden and Master of the Trade shall offer to theire Pageants uppon the day of Corpus Christi, each of them 1d."[99] Pageants are not mentioned again after this year. The Corpus Christi guild maintained its fraternal character, but in deference to Reformation sentiment it was stripped of its offensive proper name: from 1552 onward it was called simply "the Guild."[100]

Perth (Scotland)

The records of Perth strongly suggest that plays quite unlike the extant cycle dramas may have been presented on the day of Corpus Christi. For the year 1485 the Guild Book of Perth mentions a payment of 20s to Robert Douthle, chaplain, "pro suis laboribus et expensis factis In processione et ludo corporis xpi."[101] A similar entry occurs in

1486, while in 1487/8 the play alone is recorded (*in ludo corporis xpi*).[102] The nature of this play may be partly deduced from the Hammermen's Book, a manuscript which contains extracts from earlier records which are now lost. The most complete entry dates from 1518:

> The playaris on corpus christie day and quhat money sall be payt till thame that is to say
> Item in primis till adam, vjd; and ewa, vjd; Sanct eloy, vjd; The marmadin [mermaiden], viijd; The devill, viijd; his man, iiijd; The angell and the clerk, vjd; Sanct erasimus, viijd; The cord drawer, viijd; The king, xijd; The thre tormentouris, iijs; The best baner, xijd; The vthir, vjd; The stule berer and the harnes, vd; The devillis chepman, viijd; till robert hart for vestiment, iiijd; Item for [blank], ijd; Item to the menstrell, ijs.[103]

Some sense can be made of this entry, particularly with the aid of subsequent records. In 1534 items which occur in the list are specified for "corpus christis play." This connects the pageant of the Hammermen with the civic play of the preceding century. Several of the characters in the list clearly belong to a pageant of the Fall of Man. Others—the mermaid, and St. Eloy, patron of the Hammermen—seem not to fit into any particular episode. Still others distinctly belong to a St. Erasmus pageant. His tormentors put St. Erasmus to death by reeling his intestines out of his belly onto a drum: hence the "cord drawer," and an entry in 1520, "Item for sancterasmus cord, iijd."

The numerous payments to actors distinctly suggest a dramatic play. But Perth also mounted a procession on Corpus Christi. On 13 June 1520, 5s 8d was "gadderit about the toun to furneis the play affoir the processioun." This may be interpreted to mean that the dramatic play was performed before the procession; more likely it means that the money was gathered in advance. In any case, the banners mentioned in 1518 and in other years were probably for the procession. It may well be that all the players marched in the procession, and that several different plays were performed afterwards. It is difficult to believe that all these various characters could have been brought together into a single connected play or cycle. And indeed in later years some of the material was evidently purged. In 1553 the players included the Trinity, Adam, Eve, "The mekle devill," the serpent, one angel and two little angels, "the devillis chepman," St. Eloy, and the "marmadin." St. Erasmus, the tormentors, and the king have disappeared. Two persons "to beat [? bear] the bannerris" remain.

Records from the Wrights' Company supplement our information

slightly. Many processional items are recorded for 1530, and for
another unknown year. The craft spent 8d "for menden of the castell,"
and other sums "for ane crownn to sir Iohne farguson" and "for
ympis." This is too little information to allow us to reconstruct the play.
We may be certain, however, that the Corpus Christi play of Perth was
quite unlike Kolve's "protocycle."

The Perth Corpus Christi play proved remarkably tenacious. The
Kirk Session Minute Books include the following memorandum for 1
July 1577:

> Becaws certane inhabitantis of this town alsweill aganis the expres
> commandement of the ciuill magistratts in cowncall as aganis the
> Ministeris prohibitioun in pulpitt hes playit corpus christeis play
> vpon thrusday the vj of Iunij last quhilk day ves vovnt to be
> callit corpus christeis day to the great sklander of the kirk of
> god and dishonour to this haill toun; And becaws the said play is
> idolatrous superstitiows and also sclanderows alsweill be ressoun
> of the Idell day . . . [breaks off].

An entry in the Perth civic records for 1577/8 concerning the restitution
of a garment confirms this production of "corpus cristies play."[104]

The kirk brought tremendous pressure against the players to prevent
the play from ever being performed again. In particular, baptism was
refused to the children of participants who did not swear to refrain in
the future. Sanctions were evidently effective against the Corpus
Christi play, which after all required a cooperative effort among many
parties. Other customs, such as "passing to the draggoun holl" in May,
St. Robert's play in December, and going about in disguise, were more
difficult to eradicate, and occupied the kirk's attention for many years
after.[105]

Towns with Corpus Christi Cycle Plays
Preston, Lancaster, Kendal

Corpus Christi cycle plays were not confined to York, Wakefield,
and the other towns which we have studied at length. In 1631 John
Weever compared the London Clerkenwell plays to "Corpus Christi
play in my country, which I haue seene acted at Preston, and Lancaster,
and last of all at Kendall, in the beginning of the raigne of King
Iames."[106] Little is known about the Preston play, but in the eighteenth
century Preston had a procession which included such figures as the
Tailors' Adam and Eve and the Smiths' Vulcan.[107] However, these are
so similar to the late Shrewsbury show, even to the names of the
respective guilds, that we may suspect some late borrowings. Nothing is

known about the Lancaster plays, but Kendal had a Corpus Christi procession with pageants. On 14 February 1575 the corporation suppressed certain sumptuous feasts, excepting "Such lyke . . . as have bene comonlye used at . . . metyings of men off Occupacyons aboute orders for their severall pagiands of Corpus xpi playe."[108] The tolerance for these plays was not enduring, however, as may be seen in a memorandum of 1586:

> Whereas very many of the common inhabitants of the borough, preferring their own private commodities and the customs of usage to the benefit and common wealth of all others, covet and earnestly cry for the having of Corpus Christi play yearly as in former time, without allowing for the omission thereof in any year, it is ordained that the Alderman or his deputy shall not have power to give licence for the play of Corpus Christi, or for any other stage play, without the consent of the majority of the Burgesses.[109]

In this case the play seems to be classed as one of several stage plays. This implies that the dramatic play must have been stationary, and thus distinct from the processional pageants.

Canterbury

A Canterbury statute of 1490 flatly contradicts the traditional scholarly assertion that the Corpus Christi play was unknown in the south of England. The order recalls that:

> before this tyme ther hath bene by the most honourable and worshipfull the Cite of Canterbury used and continued within the same cite a play called Corpus Xpi Play, as well to the honour of the same, as to the profite of all vitelers and other occupacions within the same; which play before this tyme was maynteyned and plaide at the costs and charg of the crafts and misteris within the same cite; and wheras nowe of late daies it hath bene left and laide a part, to the grete hurt and decay of the seide cite . . . .[110]

Plans were laid for the immediate revival of the play.

It is not known for certain whether the Corpus Christi play was spectacular, dramatic, or both. In 1520, however, the churchwardens of St. Dunstan's inventoried "a booke of Abraam and Isaacke belonging to the stocke of the Schaft in the kepyng of the Church Wardeyns in the chest in the qwere there layde in the monythe of May the xxiiij day Anno Regis H. vij sexto [1491]." This may conceivably have been one of the plays from the Corpus Christi cycle. Other inventories list other books and stories which may also have been part of the Corpus Christi play.[111]

Records concerning other Canterbury pageants are more informative. In 1501/2 the council incurred expenses "for makyng of the
bankett in the Courte Hall." The banquet was held on 5 January, the
eve of Twelfth Night. One of the participants was evidently "the
lorde Prior of Cristischurche [Canterbury Cathedral]." The "barre in
the yeldehall" was removed for the occasion, and "scaffoldes" built. A
"Towre" and a "castell" were also constructed "in the yeldehall." The
play naturally enough included "the iij kynges of Coleyn," an unknown
number of "hensshemen," and a "Starre," gilded. The "pleyers" were
treated to supper "the same nyght at the Swanne," an inn.[112]

The discovery of a biblical play performed indoors at a civic banquet
before high dignitaries is of course of great importance for us. It is also
useful to discover entries which clearly demonstrate that the steeds of
the three kings were fabricated rather than live horseflesh:

> fyrst paied to Richard Inner for the makyng of ij bestes and for the
>   Towre in the yeldehall, xs.
> Item for xij elles of canvas for the iij bestes, iiijs.
> Item for payntyng of the same iij bestes, iijs.
> Item for hoopys lathe and nayle for the same iij bestes, iijs.

This shows that it was quite possible to mount a play requiring
horses indoors.

Records for an entirely different spectacle begin in 1505/6 and last
until 1537/8. These are for the watch on the eve of the Translation of
St. Thomas (2 July). St. Thomas was a fabricated image mounted on a
wheeled pageant wagon. An altar was also situated on the wagon,
together with an angel who was evidently made to move by a "vyce"
hidden within the pageant: part of the cost of the pageant was for a
"candell to lyght the turnyng of the vyce."[113] Around the pageant
marched a number of knights (no doubt four) played by children. This
pageant was part of a marching watch and was not, so far as we can
tell, associated with a dramatic play.

A play of some kind was mounted in 1542/3. Since it included four
"tormentors," it may have been a martyrdom or a play of the Passion.
Forty shillings was "receyved of master Batherst for the hole stage of
the pley to hym sold," suggesting that the play was broken up after this
year.[114]

Newcastle upon Tyne

Newcastle guilds are not listed among the returns of 1389. A 1426
indenture of the Coopers' guild shows, however, that the guilds

marched in procession and mounted plays: "the coupers shall amy-
abilly yerly atte the fest of Corpus Xpi go to gedder in procession as
other Craftes doyes; And play ther play at ther costes . . . And that
euery man of the seid craft shalbe atte the procession whanne his oure
is assigned by the seyd wardens."[115]

This is the earliest of a long series of guild indentures, some of which
still exist in the original, others surviving in mid-seventeenth-century
transcripts. Several indentures extend and clarify the information
contained in the Coopers' ordinance. The Merchant Adventurers' 1480
"ackit of the prosescion of corpus xpe day" stipulates that the
members were to appear "in [?]Bigg Marcath by vij of clok in the
mornyng . . . the lattast mayd burges to go formest in procession . . .
Provyded always that al those of the said felleship that shalbe Mair
Shereff and aldermen with thaire officers and seruandes than beyng,
attend wppon the Holy Sacramente."[116] This 7:00 A.M. march was the
morning liturgical procession.

According to the Barbers' indenture of 1442 the members were to
gather for the procession "at the Newgate,"[117] situated in the north
quarter of the city. Evidently the procession made its way from
Newgate to St. Nicholas cathedral, situated near the river at the city
center. The Tailors' indenture of 1536 confirms the starting point: "if
[a fellow] come not to the fellowshipp before the procession passe the
newgate to pay j[lb] of wax and if he come not afore the procession
ended to pay two pound of wax."[118]

The Curriers' indenture of 1546 names "the Lightes pagiant and
plaie" on Corpus Christi,[119] a formula we have seen elsewhere. The
precise relationship between the lights and pageants is defined by the
invaluable but previously unpublished indenture of the Saddlers, dated
1533. The Saddlers agreed:

> to goe in the said procession from the time of the setting forth of
> the same procession unto the comeing againe of the said pro-
> cession to the said place or places accustomed; And then Imediate-
> ly after the said procession done then their pagions to them
> accustomed and belonging to be sett furth in due order and to be
> played together at all their costs and charges after the ordynaunces
> and sessings of their wardens for time being without any contra-
> diccion or any delay . . . And that euery man of the said crafte of
> Sadlers shall meet together in his or their best array and apparrell
> att the procession . . .[120]

Like several other cities, then, Newcastle mounted a liturgical procession with torches on Corpus Christi morning but presented its

pageants later the same day, in another procession. The Millers'
indenture of 1578 instructs the members of that craft "to attend upon
their said playe in decent manner in euerie place of the said towne
where antentlie the same among other plaies usalie hath bene
plaied."[121] This may indicate a true-processional production at several
stations after the manner of Coventry or Chester. It is equally possible
that Newcastle like York mounted a procession of tableau pageants
which were followed in turn by a stationary dramatic play. If this was
the case, the "Lightes pagiant and plaie" named in the Curriers'
indenture were three distinct events.

The names or subjects of twelve of the Newcastle plays, recorded in
the various guild indentures, have long been known. We may extrapolate from this list to infer a normal cycle of episodes, a briefer version
of the York pageants. We may also infer from the extant though
corrupt Noah play that the cycle was characterized by plays of
moderate length and remarkable dramatic vitality.[122]

Sixteenth-century records of three guilds survive, those of the
Merchant Adventurers in the original Book of Orders, those of the
Slaters and of the Fullers and Dyers in printed transcripts only. The
earliest relevant Merchant Adventurers' record is dated 12 March
1517: Andrew Bewykes received 12s 4d from Robert Millor, "in mone
which was ressaved of the money to pay for the playes."[123] For some
reason the Merchant Adventurers had taken over responsibility for more
plays than one. In 1552 they paid the large sume of £31 1s 11d "for the
fyve playes where of the towne must paye for the ostmen [Hostlers']
playe, iiij^{li} ."[124] Evidently the Merchant Adventurers sponsored the
plays of the Hostlers, Vintners, Drapers, Mercers, and Boothmen.[125]
The plays are mentioned once again in 1561: "Paid for the settinge
fowrthe of the Corpuschristye plays as apers by the bukes, xiiij^{li} ixs
xjd."[126] In this same year the Fullers and Dyers paid 20d "for the care
and banner berryng."[127] The reference to the "care" is one of two
records which suggest that the Newcastle pageants were wheeled
wagons. The other occurs in the 1568 Slaters' book, which mentions
"the care," and "bearers of the care and baneres."[128]

In 1554 the Merchant Adventurers paid £4 2s "for the charges in
ande aboute Hoggmaggowyk," and in 1558 the craft paid 14s 2d "for
the charges of hogmagog."[129] Both of these entries occur next to
charges for the procession on Corpus Christi day, but Hogmagog,
certainly a giant, may well have gone at another festival. Charges for
the procession of Corpus Christi day occur each year from 1554 to
1559.[130] The Corpus Christi play was mounted in 1561 and evidently in

1568, but charges for the procession are no longer entered after 1559. A new pageant, much more amenable to Reformation sympathies, occurs under the year 1564: "Item paid for reparinge of gownes to the george as apears by a byll of pertekelers howe, iij[li] ixs vj[d]."[131] In Newcastle, as throughout England and Scotland, Protestantism was gaining the upper hand.

Appendix A/ Formulas for True-Processional Productions

In all formulas below, let

T = the total length of a true-processional production

N = the number of plays in a cycle

S = the number of stations

Q = the number of acting times

P = the length of any play

$P^{\max}$ = the length of the longest play in a cycle

$p^{\max}$ = the length of the longest play performed at a given time

J = Journey: the time required to move from one station to the next, and to prepare to play there

I = Interval: the time required to prepare for performance when a play, instead of being required to move from one station to the next, is simply "waiting in the wings" at any station

1. Formula for uniform advances:

$$T_u = Q(P^{\max}) + (Q\text{-}1)J,$$

where

$$Q = N + S\text{-}1.$$

The number of acting times (Q) is equal to the number of plays (N) plus the number of stations after the first (S-1). The minimum length of the uniform acting time is equal to the length of the longest play, $P^{\max}$. The combined length of all acting times is therefore $Q(P^{\max})$. All plays begin simultaneously, and thus no acting time can begin until all plays have made their journeys to the next station. Since no pause is counted after the last acting time is finished, the number of journeys is one less than the number of acting times, that is, (Q-1), and the time spent on journeys is (Q-1)J. The assumption here is that J is constant for all stations, or that J represents the longest journey required between any two stations.

2. Formula for synchronized advances (approximate):
$$T_s = p_1^{max} + p_2^{max} + \ldots + p_Q^{max} + (Q\text{-}1)J.$$
The total length of production is the sum of all acting times, from 1 to Q, that is, from first to last, plus all journeys between acting times. Since acting times vary, there is no alternative to simple addition based on actual scrutiny of play lengths. The length of each acting time is equal to the longest play performed at that time. This may be determined by establishing which plays (up to twelve, all contiguous) are mounted during each acting time. The factor for pauses $(Q\text{-}1)J$ is explained above. There are, in fact, cases when the shorter rather than the longer pause will govern. For example, the plays following the longest may be able to finish and then complete their journeys while the longest is still playing at the last station. In general, the production will be speeded slightly after each longer play is finished performing. Unlike uniform advances, if J is variable, the longest journey does not necessarily govern. It would be most practical to add the respective journeys to the appropriate plays, and to calculate on the basis of the longest combined journey plus play.

3. Formula for free advances:
$$T_f = p_1 + p_2 + \ldots$$
$$+ p_N + (S\text{-}1)P^{max} + (S\text{-}1)J + (N\text{-}1)I.$$
This formula is basically simple but more difficult to explain. For the moment disregard pauses for movement. Consider first all plays in the cycle up to and including the longest. (If the first play is the longest, it alone is considered.) Each play can advance to the first station as soon as the station has been cleared by the play ahead of it. Therefore the time taken by these plays at the first station is simply the sum of their individual lengths: $T' = p_1 + p_2 + \ldots + P^{max}$. Consider second the behavior of the longest play as it proceeds from the first station to the last. Since it performs its full length at each station in turn, the time taken from the moment it leaves the first station to the moment it leaves the last (not counting pauses) is $T'' = (S\text{-}1)P^{max}$. Consider third the behavior of the remaining plays after the longest play has finished at the last station. These plays will simply be able to perform one after the other without interruption, or gaps between them. This is because no other plays can hinder those behind them as much as the longest play hinders those behind it. Plays will have "piled up" behind the longest, and will play immediately each time the last stage has been cleared. (Certainly they could perform no faster!) The time lapse for this last group of plays is therefore
$$T''' = p_{max+1} + p_{max+2} + \ldots + p_N.$$
(If P^{max} is the last play in the cycle, then this summation is equal to zero.)

The total time devoted to acting the plays is simply the sum of these three summations: $T_f = T' + T'' + T'''$. But since the sum of T' and T'''

is simply the sum of all the individual plays in the cycle, then $T_f = (T' + T''') + T''$, or, $T_f = p_1 + p_2 + \ldots + p_N + (S\text{-}1)P^{\max}$. In other words, the total length of the production is the length of the cycle as peformed at the first station, plus the length of the longest play multiplied by the number of stations at which it must perform after it is finished at the first. It is important to note that the position of the longest play in the series makes no difference to the production time.

The longest play must actually make a journey from station to station between its performances. But all plays performing at the first station and the remaining plays at the last station will simply "wait in the wings." The accumulated time spent on journeys by the longest play is the sum of all the journeys (J) as the play travels between all the stations, a total of $(S\text{-}1)$ journeys. As for the plays at the first station, and those after the longest at the last station, each play requires only enough time to set up its stage (I), and since no interval is counted before the first play at the first station or after the last play at the last, the total number required is $(N\text{-}1)$. If journeys are irregular it is necessary to add up all the various journeys required of the longest play, and to substitute this summation for the factor $(S\text{-}1)J$.

Appendix B/ Doubling in True-Processional Productions

One of the obvious difficulties in dividing a single long action, like the sacred history of the world with its most salient features, into many plays presented by different casts is that the number of actors required for the entire production quickly climbs to astronomical heights. From a count of the dramatis personae in Miss Smith's text, the York cycle, excluding the last fragment, requires 352 actors for speaking roles. Additional actors are required for silent roles, and additional singers for the choirs. The production includes eight actors playing God, fourteen for the Virgin, and twenty-two for Christ. This does not even make provision for the silent Jesus in several of the trial plays.

If doubling were permitted, the number of actors could be reduced considerably. But when plays are performed simultaneously at different stations, an actor with two roles may find that, like the all-around athlete at a track-and-field meet, one of the events may have to go on without him.

In addition to doubling two or more roles in the same play, an actor performing in a cycle can take roles in several plays. In the case of a single-stage production, no limit can be set to the number of plays in which an actor can participate. In the York cycle he can take forty-eight parts. But in a true-processional performance each role requires an actor to stay with a particular play for all its performances at all stations. After finishing with one play he can then begin with another. This practice I shall call terminal doubling.

With uniform or synchronized advances it is quite easy to specify the number of plays in which an actor can perform: simply divide the number of plays by the number of stations. In the case of York, with forty-eight plays at twelve stations, an actor can take roles in four different plays. The only condition is that at least eleven plays intervene between each two successive plays in which he performs.

212

Since the free-advance mode is internally irregular, and since staggering is also irregular, opportunities for terminal doubling here are more difficult to stipulate. Tables 5 and 6, however, will facilitate an analysis for the two types of production. If an actor takes a role in the first York play in a system of unmodified free advances, he finishes at the last station after a virtual 3,020 lines have been spoken. He can then join play 15, which begins at 3,161 and ends at 8,858. Next he can join play 33, which begins at 9,025 and ends at 16,520. But the last play in the cycle has already begun at 13,835, so there is no possibility of taking a fourth role. The following chart shows the first and last play in which an actor can begin if he wishes to take three roles by terminal doubling:

Earliest Play

Play	Lines
1	0–3,020
15	3,161–8,858
33	9,025–16,520

Latest Play

Play	Lines
8	1,062–4,238
26	6,142–13,782
48	13,835–21,321

Terminal doubling is more restricted in a schedule of 646-line advances because the early plays are slower in their progress and cannot release their actors until relatively later, as shown in the following chart:

Earliest Play

Play	Lines
1	0–7,266
29	7,293–14,700

Latest Play

Play	Lines
26	6,124–13,793
48	13,835–21,321

Terminal doubling is not the only way to reduce the number of actors required for a true-processional production with free advances. An actor can also take roles in two contiguous or nearly contiguous plays as long as the sum of the lengths of these plays does not exceed the length of the longest play ahead.

If an actor is able to take roles in contiguous plays, the plays must behave as if they were bunched. In short plays following very long plays there is a natural and an inevitable bunching, something like the artificial bunching at the beginning of a production with modified advances. Taking two or more roles in bunched plays I shall call internal doubling.

In the York cycle, with modified advances, an actor can take roles in any contiguous plays as long as they do not total more than 546 lines, including intervals. Moreover, an actor can combine terminal and internal doubling. But the conduct of an actual production would not be entirely predictable, as with uniform or synchronized advances, and so in practice a very large margin would have to be made for error.

Transcribed from Ipswich Borough Records MS C4/2 (White Doomsday Book), and published by permission of the Ipswich and East
Suffolk Record Office, County Hall, Ipswich, Suffolk. Erasures are
indicated by half brackets; words added subsequent to the original
composition of the manuscript are indicated by pointed brackets.

Folio 1 (?Early sixteenth century)

Howe euery occupacion or Craftes men shuld order them selffes in
ther goung with ther pagauntes in the procession of Corpus Xpi

Generosi ⎫
pewterars ⎪
plomars ⎪
Sadlars ⎬ Seint Gorge
Masons ⎪
Tylers ⎪
Armorars ⎭

Taylors Seint John

Goldsmythes ⎫
Bladsmythes ⎪ Seint
loksmythes ⎬ Eligius
Blaksmythes ⎭

Barbours ⎱ Seint
Waxchandelers ⎰ Thomas

Glasiors peyntours ⎫
Carpenters/Carvers ⎪
Bowars Flechers ⎬ Seint
Whilwrites Coupers ⎪ luke
patenmakers Turnars ⎪
⟨Screveners⟩ ⎭

Weuers Fullars ⎱
Cappers Hadmakers ⎰

Shomakers ⎱
Tannars ⎰

Fyschmongers/a Dolphyn

Bochars ⎱
Tallowchandel[e]rs ⎰

Skynners Glovers ⎱
pursers/Cardmakers ⎰

Clothmakers Drapers ⎱ Assumpcion
Diars & Sharmen ⎰ of our Lady

Mercers pounters ⎱
habirdashars ⎰

Marchauntes mariners ⎱ a Ship
Brewars ⎰

Bakers & waferas

Friers Carmelites
Friers Minors
Friers Prechors

Folio 72 (List antedates 1461)

lez pagentz

Saynt George
Saynt Ion
Saynt Thomas
Wryghtes
Wevveres
<fulleres>
Cordwaneres
Tayloures
Fysshemongeres
Bocheres
Skynneres
Draperes
Merceres
Shypmen
Bakeres

Fratres Carmelitores
Fratres predicatores
Fratres Minores

Tabernaclum
Priores Trinitatis & Scancti Petri

Ballius cum portmannis

Folio 72ᵛ (List evidently written after list of "lez pagentz" on fol. 72, but prior to 1473, the year of the next dated entry.)

Lez pagent pro corpore xpi

Generosi ⎫
Pewtereres ⎪
Plomeres ⎪ pro Sancto
Sadeleres ⎬ Georgio
Masounys ⎪
Tyleres ⎪
Armereres ⎭

Tayloures pro Sancto Johanne

Goldsmythis ⎫
Blaksmythis ⎬ pro Sancto
loksmythis ⎪ Elegio
Bladsmythis ⎭

Barboures ⎫ pro Sancto
Wexchaundeleres ⎬ Thoma

Carpenteres ⎫
Kerveres ⎪
Bowyeres ⎪
Fletcheres ⎪
Wheelwryghtes ⎬ pro Sancto
Cowperis ⎪ luca
Patynmakeres ⎪
Turnoures ⎭
Weuerys ⎫
Hatmakeres ⎬
Fulleres ⎪
Capperes ⎭

Shomakeres ⎫
Tanneres ⎬

Fysshmongeres

Bocheres ⎫
Talwechaundeleres ⎬ le Culle

Skynneres ⎫
Gloueres ⎪
Cardmakeres ⎬ ⌐fullers¬
Purseres ⎭ ⌐cappers¬

Clothmakers ⎫
Dyeres ⎪ pro Imagine
Shermen ⎬ Assumpcionis
Draperes ⎭ beate marie

Merceres ⎫
Habyrdassheres ⎬
Poynteres ⎭

Marchauntes ⎫
Maryneres ⎬ < pro Nave >
<Brewers> ⎭

Bakerys ⎫
Wavereres ⎬

a Fratres Carmelitores
c Fratres Predicatores
v Fratres Minores

Tabernaclum

ABBREVIATIONS

For full titles of books see Bibliography. Abbreviations of manuscript references are explained in the respective chapters. Three abbreviations relevant to manuscripts are used throughout this book: MS=manuscript; BM=British Museum; PRO=Public Record Office, London.

BTD	*Beverley Town Documents,* ed. Leach
EES	Wickham, *Early English Stages, 1300–1660*
EETS	Early English Text Society (o.s.=original series; e.s.=extra series; s.s.=supplementary series)
EG	Smith, *English Gilds*
EMP	Woolf, *English Mystery Plays*
EP	Withington, *English Pageantry*
ERD	Craig, *English Religious Drama*
HMC	Historical Manuscripts Commission
JEGP	*Journal of English and Germanic Philology*
MDC	Salter, *Medieval Drama in Chester*
ME	Gardiner, *Mysteries' End*
MLN	*Modern Language Notes*
MPS	Mill, *Medieval Plays in Scotland*
MS	Chambers, *Mediaeval Stage*
NCP	*Non-Cycle Plays and Fragments,* ed. Davis
OED	*Oxford English Dictionary*
PGME	Westlake, *Parish Gilds of Medieval England*
"SEPP"	Leach, "Some English Plays and Players"
TCP	*Two Coventry Corpus Christi Plays* [*Two Coventry Plays*], ed. Craig
YAARS	York Archaeological Association, Record Series
YCCG	*The Register of the Guild of Corpus Christi in the City of York* [*York Corpus Christi Guild*]

YCR	*York Civic Records,* ed. Raine
YMA	*York Mercers and Merchant Adventurers* [*York Merchant Adventurers*]
YMB	*York Memorandum Book,* ed. Sellers
YP	*York Plays,* ed. Smith
YR	Davies, *Extracts from the Municipal Records of the City of York during the Reigns of Edward IV, Edward V, and Richard III.* [*York Records*]

NOTES

Abbreviations used in the notes are explained above. Full titles and publication details for all published works cited are given in the Bibliography following the notes.

CHAPTER 1

1. Chambers, *MS*, 2: 69; and *English Literature at the Close of the Middle Ages*, p. 21; Craig, *ERD*, pp. 1–18; Hardison, *Christian Rite and Christian Drama in the Middle Ages*, p. 285; Woolf, *EMP*, pp. 54–76; and Kolve, *The Play Called Corpus Christi*, pp. 33–50. For an extensive evaluation of Woolf, *EMP*, see my review in *Modern Philology*, forthcoming.

2. See also Jerome Taylor, "The Dramatic Structure of the Middle English Corpus Christi, or Cycle Plays," in *Literature and Society*, pp. 175–86, reprinted in *Medieval English Drama*, pp. 148–56; and Theo Stemmler, *Liturgische Feiern und geistliche Spiele*, esp. pp. 167–208. Woolf, *EMP*, p. 73, argues as I do that "the feast had little effect upon the subject-matter of the plays."

3. *Play*, p. 49.

4. Ibid., pp. 47–48.

5. *MLQ* 29 (1968): 95. See Woolf, *EMP*, p. 69, for Continental Eucharist plays performed on or about the feast of Corpus Christi.

6. *NCP*, p. 60.

7. *Play*, p. 48.

8. Review of Kolve, p. 96.

9. Editions used for this study are *The Towneley Plays* [Wakefield cycle], ed. George England and Alfred W. Pollard; *The Wakefield Pageants in the Towneley Cycle*, ed. A. C. Cawley; *York Plays*, ed. L. Toulmin Smith; and *Chester Plays*, ed. H. Deimling and G. W. Matthews.

10. *Ludus Coventriae,* ed. K. S. Block, p. 16.

11. Review of Kolve, pp. 96–97.

12. John Lydgate, *Minor Poems, I,* ed. H. N. MacCracken, pp. 35–43.

13. Kolve, *Play,* pp. 44–46.

14. Ibid., p. 48.

15. Ibid., pp. 52–54.

16. Ibid., p. 57.

17. Ibid., p. 49.

18. On the Cividale cycle, see Chambers, *MS,* 2: 77–78; and Karl Young, *Drama of the Medieval Church,* 2: 540–41. On Florence, see A. D'Ancona, *Origini del teatro italiano,* 1: 202–4. On Le Puy, see L. Petit de Julleville, *Histoire du théâtre en France: Les Mystères,* 2: 197. On the London plays, see below, chap. 10. On the Cornish cycle, see *Ancient Cornish Drama,* ed. and trans. Edwin Norris. On the paucity of historical evidence, see Robert Longsworth, *The Cornish Ordinalia: Religion and Dramaturgy,* pp. 1–12. See also *The Cornish Ordinalia: A Medieval Dramatic Trilogy,* trans. Markham Harris, pp. viii–x.

19. *Play,* p. 46.

20. Ibid., p. 37.

21. Ibid., p. 33.

22. Ibid., p. 49.

23. Taylor, "Dramatic Structure," in *Medieval English Drama,* p. 149.

24. *Christian Rite,* p. 292.

25. Harry Berger, Jr., "Theater, Drama, and the Second World: A Prologue to Shakespeare," *Comparative Drama* 2 (1968): 10. Two recent studies, Woolf, *EMP,* and Stemmler, *Liturgische Feiern,* are more concerned with the prehistory of the plays, but neither undertakes a serious assessment of the traditional histories. Major arguments of both works, but particularly of Stemmler's, must be dismissed as invalid.

26. *ERD,* p. 134. Craig first took this position in "The Corpus Christi Procession and the Corpus Christi Play," *JEGP* 13 (1914): 589–602. Craig has been defended by Merle Pierson, "The Relation of the Corpus Christi Procession to the Corpus Christi Plays," *Transactions of the Wisconsin Academy of Sciences, Arts, and Letters* 18 (1915): 110–65; and Lawrence Blair, "A Note on the Relation of the Corpus Christi Procession to the Corpus Christi Play in England," *MLN* 55 (1940): 83–95. Woolf, *EMP,* p. 75, agrees that "In England, . . . what evidence there is suggests that the plays came first." Opposing Craig are Charles Davidson, *Studies in the English Mystery Plays,* pp. 83–102; and "Concerning English Mystery Plays," *MLN* 7 (1892): 339–43; Chambers, *MS,* 2: 160–76; Matthew Lyle Spencer, *Corpus Christi Pageants in England,* pp. 61–82; and Glynne Wickham, *EES,* 1: 147–48.

27. Craig, *ERD*, pp. 128–29.

28. *MDC*, pp. 32–42. Cf. Theo Stemmler, "Zur Datierung der *Chester Plays*," *Germanisch-Romanische Monatschrift* 49 (1968): 308–13. See also below, chap. 9, n. 2.

29. *ERD*, p. 137.

30. Ibid., pp. 154–55.

31. See Woolf, *EMP*, pp. 61–63, 75–76. Neil C. Brooks, "An Ingolstadt Corpus Christi Procession and the *Biblia Pauperum*," *JEGP* 35 (1936): 1–16, has identified a tableau procession which was taken directly from a pictorial source. See also Brooks, "Processional Drama and Dramatic Procession in Germany in the Late Middle Ages," *JEGP* 32 (1933): 141–71. Wolfgang F. Michael, *Die geistlichen Prozessionsspiele in Deutschland*, argues that the German processional plays developed not out of iconographical traditions but directly from liturgical drama. I find his crucial derivation of the Innsbruck *Frohnleichnamsspiel* from the *Processus prophetarum* quite unconvincing, particularly as many motifs in the Innsbruck play (Prophets paired with Apostles, for example) were established in pictorial art, but not in liturgical drama.

32. *Play*, pp. 1, 6.

33. Ibid., p. 23.

34. Craig, *ERD*, p. 129. For an extensive analysis of the Corpus Christi procession and the documents which promulgated it, see Stemmler, *Liturgische Feiern*, pp. 188–99.

35. See Paul Murray Kendall, *The Yorkist Age*, pp. 64–70.

36. John Stow, *A Survey of London*, pp. 95–96: the citizens of London "according to their seuerall trade, made their seuerall shew, but specially the Fishmongers, which in a solemne Procession passed through the Citie, having amongst other Pageants and shews, foure Sturgeons guilt, caried on four horses: then foure Salmons of silver on foure horses, and after them six and fortie armed knights riding on horses, made like Luces of the sea, and then one representing *Saint Magnes*, because it was vpon S. Magnes day, with a thousand horsemen."

37. Stemmler, *Liturgische Feiern*, pp. 167–80.

38. Newcastle upon Tyne Archives Office, MS Enrollment Book IV, fol. 56ᵛ (see below, chap. 11, no. 117). Ordinance dated 1536, but may refer to disorders mentioned in the Coopers' ordinance of 1426.

39. See below, chap. 9.

40. On "public spectacle as an instrument of policy," see Sydney Anglo, *Spectacle, Pageantry, and Early Tudor Policy*, p. 204.

<h2 style="text-align:center">CHAPTER 2</h2>

1. *Guide to English Literature from Beowulf through Chaucer and Medieval Drama*, p. 273.

2. Thomas Sharp, *Dissertation on the Pageants or Dramatic*

Mysteries Anciently Performed at Coventry, pp. 17 ff.; text of Rogers's description in *The Trial and Flagellation, with Other Studies in the Chester Cycle,* ed. W. W. Greg and F. M. Salter, pp. 147-60, 166; William Dugdale, *Antiquities of Warwickshire,* p. 116.

3. Brooks, "Processional Drama," pp. 142-44, documents eight different methods.

4. Thomas Warton, *History of English Poetry,* 2: 222: "This practice of acting plays in churches, had at last grown to such an enormity . . ."

5. Dugdale, *Antiquities,* p. 116. See also Woolf, *EMP,* p. 73.

6. Martial Rose, *Wakefield Mystery Plays,* pp. 23-24.

7. Account printed in *TCP,* pp. 74-75.

8. Ibid., pp. xiii-xiv.

9. Craig reconsidered his original position in *ERD,* pp. 284-85: see below, chap. 8, n. 44.

10. Rose, *Wakefield,* pp. 23-24.

11. See table 5 for line lengths of York cycle plays. All textual references are to *YP.*

12. W. W. Greg, *Bibliographical and Textual Problems of the English Miracle Cycles,* pp. 24-25, is one of a very few writers who have recognized uneven play lengths as a source of difficulty.

13. See below, chap. 3.

14. At 1,000 lines per hour, 20 lines take one minute twelve seconds, while 100 lines take six minutes. Martial Rose estimates the pauses at five and ten minutes.

15. I count 13,275 lines for the cycle, making an average of 279 lines per play. Rose counts 13,121 lines, for an average of 273. See table 5 and its footnotes for the basis of my calculations.

16. This is because all acting times in a production of uniform or synchronized advances are separated by the long journey, that is, 100 lines. For a qualification of this statement, see Appendix A, under "Formula for synchronized advances."

17. See below, chap. 3.

18. See Salter, *MDC,* p. 29; and Rose, *Wakefield,* p. 23.

19. See below, chap. 3.

20. See below, chap. 3.

21. Maurice Hussey, *The Chester Mystery Plays,* pp. x-xi.

22. In the formula (see Appendix A) the increase is reflected in the factor $(S\text{-}1)\,P^{max}$, and also in the summation. It is important to keep this in mind in discussing the effect of the longest play on the total production length. Changes in any other play (unless it should become the longest) are reflected only onefold in the total production time.

23. Nobody, as far as I know, has ever imagined that the N-Town text was intended for true-processional production in its present state. This suggests that there has always been an implicit, though not an exact, understanding of the consequence of lengthy individual plays for a processional performance.

24. But see George R. Kernodle, *From Art to Theatre,* p. 61.

25. *Rites of Durham,* ed. J. T. Fowler, pp. 107–8.

26. See H. F. Westlake, *PGME,* pp. 49–59, 162 (Grantham), 220 (Northampton). See also below, introduction to chap. 11; Kendall, *The Yorkist Age,* pp. 64–68; and Anton Dörrer, *Tiroler Umgangsspiele,* p. 72.

27. Petit de Julleville, *Les Mystères,* 2: 186–88. On the royal entry, see Bernard Guenée and Françoise Lehoux, *Les Entrées royales françaises de 1328 à 1515;* Anglo, *Spectacle;* Kernodle, *From Art to Theatre,* pp. 52–108; Wickham, *EES,* 1: 51–111; and Robert Withington, *EP,* 1: 124–97.

28. Petit de Julleville, *Les Mystères,* 2: 190 (translation mine).

29. See ibid., 1: 190–200, 2: 191, 194, 195.

30. See Kernodle, *From Art to Theatre,* pp. 63–64. See also Enid Welsford, *The Court Masque,* pp. 51–52.

31. Petit de Julleville, *Les Mystères,* 2: 209.

32. *ERD,* p. 136.

33. Franz Joseph Mone, *Altteutsche Schauspiele,* pp. 145–64.

34. Michael, *Geistliche Prozessionsspiele,* pp. 31–33.

35. Brooks, "Processional Drama," pp. 141–71. Brooks, pp. 169–71, anticipates many of my observations concerning the English Corpus Christi plays; he makes his inferences, however, entirely from his experience with the German plays. See also French processions, particularly the procession of Béthune, discussed in Petit de Julleville, *Les Mystères,* 2: 212–13, and in Davidson, *English Mystery Plays,* pp. 95–102; and Spanish processions, discussed in Francis George Very, *The Spanish Corpus Christi Prosession: A Literary and Folkloric Study.*

36. See also Anna J. Mill, *MPS,* pp. 65–66.

CHAPTER 3

1. See *A History of Yorkshire: The City of York,* pp. 69–75; and *Encyclopaedia Britannica,* 11th ed., s.v. York. Arthur Brown, "York and Its Plays in the Middle Ages," in *Chaucer und seine Zeit,* pp. 407–18, has gathered much useful information of the production of York plays, though many of his assumptions are challenged in this chapter.

2. *Eboracum; or the History and Antiquities of the City of York,* esp. p. 223, and Appendix, pp. xxix–xxxii.

3. *YR,* esp. pp. 236–37.

4. *PGME,* p. 57.

5. *YP,* Introduction; Chambers, *MS,* 2: 399–406; Craig, *ERD,* pp. 199–238. See also Davidson, *Studies,* pp. 83–102; Wilhelm Creizenach, *Geschichte des neueren Dramas,* 1: 281–87; and Spencer, *Corpus Christi Pageants,* pp. 1–18.

6. For the date of the second list I follow Mendal G. Frampton, "The Date of the 'Wakefield Master': Bibliographical Evidence," *PMLA* 53

(1938): 101-3, n. 79. For Smith's version of the first list, see *YP,* pp. xix-xxvii. In listing pageants only, Smith follows Sharp, *Dissertation,* pp. 135-39. Only Drake, *Eboracum,* pp. xxx-xxxii, has printed the complete first list. *YMB,* 2: 118, omits the pageants but clearly refers the reader to the lists in *YP* and in *YR,* pp. 223-36. Davies prints the second list (pageants only). Stevens's early comments are recorded in "Informal Minutes of Conference 53," *Research Opportunities in Renaissance Drama* 12 (1969): 91-92. Stevens has reedited both lists and will publish them in a forthcoming issue of *Modern Philology.*

The lists are found in the York Memorandum Book, MS A/Y, fols. 254 ᵛ and 255. This manuscript and all other manuscripts cited in this chapter are, except where noted, in the York City Archives in the York City Library, transcribed and published by permission of the York City Library. Transcriptions of documents are printed in *YMB, YR, YP, YCR,* and *YCCG.*

7. MS A/Y, fol. 254ᵛ ; translation based on Drake, *Eboracum,* p. xxxii.

8. MS A/Y, fols. 278-278ᵛ. Translation based on Drake, *Eboracum,* pp. xxix-xxx. Sharp, *Dissertation,* pp. 133-35, reproduces Drake's translation. A transcription of the original Latin is given in *YMB,* 2: 156-58; for related decrees, see pp. 158-59.

9. MS A/Y, fol. 252ᵛ; cf. *YP,* p. xx. Translation mine.

10. MS A/Y, fol. 19ᵛ; cf. *YMB,* 1: 50-52. Translation from Spencer, *Corpus Christi Pageants,* p. 47. The complaint is not dated, but Anna J. Mill, "The Stations of the York Corpus Christi Play," *Yorkshire Archaeological Journal* 37 (1948-51): 493, argues that this must have been the immediate cause of the council decree dated 1398/9.

11. MS A/Y, fols. 4ᵛ, 10ᵛ, 19; cf. *YMB,* 1: 10, 29, 50. See also MS A/Y, fols. 163ᵛ, 164; cf. *YMB,* 1: 32.

12. MS A/Y, fol. 17ᵛ; cf. *YMB,* 1: 47.

13. MS A/Y, fol. 19ᵛ; cf. *YMB,* 1: 51-52: Sellers prints "pagina" for "vigilia." The word is legible under ultraviolet light. *YR,* p. 232, has a correct reading.

14. MS Roll C1:1: "Et pro ij pellibus pergamenti tempore billarum corporis xpi, vjd"; cf. Margaret Dorrell, "The Mayor of York and the Coronation Pageant," *Leeds Studies in English,* n.s. 5 (1971): 36. Shearmen's ordinance is in MS A/Y, fol. 43; cf. *YMB,* 1: 107.

15. MS A/Y, fols. 254ᵛ-255; cf. *YP,* p. xxxiv. Translation of the title mine. I have relied heavily on Martin Stevens's transcription of this partly illegible document.

16. Roger Burton, MS A/Y, fol. 255, notes that the Corpus Christi guild carried ten torches in the procession. On the history and ordinances of the guild, see *YCCG,* pp. v-xii, 1-9; and Westlake, *PGME,* pp. 53-59. The 1415/6 roll is MS Corpus Christi guild 99:1 and 99:2; cf. Angelo Raine, *Medieval York,* p. 314.

17. On the route of the pageants, see *YR*, p. 232; and Mill, "Stations," pp. 492–502. For evidence that torchbearing guildsmen followed the procession only to the minster, see *YCR*, 2: 97.

18. MS A/Y, fol. 247; cf. *YMB*, 2: 102–3. Translation mine. For another attempt to shorten the pageants, see *YMB*, 2: 123–34, 171–73.

19. MS A/Y, fol. 278ᵛ; cf. *YMB*, 2: 158.

20. Marshals' and Smiths' ordinance in L. Toulmin Smith, "Ordinances of the Companies of Marshals and Smiths at York, A.D. 1409–1443," *Antiquary* 11 (1885): 108. Corpus Christi guild agreement in MS B/Y, fol. 117; cf. *YCCG*, p. 252.

21. The Mercers' records are presently in the care of B. P. Johnson, Archivist for the Company of Merchant Adventurers of the City of York, Merchant Adventurers' Hall, Fossgate, York. Records cited by permission of the Governor and Court of the Company of Merchant Adventurers. The records cited are transcribed in *YMA*, pp. 49–52. Marshals' and Smiths' records are from Smith, "Ordinances," p. 108.

22. Chamberlains' Rolls beginning with MS C1:2 (1433/4); cf. Dorrell, "Mayor of York," pp. 37–42.

23. MS HB, 1, fol. 19ᵛ; cf. *YCR*, 1: 5–6. My translation.

24. MS Corpus Christi guild Roll 99: 5.

25. MSS C3:4, C3:3.

26. MS A/Y, fol. 38; cf. *YMB*, 2: 295.

27. *YCCG*, pp. viii–ix.

28. On Spofford, see *YR*, p. 248. See *YMB*, 2: 215, for a reference to the shrine in procession. The inventory of the shrine is in BM MS Lansdowne 403, fol. 1; cf. *YCCG*, pp. 296–98, and pp. 295–96. Another shrine was carried in earlier days (ca. 1431); see *YCCG*, p. 252.

29. MS HB, 17, fol. 51; cf. *YCR*, 4: 109.

30. Guild declaration cited from *YCCG*, p. 285. On dissolution, see Westlake, *PGME*, p. 58.

31. Chamberlains' Rolls cited here are MSS C1:2 and C1:3; cf. Dorrell, "Mayor of York," p. 37. Mercers' document is MS Roll 15; cf. *YMA*, p. 63. See also Mercers' contract for 1453/4; cf. *YMA*, pp. 58–59. On Mercers' documents, see n. 21 above.

32. MS HB, 1, fol. 14ᵛ; cf. *YCR*, 1: 5.

33. MS HB, 7, fol. 109ᵛ; cf. *YCR*, 2: 105.

34. MS B/Y, fol. 140; cf. *YCR*, 3: 178 (Raine fails to transcribe a large part of this entry).

35. MS HB, 25, fol. 32ᵛ; cf. *YCR*, 7: 58.

36. MS HB, 21, fol. 46ᵛ; cf. *YCR*, 5: 108.

37. MS HB, 20, fol. 50; cf. *YCR*, 5: 53. MS HB, 23, 74ᵛ; cf. *YCR*, 6: 48.

38. MS HB, 19, fol. 69ᵛ; cf. *YCR*, 5: 15.

39. MS HB, 20, fol. 17; cf. *YCR*, 5: 37.

40. MSS HB, 9, fol. 93ᵛ, 10, fol. 19ᵛ; cf. *YCR*, 3: 63, 75.

41. MS HB, 25, fol. 27ᵛ; cf. *YCR,* 7: 55. See Drake, *Eboracum,* p. 217, on origin of Yule ceremony. See also *YCR,* 7: vi.

42. MS HB, 13, fol. 51; cf. *YCR,* 4: 5.

43. MS HB, 13, fol. 96; cf. *YCR,* 4: 21.

44. MS HB, 24, fol. 139; cf. *YCR,* 6: 148.

45. MS HB, 28, fol. 67; cf. *YCR,* 4: 150.

46. MS CC4(2), fol. 162; cf. *YR,* pp. 263–64.

47. MS HB, 7, fol. 135; cf. *YCR,* 2: 118.

48. MS HB, 7, fol. 136ᵛ; cf. *YCR,* 2: 120.

49. Woolf, *EMP,* p. 60, argues without positive evidence that the Creed play was "a sleeker version of an Old and New Testament cycle." Revetour's will is transcribed in *Testamenta Eboracensia,* p. 117. See also footnote, same page: "In 1455 Robert Lasingby 'clericus paro-chialis S. Dionisii' leaves to the fabric of his church . . . 'ludum oreginale Sancti Dionisii.' "

50. MS HB, 7, fol. 137; cf. *YCCG,* p. 308. Translation mine.

51. Inventory in BM MS Lansdowne 403, fol. 36; cited from *YCCG,* pp. 293–94. See also *YR,* p. 273. Corpus Christi cycle text is written on 222 leaves: see *YP,* p. xiii. Cf. Woolf, *EMP,* p. 60.

52. On Judas torches, see Sharp, *Dissertation,* pp. 188–92.

53. Cf. processional expenses for "castles" in *YMA,* p. 37. These were evidently torch holders.

54. MS HB, 2–4, fol 99ᵛ; cf. *YCR,* 1: 81. For an earlier reference, see MS HB, 2–4, fol 98ᵛ; cf. *YCR,* 1: 81.

55. From York Minster Library MS Chamberlains' Rolls E1/53, published here by permission of the York Minster Library. Transcrip-tion verified by Katharine M. Longley, Archivist. See Dorrell's article in *Leeds Studies in English* n.s. 6 (1972), forthcoming.

56. MS HB, 9, fol. 24; cf. *YCR,* 3: 12.

57. MS HB, 9, fol. 25; cf. *YCR,* 3: 14.

58. MS HB, 17, fol. 84; cf. *YCR,* 4: 125.

59. Printed in Harold C. Gardiner, *ME,* p. 49.

60. *The English Works of Wyclif,* ed. F. D. Matthew, p. 429.

61. Full discussions of these documents are found in Westlake, *PGME,* and Toulmin Smith, *EG.*

62. PRO MS C. 47/46/454; cf. Karl Young, "Records of the York Play of the *Pater Noster,*" *Speculum* 7 (1932): 540–42. Translation from Smith, *EG,* pp. 137–38.

63. Young, "Records," p. 544, n. 1.

64. Raine, *Medieval York,* pp. 91–95.

65. Ibid., p. 94, n. 1.

66. *YMA,* pp. 81–82 (see n. 21 above). Young, "Records," pp. 544–45, suggests that when the Mercers had the Pater Noster play, they gave up their Corpus Christi pageant and play. In fact they neither had the one nor gave up the other.

67. MS HB, 13, fol. 35ᵛ; cf. *YCR*, 3: 174.

68. MS HB, 13, fol. 50ᵛ; cf. *YCR*, 4: 5.

69. See preamble to order concerning the feasts, *YCR*, 5: 177; see also pp. 172, 175, 180, 183.

70. MS HB, 22, fol. 118ᵛ; cf. *YCR*, 5: 177–78.

71. MS HB, 22, fol. 120; cf. *YCR*, 5: 179.

72. MS HB, 22, fol. 125ᵛ; cf. *YCR*, 5: 181–82.

73. MS HB, 22, fol. 129; cf. *YCR*, 5: 183.

74. MS HB, 23, fol. 10; cf. *YCR*, 6: 8.

75. MS HB, 23, fol. 16; cf. *YCR*, 6: 15.

76. MS HB, 23, fol. 19ᵛ; cf. *YCR*, 6: 17.

77. See Gardiner, *ME*, p. 84, n. 104.

78. MS HB, 23, fol. 49ᵛ; cf. *YCR*, 6: 35.

79. MS HB, 23, fol. 50; cf. *YCR*, 6: 35.

80. MS HB, 23, fol. 52; cf. *YCR*, 6: 36.

81. See MS HB, 23, fols. 92ᵛ, 145; cf. *YCR*, 6: 56, 83.

82. MS St. Thomas Hospital Register, Book 66, p. 48; cf. *YCCG*, pp. 307–8.

83. *YCCG*, pp. xii–xiii.

84. MS HB, 23, fol. 166; cf. *YCR*, 6: 94.

85. MS HB, 24, fol. 69ᵛ; cf. *YCR*, 6: 124.

86. MS HB, 24, fol. 82; cf. *YCR*, 6: 128.

87. MS HB, 24, fol. 104ᵛ; cf. *YCR*, 6: 133–34.

88. MS HB, 24, fol. 106ᵛ; cf. *YCR*, 6: 134. Dean Hutton's letter is printed in Gardiner, *ME*, p. 73.

89. MS HB, 24, fol. 108ᵛ; cf. *YCR*, 6: 135.

90. MS HB, 24, fol. 130; cf. *YCR*, 6: 144.

91. MS HB, 24, fol. 140; cf. *YCR*, 6: 149.

92. MS HB, 24, fols. 130–31; cf. *YCR*, 6: 144–45.

93. MS HB, 24, fol. 139; cf. *YCR*, 6: 148.

94. MS HB, 25, fol. 6; cf. *YCR*, 7: 46.

95. MS HB, 25, fol. 12ᵛ; cf. *YCR*, 7: 47.

96. MS HB, 25, fol. 15; cf. *YCR*, 7: 48.

97. Gardiner, *ME*, p. 74, claims that the last production of the Corpus Christi play was in 1569. This was evidently the last production of the dramatic cycle but not of the processional pageants.

98. MS HB, 25, fol. 19; cf. *YCR*, 7: 52.

99. MS HB, 26, fol. 25; cf. *YCR*, 7: 107.

100. MS HB, 26, fol. 27; cf. *YCR*, 7: 108.

101. MS HB, 27, fol. 151; cf. *YCR*, 8: 7.

102. MS HB, 27, fol. 219; cf. *YCR*, 8: 26.

103. MS HB, 25, fol. 15ᵛ; cf. *YCR*, 7: 49.

104. Ibid.

105. MS C3:7; cf. *YR*, pp. 74–77. Davies's translation. The original reads:

Expence in festo corporis xpi et vigilia sancti Blasij Episcopi
Et in expensis factis hoc anno per maiorem aldermannos ac
quampluros alios de consilio camere in festo corporis xpi videntes
& intendentes ludum in hospico Nicholi Bewyk ex consuetudine. . .
necnon ixs solutis pro firma camere . . .

106. MSS C4:1; C4:3; C5:1; C5:2; C5:3; C6:3; C6:4; C6:15; C7:1.

107. MS CC1A, fol. 132ᵛ.

108. MS CC2, fol. 29ᵛ; cf. *YR*, pp. 261–62, where the entire entry
is transcribed.

109. For 1520/1 to 1525/6, see MS CC2, fols. 29ᵛ, 66, 108, 154ᵛ,
197ᵛ, 240.

110. 1538/9: MS CC3(3), fol. 27ᵛ; 1542/3: MS CC4(1), fols. 88–88ᵛ;
1554/5: CC4(2), p. 107 (see also pp. 132–33).

111. MS HB, 22, fol. 127.

112. *YCR*, 5: 182.

113. MS HB, 2–4, fol. 116; cf. *YCR*, 1: 90.

114. MS CC2, fol. 240.

115. MS HB, 10, fol. 122ᵛ; cf. *YCR*, 3: 104.

116. MS CC2, fol. 246.

117. MS CC3(2), p. 51; cf. MS C6:7.

118. MS CC3(2), p. 126: see also p. 153; and MS HB, 13, fol. 24; cf.
YCR, 3: 172.

119. MS HB, 6, fols. 99, 104ᵛ, 107; cf. *YCR*, 2: 23, 25, 27–28.

120. MS HB, 27, fol. 246; cf. *YCR*, 8: 36.

121. See MS HB, 28, fols. 53, 99ᵛ; cf. *YCR*, 8: 57, 68. The Skinners'
ordinances of 1582 refer in the traditional manner to pageants and
pageant masters (*YCR*, 8: 61–62), but this was probably a mere
holdover from earlier times.

122. MS HB, 28, fol. 143; cf. *YCR*, 8: 76–77.

123. MS HB, 28, fol. 144; cf. *YCR*, 8: 77.

124. MS HB, 28, fol. 144ᵛ; cf. *YCR*, 8: 77.

125. MS CC6(1), paper note bound between fols. 70 and 71.

126. MS CC5(3), fol. 74; cf. *YR*, p. 274; see also "Chardges of the
shewe on mydsomer even," MS CC5(3), fol. 73.

127. MS HB, 29, fol. 20; cf. *YCR*, 8: 101.

128. MS HB, 29, fol. 23ᵛ; cf. *YCR*, 8: 103.

129. MS CC6(1), fols. 50, 70ᵛ (see also fols. 51, 63); cf. *YR*, p. 276.

130. Printed in *YR*, pp. 275–76. Original cannot be found.

131. MS CC6(1), fol. 71. See also two bills for work on pageants,
pasted on fols. 71ᵛ and 72; and list of assessments on fol. 90.

132. *Register of the Freemen of the City of York, I, 1272–1558,* p.
189.

133. Raine, *Medieval York,* p. 153; and Bewyk's will in the York
Borthwick Institute, listed in *Wills, 1389–1514,* YAARS, p. 17.

134. MS C3:6.

135. *Register of the Freemen,* p. 239; and MS HB, 15, fol. 30; cf. *YCR,* 4: 56.

136. *Wills, 1514–1553,* YAARS, p. 63.

137. MSS CC2, fol. 187ᵛ (1524); CC3(1), fol. 133 (1527).

138. *Wills, 1568–1585,* YAARS, p. 6 (Ayneley); and *Wills, 1585–1594,* YAARS, p. 29 (Colthurst).

139. See above, n. 137.

140. MSS CC3(3), fol. 9; CC4(1), fol. 37; CC4(2), p. 59; cf. Mill, "Stations," pp. 495–98.

141. Raine, *Medieval York,* pp. 134–44; and *History of Yorkshire, City of York,* pp. 542–44 (photograph of Mansion House, p. 545).

142. MS Acc. 104/3: "A manuscript transcript of Hilyard's Catalogue of Mayors and Sheriffs of York, published in 1664 with additional notes continued up to 1727, by Thomas Hammond."

143. MS E/101, p. 87 (for 21 Jan. 1722/3).

144. MS E/101, p. 89 (for 13 Jan. 1723/4). I have this information from Mrs. Rita Green, Archivist, who, however, argues that the inn must have been to the south of the passage and the Chapel of St. Christopher to the north.

145. Drake, *Eboracum,* p. 330.

146. Information supplied by the York City Library.

147. MSS CC4(2), p. 107; CC5(3), fol. 74.

148. MS HB, 29, fol. 30.

149. MS HB, 28, fol. 144ᵛ; cf. *YCR,* 8: 77; and MS HB, 29, fol. 23ᵛ; cf. *YCR,* 8: 103.

150. MSS C1:2; C3:4; C3:6.

151. MS C1:1; cf. *YR,* pp. 230–31. My translation.

152. I have established by personal experience that at York on Midsummer eve, effective darkness sets in about 10:30 P.M.

153. Citations in this and subsequent paragraphs from *YP.*

154. See Craig, *ERD,* pp. 227–28.

155. See, for example, MS CC3(1), fol. 232: "Item sexto loco coram domino maiore & sociis suis ac de John Archebald foster ex altera parte strati, viijd."

156. This item should be added to the catalogue in my "Six-Wheeled Carts: An Underview," *Technology and Culture* 13 (1972): 413–15.

157. I have consulted the original MS (see n. 21 above). Transcription cited from "The Doomsday Pageant of the York Mercers, 1433," *Leeds Studies in English,* n.s. 5 (1971): 29–30.

CHAPTER 4

1. For studies of the relationship between the York and Wakefield cycles, see bibliography in *Wakefield Pageants,* ed. Cawley, p. xxxvi.

2. Published in J. W. Walker, *Miscellanea II,* pp. 18–32. For other interpretations of the Wakefield records, see Martial Rose, *Wakefield,*

pp. 17–30; and Chambers, *English Literature at the Close of the Middle Ages,* pp. 34–36.

3. Citations from the Burgess Court Rolls are from Walker, *Miscellanea II,* pp. 18–24.

4. The first item (ibid., p. 18) is a demand for payment of debts "at the feast of seynt Androo [30 November] next."

5. In a paper written for the Medieval Drama Seminar of the 1969 MLA convention, Cawley noted parallels between these items and several found in other cities for Corpus Christi day: "priests," St. John's Bristol (1536), in Blair, "A Note," p. 86; "great banner [*magno vexillo*]," St. Edmund's Sarum (1501), in J. C. Cox, *Church-Wardens' Accounts from the Fourteenth Century to the Close of the Seventeenth Century* (London, 1913), p. 72; "for ryngyng of the bells against the procession," St. John's Bristol (1555), and "Rosse garlonds," St. Mary Magdalene, London (1545), in Blair, "A Note," pp. 87, 90.

6. Rose, *Wakefield,* p. 20.

7. See above, chap. 3, n. 122.

8. The 1554 entry includes an order "that gyles Dolleffe shall brenge In or Causse to be broght the regenall of Corpus Xty play before [i.e., between] this and wytsonday."

9. Cited in *Wakefield Pageants,* ed. Cawley, p. 125.

10. See Martin Stevens, "The Missing Parts of the Towneley Cycle," *Speculum,* 45 (1970), 261–64.

11. Rose, *Wakefield,* p. 24.

12. Ibid., pp. 31–33.

13. Citations from *Towneley Plays,* ed. England and Pollard.

14. Information on the bell tower from J. W. Walker, *Wakefield,* 1: 177–84.

15. For further speculation, see my essays cited in the footnote on the first page of this chapter.

CHAPTER 5

1. PRO MS C. 47/46/448; cf. Westlake, *PGME,* p. 233. Translation from Smith, *EG,* pp. 149–50.

2. PRO MS C. 47/46/446; cf. Westlake, *PGME,* p. 233. Translation from Smith, *EG,* p. 148.

3. MS GGB (Great Guild Book), fol. 12ᵛ; cf. *BTD,* p. 34. Leach prints Latin transcriptions on the left-hand page and English translations on the right, assigning the same number to both pages. I use Leach's translations throughout this chapter except where noted. The Beverley town documents are in the care of the Beverley Town Clerk, Municipal Offices Building, and are transcribed and published here by permission of the Town Clerk.

4. MS GGB, fol. 77; cf. HMC, *Report on the Manuscripts of the Corporation of Beverley,* ed. A. F. Leach, p. 99.

5. MS GGB, fol. 42ᵛ; cf. *BTD*, p. 115. From a translation made in 1539. Original Latin on facing page in *BTD*.

6. MS Roll for 1502/3; cf. *HMC*, Beverley, p. 169.

7. PRO MS C. 47/46/445; cf. Westlake, *PGME*, p. 232. On the ordinances and composition of the guild, see A. F. Leach, [no title], *Proceedings of the Society of Antiquaries of London*, 2d ser. 15 (1893–95): 103–18; and *BTD*, p. lix.

8. MS GGB, fol. 12ᵛ; cf. *BTD*, pp. 35–36.

9. MS GGB, fol. 26; cf. *BTD*, p. 62.

10. MS GGB, fol. 12ᵛ; cf. *BTD*, p. 45, where Leach translates "pagine" as "stage."

11. MS GGB, fol. 12ᵛ; cf. *BTD*, pp. 33–34.

12. MS GGB, fol. 13; cf. *BTD*, p. 37. Inventory transcribed directly from MS.

13. MS GGB, fol. 13; cf. *BTD*, p. 39.

14. MS GGB, fol. 12ᵛ; cf. *BTD*, p. 35. My translation.

15. MS Roll for 1423/4; cf. HMC, Beverley, p. 160; and Leach, "SEPP," p. 216.

16. MS Governors' Minute Book, fols. 96, 106ᵛ; cf. HMC, Beverley, p. 135.

17. MSS Rolls for 1449/50, 1450/1, 1459/60, 1502/3; cf. Leach, "SEPP," pp. 214–16; and HMC, Beverley, p. 170. Translations of the 1502 account mine.

18. MS Governors' Minute Book, fols. 117ᵛ, 139, 153; cf. Leach, "SEPP," p. 216; and HMC, Beverley, pp. 136, 139.

19. MS GGB, fol. 1; cf. Leach, "SEPP," pp. 218–19.

20. *BTD*, p. 36; HMC, Beverley, pp. 87, 100.

21. *BTD*, p. 109.

22. HMC, Beverley, pp. 102–3, 89. The Braziers were the same as the Cutlers who produced the pageant in 1520/1: see ibid., p. 102.

23. Ibid., p. 103.

24. Ibid., p. 98.

25. Ibid., p. 99.

26. MS GGB, fol. 81; cf. *BTD*, p. 99. In "SEPP," p. 213, Leach dates this 1498 instead of 1493, probably by a printer's error. The new names are from the sixteenth-century list.

27. HMC, Beverley, p. 172.

28. MS Governors' Minute Book, fol. 49ᵛ; cf. HMC, Beverley, pp. 128–29.

29. MS Governors' Minute Book, fols. 204–204ᵛ; cf. HMC, Beverley, pp. 142–43. Leach, "SEPP," gives the date (in error) as 1469.

30. MS Governors' Minute Book, fol. 205ᵛ; cf. HMC, Beverley, pp. 143–44. My translation.

31. MS Roll for 1445/6: "Et in pane & cervisia datis hominibus de Riston post proclamacionem ludi sui in foro bladi ad honorem ville,

vjd. . . . Et in pano [*sic*] & ceruisia datis hominibus de Cocyngham post proclamacionem ludi sui in communo mercato ville, ixd."

32. MS Roll for 1520/1; cf. Leach, "SEPP," p. 172.

33. MS Roll for 1519/20; cf. HMC, Beverley, p. 171.

34. MS GGB, fol. 43; cf. *BTD,* pp. 117–18.

35. *MS,* 2: 341.

36. *BTD,* p. 119.

CHAPTER 6

1. Craig, *ERD,* pp. 239–80; and "Mystery Plays at Lincoln—Further Research Needed," *Lincolnshire Historian* 2 (1964): 37–41; Kenneth Cameron and Stanley J. Kahrl, "The N-Town Plays at Lincoln," *Theatre Notebook* 20 (1965/6): 61–69; and "Staging the N-Town Cycle," *Theatre Notebook* 21 (1967): 122–38, 152–65.

2. Mark Eccles, "*Ludus Coventriae:* Lincoln or Norfolk?" *Medium Aevum* 40 (1971): 135–41.

3. Christopher Wordsworth, *Notes on Mediaeval Services in England,* p. 141. The square brackets are Wordsworth's.

4. Virginia Shull, "Clerical Drama in Lincoln Cathedral, 1318–1561," *PMLA* 52 (1937): 946.

5. Ibid., pp. 948–66. These and all MSS cited in this chapter are, except where noted, in the Lincolnshire Archives Office, Lincoln Castle, transcribed and published by permission of the Dean and Chapter of Lincoln, and the Lincoln Corporation. Stanley J. Kahrl plans to reedit all the Lincoln dramatic records for the Malone Society Collections series.

6. MS Bj/2/9, fol. 11; cf. Shull, p. 953. For similar rites, see Young, *Drama,* 2: 531, 537–38.

7. MS Bj/2/16, 1458/9, *allocationes;* cf. Shull, p. 955.

8. Cited in *MS,* 2: 137, n. 4. Wells Cathedral has a fine example of such a clock. See also Wickham, *EES,* 1: 165–66, 304.

9. Records cited in Shull, pp. 956–57.

10. MS A/2/36, fol. 32; cf. Shull, p. 957.

11. MS A/2/37, fol. 27; cf. Shull, p. 958. Translation from Leach, "SEPP," p. 225.

12. MS A/2/37, fol. 46; cf. Shull, p. 961.

13. Records cited in Shull, pp. 963–64.

14. Record cited ibid., pp. 960–61.

15. Leach, "SEPP," pp. 225–26; Loomis, "Lincoln as a Dramatic Centre," *Mélanges d'histoire du théâtre du moyen âge et de la Renaissance, offerts à Gustave Cohen,* p. 247. See also A. C. Cawley, in "Informal Notes of Seminar 17," *Research Opportunities in Renaissance Drama* 13–14 (1970/1): 205.

16. Most forms of the word signified "artifice, trick," or "contrivance, machine": see R. E. Latham, *Revised Medieval Latin Word List,* s.v. *ingenium.* See also *OED,* s.v. Ingenio (obs.): "L. *ingenium* clever thought, invention, in med. L. and Romantic, clever device, machine, engine." Cf. *Ingenious.*

17. Wickham, *EES,* 1: 55. Wickham's translation.

18. Ibid., p. 70. Wickham's translation.

19. For analogous mechanical devices, see Anglo, *Spectacle,* pp. 34, 201, 258.

20. MS A/3/3, fol. 87; cf. Shull, p. 963. My translation.

21. PRO MS C. 47/40/137; cf. Westlake, *PGME,* p. 168.

22. The Minute Books are MSS L1/1/1/1–3, here cited as MSS MB, 1–3. The entries cited in this paragraph are from MS MB, 1, fol. 42^v. Selected transcriptions from the Minute Books may be found in "The Manuscripts of the Corporation of Lincoln," ed. William Dunn Macray, HMC, *Fourteenth Report,* Part 8, pp. 24–75. Entries are easily located by date. See n. 5 above.

23. MS MB, 1, fol. 72^v.

24. Ibid., fol. 81.

25. HMC, Lincoln, pp. 26–27.

26. MS MB, 1, fol. 97.

27. Ibid., fol. 97^v.

28. Ibid., fol. 132.

29. Ibid., fol. 142^v.

30. Ibid., fol. 179^v.

31. Cameron and Kahrl, "Staging," p. 130.

32. MS MB, 1, fol. 178.

33. Ibid., fol. 179^v.

34. Ibid., fol. 198.

35. Ibid., fol. 132.

36. Ibid., fol. 273^v.

37. Ibid., fol. 276.

38. Ibid., fol. 278^v.

39. MS MB, 2, fol. 48^v.

40. PRO MS C. 47/41/152; cf. Westlake, *PGME,* pp. 172–73.

41. MS 5009 in the collection at the Lincoln City Library, transcribed and published by permission of the Director. Much of this material has been edited by Hardin Craig, "The Lincoln Cordwainers' Pageant," *PMLA* 32 (1917): 605–15. As Craig's citations are identifiable by date, I will give references only to the original manuscript, from which I made my transcriptions. (See n. 5 above.)

42. MS 5009, fols. 1–2^v.

43. Ibid., fol. 3.

44. Ibid., fol. 26.

45. Ibid., fol. 22.

46. Cited from Wickham, *EES,* 1: 225. For another example of a glass lantern, Middleton's "Crystal Sanctuary" of 1623, see ibid., pp. 221-22 and n. 41.

47. Cf. Craig, "Lincoln Cordwainers' Pageant," pp. 610-11, and *ERD,* p. 273; M. D. Anderson, *Drama and Imagery in English Medieval Churches,* pp. 135, 141; and Cameron and Kahrl, "N-Town Plays," p. 67.

48. Lincoln City Library MS 5009, fol. 38.

49. Ibid., fol. 54.

50. Ibid., fol. 86.

51. Ibid., fol. 120^v. Although no date is given for this entry, the hand and particularly the word "Pamentes" are identical to those of the subsequent entry dated 3 and 4 Philip and Mary.

52. Ibid., fol. 86.

53. Ibid., fols. 120^v, 121.

54. MS MB, 2, fol. 110.

55. Ibid., fol. 119^v.

56. MS Diocesan Records, Misc. Rolls, 1; cf. J. W. F. Hill, "Three Lists of the Mayors, Bailiffs, and Sheriffs of the City of Lincoln," *Reports and Papers of the Associated Architectural and Archaeological Societies* 39 (1929): 231-38. Leach, "SEPP," p. 223, transcribes "hoc anno" in the first entry as "lvi anno." He also drops four entries. The last two items in my list are dated from mayoral years rather than the confusing regnal years.

57. MS Bj/5/7, 1473/4, *allocationes.*

58. Ibid., 1474/5, *curialitates;* cf. Craig, *ERD,* p. 275.

59. MSS Bj/5/7, 1477/8; and Bj/3/1, 1478/9; both under *curialitates.*

60. MS Bj/3/2, 1480/1, *curialitates,* contains an entry identical to the 1478/9 entry, except that it is followed by "nihil hoc anno."

61. The Account Books for 1480/1 to 1495/6 are bound in one volume, MS Bj/3/2. The entries are listed under *curialitates* or *allocationes.* On 1480/1, see n. 60. The Pater Noster play was given in 1482/3 and 1489/90. The Corpus Christi play was given in 1486/7, 1487/8, and 1495/6. John Sharp's house is not named after 1480/1.

62. MS Bj/3/2, 1482/3, *allocationes;* 1489/90, *curialitates.*

63. See Alan H. Nelson, "Some Configurations of Staging in Medieval English Drama," in *Medieval English Drama,* pp. 131-47.

64. PRO MSS C. 47/41/157-59; and C. 47/40/134-35; cf. Westlake, *PGME,* pp. 167-68, 173-74; and Smith, *EG,* pp. 179-84.

65. PRO MS C. 47/40/135; translation from Smith, *EG,* p. 179. See also J. W. F. Hill, *Medieval Lincoln,* p. 298.

66. Quoted from Cameron and Kahrl, "N-Town Plays," p. 65, n. 29.

67. Cf. ibid., p. 68.

68. MS MB, 1, fol. 273^v.

69. Ibid., fol. 216.

70. MS MB, 3, fol. 33^v.

71. MS MB, 2, fol. 185.

72. Ibid., fol. 193^v.

73. MS MB, 3, fol. 10^v.

74. Ibid., fol. 22^v.

CHAPTER 7

1. Chambers, *MS,* 2: 386, entitles his section on Norwich, *"Whitsun Plays."* Craig, *ERD,* p. 298, entitles a textual subdivision, "Norwich Whitsun Plays."

2. With exceptions noted, all MSS cited in this chapter are located in and are transcribed and published by permission of the Norwich and Norfolk Record Office, Norwich. The 1527 petition is in MS Assembly Book 1510–1550, fols. 120–120^v; cf. Henry Harrod, "A Few Particulars concerning Early Norwich Pageants," *Norfolk Archaeology* 3 (1852): 6–8. Davis, in *NCP,* pp. xxvii–xxviii, prints a parallel text from MS Second Folio Assembly Proceedings 1491–1553, fols. 129^v–130.

3. This misunderstanding may be traced directly to Harrod, "A Few Particulars," p. 5, and has been taken over by virtually every scholar since Harrod's time.

4. On Tombland fair, see *Records of the City of Norwich,* ed. William Hudson and John C. Tingey, 2: cxxxv–cxxxix; and Francis Blomefield, *An Essay towards a Topographical History of the County of Norfolk,* 2d ed., 3: 170, 195. While St. Luke's procession is reminiscent of the Ipswich Corpus Christi pageants (see below, chap. 11, and Appendix C), it bears no relation to the Norwich list of biblical pageants which we shall examine below.

5. Henry Harrod, "Queen Elizabeth Woodville's Visit to Norwich in 1469," *Norfolk Archaeology* 5 (1859): 35.

6. MS Liber Albus, fol. 172^v; cf. *Records of Norwich,* 2: 312.

7. See Kernodle, *From Art to Theatre,* p. 117. St. Luke was often taken as patron by Painters: on the London Painters' guild of B.V.M. and St. Luke, see Westlake, *PGME,* p. 236.

8. See n. 2 above.

9. PRO MS C. 47/44/304; cf. Smith, *EG,* p. 30; and Westlake, *PGME,* p. 204.

10. For a full account of Norwich St. George Guild, see Mary Grace, *Records of the Gild of St. George in Norwich, 1389–1547;* on foundation date, see pp. 8–9. See also Smith, *EG,* pp. 17–18, 433–60; and [Benjamin] Mackerell, "Account of the Company of St. George in Norwich," *Norfolk Archaeology* 3 (1852): 315–74; *Records of Norwich,* 1: lxxvi, xcix–ci, 2: xlvii, cxli–cxliii, 152, 395–404; Westlake, *PGME,* pp. 116–19; Blomefield, 3: 133–34; and Withington, *EP,* 1, 26–29.

11. Mackerell, "Account," p. 331; Westlake, *PGME,* pp. 117-18.

12. *Records of Norwich,* 2: 395-401.

13. Photograph in Withington, *EP,* 1: 29; and C. Walter Hodges, *The Globe Restored,* p. 159.

14. Withington, *EP,* 1: 26-27, nn. 4-5.

15. Grace, *Records,* p. 67.

16. Ibid., p. 34.

17. Ibid., pp. 64-67; see also p. 70.

18. Ibid., pp. 140, 149.

19. Withington, *EP,* 1: 27, n. 6. Original cannot be found.

20. *Records of Norwich,* 1: 340; for a full account of the insurrection, see pp. lxxxviii-xciii.

21. MS Misc. Rolls 9c (one of several rolls, three of which contain this entry); cf. *Records of Norwich,* pp. 344-46.

22. MS Misc. Rolls 9c No. 4.

23. Blomefield, 3: 151-52.

24. William Fake, who died in 1485, was a benefactor to the library and college of the Chapel in the Fields: see ibid., 4: 179.

25. Harrod, "Queen Elizabeth Woodville's Visit," pp. 32-37. On the entries of Richard II, Henry VI, Edward IV, and Richard III, see Blomefield, 3: 112, 156, 167, 173 ("grand pageants" were erected for Richard III).

26. MS Chamberlains' Accounts 1537-1547, fols. 11^v-13^v.

27. This and subsequent citations from the Grocers' accounts are from the newly discovered early eighteenth-century transcriptions by John Kirkpatrick, MS 21f., Box 11c, No. 68, described by F. I. Dunn, "The Norwich Grocers' Play and the Kirkpatrick Papers at Norwich," *N & Q* 19 (1972): 202-3; cf. Robert Fitch, "Norwich Pageants, the Grocers' Play," *Norfolk Archaeology* 5 (1859): 24-31; and *NCP,* pp. xxxii-xxxvi.

28. MS Chamberlains' Accounts 1537-1547, fol. 12.

29. MS Mayors' Court Book 1540-1549, fol. 4^v; cf. *Records of Norwich,* 2: 168.

30. *EP,* 2: 12, n. 3.

31. MS Chamberlains' Accounts 1537-1547, fols. 155^v-156. See also Chamberlains' Accounts 1541-1549, fol. 118^v.

32. MS Mayors' Court Book 1540-1549, p. 216; cf. *Records of Norwich,* 2:171.

33. See above, n. 27; cf. *NCP,* p. xxxiv.

34. MS Chamberlains' Accounts 1537-1547, fols. 229-229^v.

35. MS Chamberlains' Accounts 1541-1549, fols. 248-49; cf. Withington, *EP,* 2: 12.

36. MS Second Folio Assembly Proceedings 1491-1553, fol. 218^v; cf. Gardiner, *ME,* p. 61, n. 69.

37. See above, n. 27; cf. *NCP,* p. xxxiv.

38. MS Second Folio Assembly Proceedings 1491–1553, fol. 225ᵛ; cf. Withington, *EP*, 1: 20, n. 8 (numbered from p. 19).

39. MS Chamberlains' Accounts 1541–1549, fols. 137ᵛ–138.

40. Withington, *EP*, 2: 16.

41. See above, n. 27; cf. *NCP*, p. xxxv.

42. MS Liber Albus, fol. 162ᵛ; cf. *Records of Norwich*, 2: 288.

43. *Records of Norwich*, 2: lii. In 1457, "This year the Mayor's Riding the Perambulation was left off (which of old time they used) during five years": cited from Goddard Johnson, "Chronological Memoranda Touching the City of Norwich," *Norfolk Archaeology* 1 (1847): 142.

44. MS First Folio Assembly Proceedings 1434–1491, fol. 28ᵛ; translation from *Records of Norwich*, 2: 92.

45. MS Second Folio Assembly Proceedings 1491–1553, fols. 170–170ᵛ; cf. *Records of Norwich*, 2: 120–21. See also p. cl.

46. MS Second Folio Assembly Proceedings 1491–1553, fol. 188ᵛ; cf. *Records of Norwich*, 2: 123–24. For prohibition, see Assembly Book 1510–1550, fol. 178ᵛ.

47. MS Chamberlains' Accounts 1537–1547, fol. 12ᵛ: "Payd in dyuers expences for the bothe at maudelyn feyer that is to saye to Capon for makyng of the same both, ijs."

48. Ibid., fols. 88, 113–116ᵛ.

49. For similar examples of public "theatres," see Wickham, *EES*, 2(1): 168, 362, n. 25; and Kenneth M. Dodd, "Another Elizabethan Theater in the Round," *Shakespeare Quarterly* 21 (1970): 125–56. On *The Castle of Perseverance*, see Richard Southern, *Medieval Theatre in the Round*. On the N-Town plays, see my "Configurations of Staging in Medieval English Drama," in *Medieval English Drama*, pp. 131–47. On Norwich, see also Blomefield, 4: 426, concerning the guild of St. Thomas and the Chapel of St. Thomas in the Wood: "at the gild days, there were grand processions made, and interludes played, with good cheer after them."

50. PRO MSS C. 47/43/290–291; cf. Westlake, *PGME*, p. 201.

51. Blomefield, 4: 170.

52. Ibid., p. 179.

53. *Records of Norwich*, 2: 176.

54. MS Old Free Book, fol. 162; cf. *NCP*, ed. Davis, p. xxx. I follow Davis's dating. Blomefield, 3: 176, cites an entry, not now in the Assembly Books, which he dates 1489: "It was ordained in Common Assembly that all the Companies should go in Procession on Corpus Christi Day before the procession."

55. On the history of the Chapel in the Fields, see Blomefield, 4: 170–84; and Nikolaus Pevsner, *The Buildings of England: North-East Norfolk and Norwich*, p. 261. On the History of the Norwich guildhall, see Blomefield, 4: 227–34. For details cited in my text, see also

Blomefield, 4: 227; *Records of Norwich*, 1: lxxvi, n. A; and Blomefield, 3: 119, 124, 149, 175, 194, and 4: 228.

56. MS Old Free Book, fol. 162; cited from *NCP*, pp. xxix–xxx.

57. For more information on Stephen Prowett, see L. G. Bolingbroke, "Pre-Elizabethan Plays and Players in Norfolk," *Norfolk Archaeology* 11 (1892): 338.

58. Grocers' records noted above, n. 27; cf. *NCP*, pp. xxxii–xxxv.

59. Cited from *Records of Norwich*, 2: 398.

60. MS 21f., Box 11c, No. 68, note among transcriptions.

61. See above, n. 27; cf. *NCP*, p. xxxiii.

62. *NCP*, pp. xxxi–xxxii.

63. See above, n. 27; cf. *NCP*, p. xxxiv.

64. See Pevsner, *North-East Norfolk and Norwich*, pp. 260–61. In 1544 the building was called "New-Hall": Blomefield, 3: 214. The Grocers held their assembly at "the Black Fryers" in 1534: *NCP*, p. xxxii. MS Chamberlains' Accounts 1537–1547, fol. 25^v, contains the following entry for 1538/9: "And payd to the Jentilmen wewing [viewing] the blak freres." See also fol. 28^v: "the late house or priory of blak freres."

65. MS Liber Albus, fol. 172^v; cf. *Records of Norwich*, 2: 312; and *NCP*, p. xxxi.

66. *Paston Letters*, ed. Norman Davis, pp. 113–14.

67. See above, n. 27; cf. *NCP*, pp. 8–18.

68. *Play*, p. 54.

69. For citations in this and the following two paragraphs, see above, n. 27; cf. *NCP*, pp. xxxii–xxxv.

70. MS Third Folio Assembly Proceedings 1553–1583, fol. 121^v; cf. *Records of Norwich*, 2: 135.

71. See above, n. 27; cf. *NCP*, pp. xxxv, 16–17.

72. *NCP*, pp. 11–13.

73. Fitch, "Norwich Pageants," p. 16 n.

74. See above, n. 27; cf. *NCP*, p. xxxvi.

75. *Records of Norwich*, 2: 188.

76. See above, n. 27; cf. *NCP*, pp. xxxiv–xxxv.

77. MS Chamberlains' Accounts 1531–1537, fol. 101.

78. MS Chamberlains' Accounts 1541–1549, fol. 36.

79. Ibid., fol. 119.

80. Ibid., fols. 249–50. Noted in Alfred Harbage, *Annals of English Drama, 975–1700*, 2d ed. rev. S. Schoenbaum, p. 28.

81. Transcribed inaccurately by J. T. Murray, *English Dramatic Companies, 1558–1642*, 2: 411–13; and by Wickham, *EES*, 2: 332–35.

82. MS Mayors' Court Book 1540–1549, p. 534; cf. *Records of Norwich*, 2: 171.

83. MS Chamberlains' Accounts 1541–1549, fol. 338.

84. Wickham, *EES*, 2: 65.

CHAPTER 8

1. J. Q. Adams, *Chief Pre-Shakespearean Dramas*, p. 378. See also Chambers, *MS*, 2: 110.

2. *A Hundred Mery Talys*, ed. Hermann Oesterley, pp. 96–100.

3. Ibid., p. iii.

4. *Antiquities*, p. 116.

5. Sharp, *Dissertation*, p. 6. Sharp states that Dugdale began to collect materials for his book ca. 1630.

6. On the history and present state of the Coventry records, see Craig, *ERD*, pp. 281–83; and *TCP*, pp. v–vi.

7. In subsequent notes Sharp, *Dissertation*, will be cited simply as Sharp. Wherever *TCP* cites Sharp and the original had perished, I cite Sharp but also give the reference in *TCP*. *The Coventry Leet Book* (the original of which survives) was edited by Mary D. Harris; for her comments on earlier use of the Leet Book, see pp. ix–xi. Sharp printed additional records in *The Presentation in the Temple, a Pageant, as originally represented by the Corporation of Weavers in Coventry*, introduction. See also "The Manuscripts of the Corporation of Coventry," ed. John Cordy Jeaffreson, HMC, *Fifteenth Report*, Part 10, p. 110.

8. See *TCP*, pp. xx–xxii.

9. Ibid., p. xxi.

10. Cited from ibid.

11. Sharp, p. 5; cf. *TCP*, xxi: Dugdale writes, "In his Mayoralty K. H. 7. came to see the plays acted by the *Grey Friers*, and much commended them."

12. Craig, *ERD*, p. 294.

13. *Ludus Coventriae*, pp. xxxvii–xxxviii.

14. Dugdale's *Antiquities* was published in a revised edition in 1730: see Hubert M. Jenkins, "Dr. Thomas's Edition of Sir William Dugdale's *Antiquities of Warwickshire*," *Dugdale Society Occasional Papers* 3 (Oxford, 1931): 3–20.

15. PRO MS C. 47/46/496; cf. Westlake, *PGME*, p. 230; and Smith, *EG*, pp. 232–33.

16. Sharp, p. 164: in 1554 the Smiths "paid the mynstrells for prosesyon and pageants . . ."

17. *TCP*, pp. xi–xii.

18. Ibid., p. 107.

19. Sharp, p. 163. See other records, pp. 163–64. Craig, *TCP*, p. 89, misquotes the Smiths' record.

20. See also Smiths' order, cited below, n. 26.

21. See Sharp, pp. 183–84, esp. act of Leet for 1549. Sharp, p. 5, notes that "Henry VII [saw] Pageants on St. Peter's day" in 1486.

22. Ibid., pp. 200–205.

23. Ibid., pp. 161–62.

24. Ibid., pp. 28, 164; cf. *TCP*, p. 86, text and n. 10.

25. *TCP*, p. 75.

26. Sharp, p. 22; cf. *TCP*, p. 85.

27. *TCP*, p. 80.

28. Sharp, p. 160; cf. *TCP*, p. 99.

29. *TCP*, p. 99.

30. HMC, Coventry, p. 143. This record has been entirely overlooked until now, as has the following record, p. 150, from 1 June, 44 Elizabeth (1602): "Lease . . . by . . . Masters and wardens of the Company of Mercers of Coventre, of a Message or tenement 'lately being a pagent house' in Gosford 'Street.' "

31. Sharp, p. 78; cf. *TCP*, p. 103, n. 5. See other references to early pageants (1427/8–40), in *TCP*, pp. 72–73, 84.

32. *TCP*, p. 73.

33. Ibid., pp. 73–74.

34. Ibid., p. 107.

35. Sharp, p. 15; cf. *TCP*, p. 83, where Craig twice prints "Colchow" for "Colclow."

36. HMC, Coventry, pp. 119–20.

37. *TCP*, pp. xi–xii. On the 1445 list, see Sharp, p. 160 n.: "It appears from this list, that the junior Company went first, and was followed by the others, in inverted order as to seniority, until the Mercers' or *eldest* Company closed the procession"; see also p. 165.

38. *TCP*, p. xii.

39. On Mercers' guild, see HMC, Coventry, p. 110.

40. Craig, *TCP*, p. xii, writes, "The fullers were made a separate craft in 1447," but in his footnotes he gives the date as 1547. The latter is correct: see Harris, *The Coventry Leet Book*, 3: 782.

41. See *TCP*, pp. xii–xiii.

42. These two plays are extant; see ibid., text.

43. Ibid., pp. xi–xiii.

44. In *TCP*, pp. xi–xix, Craig accepted the possibility that Coventry had no Old Testament plays. He changed his mind in *ERD*, pp. 284–93, persuaded by the "generic" argument.

45. Ibid., pp. xii–xiv.

46. *ERD*, p. 294.

47. *TCP*, pp. 109–14.

48. Ibid., p. xiv.

49. Ibid., pp. 114–16.

50. Ibid., pp. 116–18.

51. Ibid., p. xxi.

52. Ibid., pp. xxi–xxii.

53. Ibid., p. 114, n. 2.

54. Ibid., p. xxi.

55. Ibid., p. 74.

56. Ibid., p. xiv.

57. The extant Coventry plays are 900 and 1,192 lines long, not counting songs. If the second was the longest in the cycle, and if the remaining plays averaged the same as these two (1,046 lines), then from the formula in Appendix A, a production with free advances of ten plays at ten stations would be virtually 22,268 lines in length.

58. *TCP*, p. 106.

59. The document, cited below, chap. 9, n. 52, includes the stipulation that pageant figures should be "borne and caried during the seid wache from place to place," even though the figures were not presented dramatically.

60. Sharp, p. 21, n. k.; cf. *TCP*, p. 85.

61. *The Acts and Monuments of John Foxe*, ed. Stephen R. Cattley, 8: 170. See also Chambers, *MS*, 2: 358.

62. Sharp, p. 77; cf. *TCP*, p. 99.

63. *TCP*, pp. 95–96.

64. Ibid., p. 108.

65. Sharp, pp. 21, n. k, 48, 50; cf. *TCP*, pp. 94–95.

66. Sharp, pp. 73–74; cf. *TCP*, p. 102.

67. Cf. Craig, *ERD*, p. 294. Mary D. Harris, "The Ancient Records of Coventry," *Dugdale Society Occasional Papers* 1 (Oxford, 1924): 6–7, prints two items overlooked by Sharp: (1567) "Item paid for cullern [colouring] of a pece that beryth the worldes and the black soles face, xijd"; and "payd for the payntyng of the worldys and the pyllur, iijs iijd."

68. *TCP*, p. xxi.

69. The Weavers' pageant is 1,192 lines long. A journey of 100 lines would bring the total to a virtual 1,300 lines, or one hour and eighteen minutes if played at 1,000 lines per hour.

70. Sharp, p. 20; cf. *TCP*, p. 75.

71. *TCP*, pp. 84–85.

72. Ibid., p. 89.

73. Ibid., p. 76.

74. See orders of Leet for 1494, ibid., pp. 75–77.

75. Ibid., p. 89.

76. Sharp, p. 12; cf. *TCP*, pp. 92–93.

77. *TCP*, p. 92: "Paid to Mr Smythe of Oxford the xv[th] daye of Aprill 1584 for his paynes for writing of the tragedye, xiij[li] vjs viijd." See also pp. 90–92, 98, 102, 109; and Sharp, pp. 37–42. Sharp gives a detailed analysis of the play and its production.

78. See Sharp, pp. 125–32. This pageant, or an ancestor, may have been established in 1416: "The Pageants and Hox tuesday invented, wherein the King and Nobles took great delight"; from *TCP*, p. xx. See also Chambers, *MS*, 2: 264–66; and Gardiner, *ME*, pp. 83–85.

79. Sharp, p. 39, nn. m–n.

80. *EES,* 1: 171–74.

81. In many records, "pageant" is in the singular, while "scaffolds" is in the plural: see Craig, *TCP,* pp. 84, 91, 98, 103, 109. But see also p. 95 for the year 1568.

82. See examples in Leo van Puyvelde, *L'Ommegang de 1615 à Bruxelles;* and in George R. Kernodle, "The Medieval Pageant Wagons of Louvain," *Theatre Annual* 2 (1964): 58–62. Some of the Louvain pageants are built so that the beds cover the wheels in an I-shaped plan. This strikes me as an artist's fiction.

83. See my "Six-Wheeled Carts," pp. 391–416. Sharp, p. 38, n. 1, notes that support posts may have been supplied for the wagons. He also notes, p. 7, two records from the Drapers' accounts which concern ladders.

84. This and subsequent citations from *TCP,* texts.

CHAPTER 9

1. BM MS Harley 2125, fol. 32; cf. Rupert Morris, *Chester in the Plantagenet and Tudor Reigns,* p. 323.

2. *MDC,* pp. 32–42. Cf. Arthur Brown, "A Tradition of the Chester Plays," *London Medieval Studies* 2 (1951): 68–72, whom Salter answers in *MDC,* pp. 116–17, n. 10.

3. See Stemmler, "Zur Datierung der *Chester Plays,*" pp. 308–13.

4. Morris, *Chester,* pp. 32, 405, dates this event 1358 and 1399. The former is clearly erroneous: the dispute is dated 22 Richard II (1398/9).

5. See, for example, ibid., p. 32.

6. The Chester Coopers' MSS are presently in the care of Mr. A. E. Edwards, Steward. Citations in this chapter are transcribed and published by permission of the Aldermen of the Coopers' Company. Cf. *Trial,* ed. Greg and Salter, pp. 7–8.

7. Manuscripts cited in this chapter are, except where noted, in the Chester City Record Office, Town Hall, Chester, transcribed and published by permission of the Record Office and the City Archivist. The MSS cited here are, in order, MS MR (Mayor's Roll) 85; cf. Salter, *MDC,* p. 46; BM MS Harley 2054, fol. 36 ᵛ; cf. Salter, *MDC,* p. 47; Coopers' MS "Script and Composicion," dated 12 March, 8 Edward IV (see above, n. 6); and Salter, *MDC,* p. 122, n. 34.

8. MS MB (Mayor's Book)/5, fol. 286; cf. Morris, *Chester,* p. 572.

9. See F. M. Salter, "The Banns of the Chester Plays," *Review of English Studies* 15–16 (1939/40): 450 ff.

10. BM MS Harley 2150, fols. 86–88 ᵛ; cf. *Trial,* pp. 133–39.

11. MS MB/12, fol. 24 ᵛ; cf. Salter, *MDC,* p. 46.

12. BM MS Harley 2057, fol. 26 ᵛ: "In this yeare it apeareth the watch on Midsomer even begonn"; cf. Morris, *Chester,* p. 323.

13. See Morris, *Chester,* p. 316.

14. BM MS Harley 2150, fols. 88–88 ᵛ; cf. *Trial,* p. 139.

15. BM MS Harley 2150, fol. 86; cf. *Trial,* p. 132.

16. BM MS Harley 2054, fol. 15ᵛ; cf. Morris, *Chester,* p. 350.

17. See, for example, the lines concerning the Painters' pageant: the Painters "Haue taken on theym with full good chere / That the Sheppardes play then shall appere." Cited in *Trial,* p. 135.

18. See, for example, lines concerning the Passion pageant: "make out Christes dolefull death / his scourgeinge his whippinge, his bloodshed and passion / and all the paynes he suffered till the laste of his breathe." Cited ibid., p. 156.

19. BM MS Harley 1944, fol. 22; cf. *Trial,* pp. 146–47. See also BM MS Harley 1948, fols. 64–64ᵛ; cf. *Trial,* pp. 165–66.

20. MS MB/19, fols. 52–52ᵛ; cf. Morris, *Chester,* p. 304.

21. BM MS Harley 1948, fol. 64ᵛ; cf. *Trial,* p. 166.

22. See, for example, *YCCG,* p. 308. See also Morris, *Chester,* p. 255: "mansion place"; and Wickham, *EES,* 2: 186, 193–94.

23. Morris, *Chester,* pp. 578–81.

24. Ibid., pp. 195–96.

25. MS AB (Assembly Book)/1, fol. 52ᵛ; cf. Morris, *Chester,* pp. 236–37.

26. George Ormerod, *The History of the County Palatine and City of Chester,* 2: 503–9.

27. PRO MS Chester/3/71/9, p. 2 (Inquisition Post Mortem 1 Mary, 1533); cf. Ormerod, *History,* 2: 506, n. b. In the late nineteenth century J. P. Earwicker assembled translations of Inquisitions Post Mortem relevant to Chester. On Whitmore, see MS CR 63/1/226/j/5.

28. See transcriptions of Smiths' accounts BM MS Harley 2054, fols. 16–19; cf. Morris, *Chester,* pp. 305–23 passim, notes. See also Frank Simpson, "The City Gilds of Chester: The Smiths, Cutlers, and Plumbers' Company," *Journal of the Chester and North Wales Architectural, Archaeological, and Historic Society,* n.s. 20 (1914): 5–121.

29. BM MS Harley 1944, fol. 25; cf. *Trial,* pp. 159–60.

30. Salter, "Banns," pp. 433–34.

31. Ormerod, *History,* 2: 506.

32. BM MS Harley 2054, fol. 16ᵛ; see above, n. 28.

33. Ibid., fols. 16ᵛ, 18ᵛ, 19ᵛ, 20ᵛ.

34. The Chester Painters' Book is presently in the care of Mr. H. R. J. Swinnerton, Steward. Citations in this chapter are transcribed and published by permission of the Aldermen and Brethren of the Chester Company of Painters, Glaziers, Embroiderers and Stationers. Cf. Joseph C. Bridge, "Items of Expenditure from the 16ᵗʰ Century Accounts of the Painters, Glaziers, Embroiderers, and Stationers' Company, with special reference to the 'Shepherds Play,' " *Journal of the Chester and North Wales Architectural, Archaeological and Historic Society,* n.s. 20 (1914): 153–91. The Painters' Book is not foliated: see items under years named.

35. BM MS Harley 2054, fol. 21; see above, n. 28.

36. See Gardiner, *ME,* pp. 79–83, for another version of the demise of the Chester plays. *Trial,* pp. 15, 17, lists 1572 and 1574 as the years of the Coopers' entries for the pageant and play. The first year is correct, the second misleading. The account begins 20 November 1574 and thus covers Midsummer 1575: see above, n. 6. BM MS Add. 29777 is similarly one year out for every entry.

37. BM MS Harley 1046, fol. 166ᵛ; cf. Salter, "Banns," p. 447. By accident the year, 1575, is omitted, but the previous entry is dated 1574 and the following entry 1576.

38. MS CHB/3, fol. 28ᵛ; cf. Morris, *Chester,* p. 304.

39. BM MS Harley 2057, fol. 29; cf. Salter, *MDC,* p. 51.

40. MS AB/1, fol. 162ᵛ; cf. Morris, *Chester,* p. 319; BM MS Harley 2057, fol. 29; cf. *The Digby Mysteries,* ed. F. J. Furnivall, p. xxviii.

41. MS MB/21, fol. 187ᵛ; cf. Morris, *Chester,* p. 304.

42. MS AB/1, fol. 165ᵛ; cf. Morris, *Chester,* p. 320.

43. Ibid.

44. Cited in *Digby,* p. xxviii.

45. BM MS Harley 2125, fol. 40ᵛ; cf. Morris, *Chester,* p. 318.

46. BM MS Harley 1948, fols. 64–64ᵛ; cf. *Trial,* p. 166.

47. MS Coopers' Book (see n. 6 above); cf. *Trial,* p. 16.

48. Salter first made this declaration in *Trial,* pp. 25–26. John Butt, Rev. of *Trial,* ed. Greg and Salter, *Review of English Studies* 15 (1939): 92, notes that Salter gives no evidence for this assertion. Salter may have been influenced by Morris, *Chester,* p. 302, who writes: "The city pageants were yearly performed upon the Roodeye." Morris prints a petition from 1586 which refers to the "games, Pastymes, playes, and pleasures upon that said clausure as heretofore . . . have been used," but this probably concerns civic triumphs rather than the cycle plays.

49. Morris, *Chester,* p. 324: the Barber Surgeons were ordered "to repayer with theire showe to the barres, where it is to be sett out."

50. BM MS Harley 2054, fols. 20ᵛ–21; cf. Morris, *Chester,* p. 322.

51. BM MS Harley 1944, fols. 26–26ᵛ; cf. *Digby,* pp. xxiii–xxiv.

52. BM MS Harley 2150, fols. 207–208; cf. Morris, *Chester,* pp. 323–24 n.

53. See Morris, *Chester,* p. 328: "hier of Armour."

54. BM MS Harley 2150, fol. 204; cf. Morris, *Chester,* p. 330.

55. BM MS Harley 1944, fol. 26ᵛ; cf. *Digby,* p. xxiii; and BM MS Harley 1944, fol. 23ᵛ; cf. *Trial,* p. 155.

56. BM MS Harley 1944, fol. 26ᵛ; cf. *Digby,* p. xxiii; and *Chester Plays,* p. 329. Furnivall, in *Digby,* transcribes the subsequent entry as "god in stringes," and writes: "This is the only way that Mr C. T. Martin of the Record Office and I can read the MS." But "god" may be "goe," and the third word has no "r." "goe in stinges" may mean "walk on stilts": note the entry concerning stiltwalkers, discussed in my text immediately below.

57. Morris, *Chester,* p. 324; Salter, "Banns," pp. 454–55.

58. MS Painters' Book; see above, n. 34.

59. MS Coopers' Book (see above, n. 6); cf. *Trial,* p. 14.

60. BM MS Harley 2054, fols 16, 17ᵛ–19; see above, n. 28.

61. See above, n. 12.

62. MSS TAR/7-8; cf. Morris, *Chester,* p. 326.

63. BM MS Harley 2054, fols. 15ᵛ–16; see above, n. 28.

64. Ibid., fol. 21ᵛ.

65. MS Painters' Book; see above, n. 34.

66. MS Coopers' Book (see above, n. 6); cf. *Trial,* p. 17.

67. BM MS Harley 2125, fol. 123; cf. *Digby,* p. xxiv n.; and Morris, *Chester,* pp. 318–19.

68. *Trial,* pp. 10–11.

69. BM MS Harley 2125, fol. 43; cf. Salter, *MDC,* p. 24.

70. Salter, *MDC,* p. 25.

71. See J. H. E. Bennett, "The Hospital and Chantry of St. Ursula the Virgin of Chester," *Journal of the Chester and North Wales Architectural, Archaeological and Historic Society,* n.s. 32 (1938): 118–20.

72. MS AB/1, fol. 333ᵛ; cf. Salter, *MDC,* pp. 26–27; and Morris, *Chester,* pp. 353–54, both of whom identify this entry incorrectly.

73. Salter, *MDC,* p. 27.

Chapter 10

1. Chambers, *MS,* 2: 379–80. Translation mine.

2. W. O. Hassall, "Plays at Clerkenwell," *MLR* 33 (1938): 564–67. For a map of London showing Clerkenwell, see Wickham, *EES,* 1: 60. Woolf, *EMP,* p. 58, accepts the *Holkham Bible Picture Book* as evidence of a cycle play in London, ca. 1320–30. I find this evidence unconvincing, though the London history-of-the-world play may well have antedated 1384 (see n. 3 below).

3. Corpus Christi College Cambridge MS 197A, fol. 146, cited with the permission of the Master and Fellows of Corpus Christi College, Cambridge. Cf. Ranulph Higden, *Polychronicon Ranulphi Higden Monachi Cestrensis,* ed. Joseph Rawson Lumley, 9 [Malvern's continuation]: 49. My translation. See also Robert Dodsley, *A Select Collection of Old Plays,* 1: xii: Richard II was asked in 1378 by the scholars of St. Pauls "to prohibit some unexpert People from presenting the History of the Old Testament, to the great Prejudice of the said Clergy, who have been at great Expence in order to represent it publickly at *Christmas.*" Chambers, *MS,* 2: 380, notes, "I cannot trace the original authority."

4. Hassall, "Plays," p. 565. Woolf, *EMP,* p. 357, cites the *Calendar of Letter-Books preserved amongst the Archives of the Corporation of the City of London, "Letter-Book H,"* ed. R. C. Sharpe (London, 1907), p. 272.

5. PRO MS E 403/533; translation from Frederick Devon, *Issues of*

the Exchequer, pp. 244–45.

6. John [for Jean] Froissart, *Chronicles of England, France, etc.,* trans. Thomas Johnes, pp. 527–29.

7. Corpus Christi College Cambridge MS 197A, fol. 204; cf. Higden, *Polychronicon,* 9: 259.

8. BM MS Harley 565, fol. 60 ᵛ; cf. *A Chronicle of London, from 1089 to 1493,* ed. E. Tyrrell and N. H. Nicolas, p. 80.

9. Fol. 68 ᵛ; cf. *Chronicle of London,* p. 91.

10. "Gregory's Chronicle," in *Historical Collections of a Citizen of London,* ed. James Gardiner, p. 105; MS Cotton Julius B.1, fol. 35 ᵛ.

11. *Chronicle of the Grey Friars of London,* ed. John G. Nichols, p. 12. See Nichols's note: "Stowe places this great play under the year 1409."

12. PRO MS E/101/405/22, fol. 35 ᵛ (Partly illegible, even under ultraviolet light); translation corrected from James H. Wylie, *History of England under Henry the Fourth,* 4: 213.

13. *The Works of Geoffrey Chaucer,* ed. F. N. Robinson, pp. 48–55, esp. lines 3124, 3513–46, 3383–84; p. 81, lines 555–59, and corresponding note.

14. *Chaucer Life-Records,* ed. Martin M. Crow and Clair C. Olson, p. 472.

15. Ibid., pp. 477–89.

16. See, for example, Kolve, *Play,* pp. 36–37.

17. John Weever, *Ancient Funerall Monuments* (1631), p. 405; cf. 2d ed., p. 191.

18. *ERD,* p. 141.

19. John Stow, *A Survey of London,* ed. C. L. Kingsford, 1: 230.

20. See above, chap. 1, n. 12.

21. *Survey,* 1: 230–31.

22. *A Calendar of Dramatic Records in the Books of the Livery Companies of London, 1485–1640,* ed. Jean Robertson and D. J. Gordon, p. 135.

23. See *PGME,* pp. 50–51, 66, 183, 237, where Westlake describes two London guilds dedicated to Corpus Christi: "the little company of the Corpus Christi light," St. Giles, Cripplegate (1352); and a guild later called the Holy Trinity guild, St. Botolph's, Aldersgate (1374).

24. Blair, "Notes," pp. 88–91.

25. *Chronicle of the Grey Friars,* p. 56.

26. *The Diary of Henry Machyn,* ed. John C. Nichols, pp. 63–64.

27. Information from *Calendar,* pp. xiii–xxiv. Wickham, *EES,* 2 (1): 325–26, suggests that the pageants of the Midsummer Show may have been the survivors of a London guild cycle. No evidence of a craft cycle, either plays or pageants, has, however, been discovered.

28. Stow, *Survey,* 1: 102–3.

29. Ibid., pp. 159–60.

30. *Calendar,* p. xxii, n. 4.

31. Ibid., pp. xxi–xxii.

32. Ibid., p. 4. See also Chambers, *MS,* 2: 382, concerning a pageant borrowed from St. Sepulchre's.

33. *Calendar,* pp. xxiii–xxiv.

34. Ibid., pp. xxiv ff. See also Sheila Williams, "Les Ommegangs d'Anvers et les cortèges du Lord-Maire de Londres," in *Les Fêtes de la Renaissance,* ed. Jean Jacquot, 2: 349–57; David M. Bergeron, *English Civic Pageantry, 1558–1642;* and Richard L. Grupenhoff, "The Lord Mayors' Shows: From Their Origins to 1640," *Theatre Studies* 18 (1971/2): 13–22.

35. In the late seventeenth century the Lord Mayor's Procession was followed by dramatic entertainment, much as in earlier years at York (only briefer): see F. W. Fairholt, *Lord Mayors' Pageants,* pt. 2: 109–38, 141–76, 209–36.

36. *Calendar,* p. 136.

37. Westlake, *PGME,* pp. 84–88, and facsimile, opp. p. 88.

38. *Calendar,* p. 132; see Wickham, *EES,* 2(1): 185–86. See also Chambers, *MS,* 2: 382.

39. Both records cited from Wickham, *EES,* 2(1): 186.

40. *Diary,* p. 290.

41. *Survey,* 1: 93.

42. Chambers, *MS,* 2: 381–82.

43. Ibid., p. 381.

44. Machyn, *Diary,* p. 138.

45. Ibid., p. 145.

CHAPTER 11

1. *ERD,* p. 136.

2. Ibid., p. 112.

3. Fols. 53ᵛ–54.

4. Translation from Fairholt, *Lord Mayors' Pageants,* pt. 1: xii–xiii. For original, see Albrecht Dürer, "Tagebuch der niederländischen Reise," in Dürer, *Schriften, Tagebücher, Briefe,* ed. Max Steck, pp. 44–45.

5. On Antwerp, see Sheila Williams and Jean Jacquot, "Ommegangs Anversois du temps de Bruegel et de van Heemskerk," in *Les Fêtes de la Renaissance,* ed. Jean Jacquot, 2: 359–88, and pl. 31–37; on Brussels, see Leo van Puyvelde, *L'Ommegang de 1615 à Bruxelles;* and on Louvain, see George R. Kernodle, "The Medieval Pageant Wagons of Louvain," *Theatre Annual* 2 (1943): 58–62.

6. Hereford city MSS are in the Hereford City Library. Mr. J. F. W. Sherwood, Librarian and Curator, has kindly checked published transcriptions against the original documents, offered several improved readings, and has given me permission to publish his revised tran-

scriptions. The document cited here is MS Miscellaneous Papers 1378–1687, vol. VI, no. 12; cf. "Manuscripts of the Corporation of Hereford," ed. William Dunn Macray, HMC, *Thirteenth Report,* Part 4, pp. 304–5.

7. MS Great Black Book, fol. 27; cf. Richard Johnson, *The Ancient Customs of the City of Hereford,* p. 119.

8. MS Mayor's Book, fol. 176; cf. HMC, Hereford, pp. 288–89.

9. HMC, Hereford, p. 300.

10. "Corpus Christi Pageants at Bungay, 1514," in *The Eastern Counties Collectanea,* ed. John L'Estrange, p. 272. For records of interludes in 1558 and later years, see Bolingbroke, "Pre-Elizabethan Plays," pp. 336–38.

11. Pierson, "The Relation of the Corpus Christi Procession," p. 158.

12. Mill, *MPS,* pp. 261–63; see pp. 70–71 for a discussion of the Lanark records.

13. Smith, *EG,* p. 385.

14. Ibid., p. 407.

15. Ibid., p. 408.

16. Chambers, *MS,* 2: 398; J. O. Halliwell-Phillips, *Outlines of the Life of Shakespeare,* 1: 242–43.

17. Mill, *MPS,* p. 249; see p. 71 for a discussion of the records of Haddington.

18. Ibid., p. 74, n. 3.

19. Ibid., pp. 172–73; see p. 71 for a discussion of the records of Dundee.

20. Dublin records cited from John T. Gilbert, *Calendar of Ancient Records of Dublin,* 1: 239–42. I wish to thank the officers of the Dublin City Libraries for suggestions in making use of this material. For further commentary on Dublin's plays, see Davidson, "Concerning English Mystery Plays," pp. 170–72; Peter Kavanagh, *The Irish Theatre;* and William Smith Clark, *The Early Irish Stage.*

21. Gilbert, *Calendar,* 1: 242. Gilbert explains that this leaf is not now in the Chain Book, but was transcribed in the seventeenth century into BM MS Add. 4791, fol. 157.

22. Chambers, *MS,* 2: 365.

23. Gilbert, *Calendar,* 2: 54.

24. Chambers, *MS,* 2: 394–95; Pierson, "The Relation of the Corpus Christi Procession," pp. 147–48; and "Municipal Records of Shrewsbury," ed. William Dunn Macray, HMC, *Fifteenth Report,* Part 10, p. 10.

25. Pierson, "The Relation of the Corpus Christi Procession," p. 147.

26. HMC, Shrewsbury, p. 32.

27. Chambers, *MS,* 2: 250–55; see also pp. 394–95.

28. Ibid., 2: 163, 395.

29. Withington, *EP,* 1: 16; and Chambers, *MS,* 2: 376.

30. John Nichols, *The History and Antiquities of the County of Leicester,* 2(2): 378.

31. Quoted from Chambers, *MS,* 2: 376. See also Nichols, *History,* 2 (2): 378–79.

32. Chambers, *MS,* 2: 376.

33. Ibid., pp. 392–93.

34. Ibid., p. 344. This guild was instrumental in founding Corpus Christi College: see Westlake, *PGME,* p. 44.

35. Chambers, *MS,* 2: 393.

36. Mill, *MPS,* p. 244.

37. PRO MS C. 47/46/401; cf. Westlake, *PGME,* pp. 225–26.

38. Bury St. Edmunds and West Suffolk Record Office MS B9/1/2. K. Hall, Acting County Archivist, has kindly supplied me with a fresh transcription of this document and has given permission to publish it here. Cf. "The Manuscripts of the Corporation of Bury St. Edmunds," Historical Manuscripts Commission, *Fourteenth Report,* Part 8, ed. William Dunn Macray, p. 134. See also Chambers, *MS,* 2: 344.

39. King's Lynn Borough MSS are kept in the Muniments Room, Town Hall. Excerpts cited in this chapter are reproduced by kind permission of the King's Lynn Borough Council. Cited here is MS Chamberlains' Roll Ea38; cf. "The Manuscripts Belonging to the Corporation of the Borough of King's Lynn Co. Norfolk," ed. John Cordy Jeaffreson, HMC, *Eleventh Report,* Part 3, p. 223.

40. See, for example, MS Chamberlains' Roll Ea37 (5–6 Richard II): "Et de xxxviijs solutis tam diuersis Ministrallis domini Regis quam aliorum Comitum Baronum & dominorum ac Episcopi Norwicensis [Norwich] veniendis per diuersis vices hoc anno de dono." See also HMC, Lynn, p. 225.

41. MS Chamberlains' Roll Ea54: "Item solutis pro ij lagenis vini rubij expenditis in domo Arnulphi Tixonye . . . ad videndum quemdam ludum in festo corporis xpi"; translation from HMC, Lynn, p. 224.

42. PRO MS C. 47/43/279; cf. Westlake, *PGME,* p. 50.

43. Cited from HMC, Lynn, p. 235.

44. Cited from ibid., p. 166.

45. Cited from ibid., p. 225.

46. Chambers, *MS,* 2: 374, 384. See also HMC, Lynn, pp. 216–21.

47. "Pre-Elizabethan Plays and Players," pp. 334–36.

48. PRO MS C. 47/45/374; cf. Westlake, *PGME,* p. 219.

49. Wickham, *EES,* 2(1): 166.

50. Ibid., p. 167.

51. Mill, *MPS,* pp. 115–16; see pp. 61–68 for a discussion of the Aberdeen records.

52. *The Catholic Encyclopedia,* s.v. Precious Blood. Woolf, *EMP,* p. 69, suggests that the Aberdeen play was "a miracle of the bleeding host," that is, a eucharistic miracle. This argument, however, overlooks

the distinctive character of the Holy Blood.

53. Mill, *MPS*, p. 117.

54. Ibid., p. 116.

55. Ibid., pp. 119-20.

56. Ibid., pp. 65-67.

57. This and subsequent citations from the Aberdeen records are from ibid., pp. 121-28.

58. Chambers, *MS*, 2: 333, 336-37.

59. Mill, *MPS*, pp. 319-22; see pp. 71-73 for a discussion of the Edinburgh records.

60. Ibid., pp. 180-81.

61. Ibid., pp. 78-85.

62. Ibid., pp. 180-87.

63. Ibid., p. 179.

64. Ibid., pp. 225-35.

65. Ibid., p. 73.

66. PRO MSS C. 47/41/161, i, iii; cf. Westlake, *PGME*, pp. 174-75.

67. Louth records cited in this chapter are in the Lincolnshire Archives Office, Lincoln Castle, and are transcribed and published by permission of the Lincolnshire Archives Office and the Vicar of Louth. The record cited here is from MS Louth Parish 7/1, p. 222; cf. Reginald C. Dudding, *The First Churchwardens' Book of Louth*, p. 153. Louth records are also cited in Stanley J. Kahrl, "Medieval Drama in Louth," *Research Opportunities in Renaissance Drama* 10 (1967): 131-33.

68. MS Louth Parish 7/1, p. 219; cf. Dudding, p. 150.

69. MS Louth Parish 7/2, fol. 76.

70. Ibid., fol. 3ᵛ; MS Louth Parish 7/1, p. 299; cf. Dudding, p. 194.

71. MS Account Book of the Trinity Guild in Louth, Mon (Monson Collection) 7/2, fol. 238ᵛ. On the early history of the two guilds, see Westlake, *PGME*, pp. 174-75.

72. MS Louth Parish 7/1, p. 285; cf. Dudding, p. 198.

73. MS Louth Parish, 7/1, p. 306; cf. Dudding, p. 203.

74. MS Mon 7/28, p. 106; MS Louth Parish 7/2, fol. 4.

75. Ibid., fols. 29, 35.

76. See Kahrl, "Medieval Drama in Louth," p. 132.

77. MS Louth Parish 7/1, p. 267; cf. Dudding, p. 182.

78. MS Louth Parish 7/2, fol. 3.

79. Cited from Kahrl, "Medieval Drama in Louth," p. 133.

80. Westlake, *PGME*, pp. 21-22, 51-53.

81. MSS cited in my text are, except where noted, Ipswich borough records in the Ipswich and East Suffolk Record Office, County Hall, Ipswich, cited by permission of the Archivist. Many excerpts occur in Nathaniel Bacon, *The Annalls of Ipswiche: The Lawes Customes, and Government of the Same* (1654), ed. William H. Richardson, but some of the documents which Bacon cites are not now to be found, and many of

Bacon's transcriptions are mere summaries of the originals. In general I cite directly from the MSS where they are extant, and cite from Bacon where they are not.

82. Bacon, *Annalls,* p. 102.

83. MS Petty Pleas Court Roll, 23 Henry VI, no. 1; cf. Bacon, *Annalls,* p. 103.

84. MS C4/2 (White Doomsday Book), fols. 72, 72ᵛ, 1. The lists are mentioned but not printed in "The Manuscripts of the Corporation of Ipswich Co. Suffolk," ed. John Cordy Jeaffreson, HMC, *Ninth Report,* Part 1, p. 241.

85. At the bottom and along the right half of the same page is a long list of English kings with the length of each reign. The last king in the list is Henry VI, but here no length of reign given, so that he must still have been alive.

86. MS C5/12/7, p. 102; cf. Bacon, *Annalls,* p. 195.

87. Bacon, *Annalls,* p. 181.

88. MS C5/12/2, p. 116; cf. Bacon, *Annalls,* p. 116.

89. BM MS Add. 24435, fol. 153ᵛ; cf. Bacon, *Annalls,* p. 194; and MS C5/12/8, p. 28; cf. Bacon, *Annalls,* p. 205.

90. MS C5/12/2, p. 57; cf. Bacon, *Annalls,* p. 164.

91. BM MS Add. 24435, fol. 33; cf. Bacon, *Annalls,* p. 188.

92. MS C5/12/2, p. 56; cf. Bacon, *Annalls,* p. 164.

93. BM MS Add. 24453, fol. 33; cf. Bacon, *Annalls,* p. 166.

94. BM MS Add. 24453, fol. 52.

95. Ibid., fol. 53ᵛ.

96. Ibid., fol. 153; cf. Bacon, *Annalls,* p. 177: "the play and Dinner shall hold this year." The entry actually reads: "Et quod prandium vocatum Corpus Xpi Dynner hoc anno tenetur & custoditur; Et quod ludus vocatus Corpus Xpi Playe pro hoc anno ludetur nec tenetur."

97. MS C5/12/8, p. 28; cf. Bacon, *Annalls,* p. 205.

98. Bacon, *Annalls,* p. 177. This is from MS C5/14/4, p. 570, but the left half of the page is now torn away, leaving only a reference to "lusores," and to "ornamenta pro eodem ludo."

99. Bacon, *Annalls,* p. 219.

100. Ibid., p. 237.

101. Mill, *MPS,* pp. 264–65; see pp. 68–70 for a discussion of the records of Perth.

102. Ibid., p. 265.

103. This citation and subsequent citations in the next three paragraphs are from ibid., pp. 271–74.

104. Ibid., p. 277. See also Register of Acts for 23 June 1603, pp. 266–67, concerning "the play to be plyit on tuyday in the playfield." The day of the agreement was Corpus Christi.

105. Ibid., pp. 275–83.

106. *Ancient Funerall Monuments,* p. 405.

107. Chambers, *MS,* 2: 164, 392.

108. Ibid., 2: 373.

109. *A Boke of Recorde or Register of Kirkby Kendall,* ed. R. S. Ferguson, p. 136.

110. The published transcripts of the Canterbury records which I cite in my text have been verified for me by Anne M. Oakley, Archivist of the Cathedral Archives and Library, Canterbury. The record cited here is from "The Records of the City of Canterbury," ed. J. Brigstocke Sheppard, HMC, *Ninth Report,* Part 1, p. 174.

111. Citations from J. Meadows Cooper, "Accounts of St. Dunstan's Church, Canterbury," *Archaeologia Cantiana* 17 (1887): 80. (24 May 1491 was the Tuesday after Whitsunday.) See also Cooper, *The Accounts of the Churchwardens of St. Dunstan's, Canterbury, A.D. 1484-1580,* pp. 27, 28, 30, 39; and V. S. D. [John Bowes Bunce, Vicar of St. Dunstan's], letter in *Gentleman's Magazine* (December 1837), pp. 569-71.

112. Citations in this and in the next following paragraph are from Giles E. Dawson, ed., *Records of Plays and Players in Kent,* 1450-1642, pp. 189-90.

113. Ibid., pp. 191-98; see also pp. 188-89, and cf. Chambers, *MS,* 2: 344-45.

114. Dawson, *Records,* p. 198.

115. Newcastle MSS cited in my text are, except where noted, in the City Archives Office, 7 Saville Place, Newcastle upon Tyne, transcribed and published by permission of the Lord Mayor and citizens of Newcastle upon Tyne. The Coopers' Indenture is MS 151/3/1. It was written in 1497, but is a transcription of an earlier indenture dated 20 January 1426/7. For summaries of guild ordinances, see John Brand, *History and Antiquities of the Town and County of the Town of Newcastle upon Tyne,* 2: 315-59. See also Chambers, *MS,* 2: 424; and Craig, *ERD,* pp. 303-5.

116. Newcastle upon Tyne Merchant Adventurers' MS Book of Orders, 1480-1568, fol. 3. This MS is now in the care of Mr. John Stephenson, Clerk to the Company, Milburn House, Dean Street. I am grateful to the Governor and the Company of Merchant Adventurers of Newcastle upon Tyne for permission to transcribe and publish extracts from the Book of Orders. Cf. *Extracts from the Records of the Merchant Adventurers of Newcastle upon Tyne,* ed. J. R. Boyle and F. W. Dendy, 1: 4-5.

117. In addition to the Indentures of the Coopers and Merchant Adventurers already cited, only one original indenture survives, that of the Curriers, MS 151/1/1, dated 1 October, 37 Henry VIII. Other indentures were transcribed in the mid-sixteenth century, and survive in MSS Enrollment Book III 1659-1669, and Enrollment Book IV 1661-1675. The transcriptions are bound in at the back of these two

volumes, upside down, so that the back cover becomes the front cover for the transcriptions. The Barbers' indenture occurs in MS EB (for Enrollment Book) III, fols. 64^v–65.

118. MS EB III, fol. 57^v.

119. MS 151/1/1.

120. MS EB IV, fols. 5–6.

121. MS EB III, fols. 54^v–55.

122. See *NCP*, p. xliii, for list of pageants; for play text see pp. 19–31.

123. MS Book of Orders, fol. 8^v. For subsequent entries from the Book of Orders, cf. *Extracts*, 2: 161–74.

124. MS Book of Orders, fol. 36.

125. See ibid., fols. 34, 38.

126. Ibid., fol. 49.

127. Brand, *History*, 2: 371 n.

128. Ibid., p. 370 n.

129. MS Book of Orders, fols. 38^v, 44^v.

130. Ibid., fols. 38–45^v passim.

131. Ibid., fol. 52^v.

BIBLIOGRAPHY

Adams, Joseph Quincy. *Chief Pre-Shakespearean Dramas*. Boston: Houghton Mifflin, 1924.

The Ancient Cornish Drama. Ed. and trans. Edwin Norris. 2 vols. Oxford, 1859.

Anderson, M. D. *Drama and Imagery in English Medieval Churches*. Cambridge: Cambridge U. P., 1963.

Anglo, Sydney. *Spectacle, Pageantry, and Early Tudor Policy*. Oxford: Clarendon Press, 1969.

Bacon, Nathaniel. *The Annalls of Ipswiche: The Lawes Customes and Government of the Same* (1654). 2d ed. Ed. William H. Richardson. Ipswich, 1884.

Bennett, J. H. E. "The Hospital and Chantry of St. Ursula the Virgin of Chester." *Journal of the Chester and North Wales Architectural, Archaeological and Historic Society*, n.s. 32 (1938): 98–129.

Berger, Harry, Jr. "Theater, Drama, and the Second World: A Prologue to Shakespeare." *Comparative Drama* 2 (1968): 3–20.

Bergeron, David M. *English Civic Pageantry, 1588–1642*. London: Edward Arnold, 1971.

Beverley Town Documents. Ed. A. F. Leach. Selden Society 14. London, 1900.

Blair, Lawrence. "A Note on the Relation of the Corpus Christi Procession to the Corpus Christi Play in England." *MLN* 55 (1940): 83–95.

Blomefield, Francis. *An Essay towards a Topographical History of the County of Norfolk*. 2d ed. 11 vols. London, 1805–1810.

A Boke of Recorde or Register of Kirkby Kendall. Ed. R. S. Ferguson. Kendall, 1892.

Bolingbroke, L. G. "Pre-Elizabethan Plays and Players in Norfolk." *Norfolk Archaeology 11* (1892): 332–51.

Brand, John. *History and Antiquities of the Town and County of the Town of Newcastle upon Tyne* . . . London, 1789.

Bridge, Joseph C. "Items of Expenditure from the 16th Century Accounts of the Painters, Glaziers, Embroiderers, and Stationers' Company, with Special Reference to the 'Shepherds Plays.'" *Journal of the Chester and North Wales Architectural, Archaeological and Historic Society,* n.s. 20 (1914): 153–91.

Brooks, Neil C. "An Ingolstadt Corpus Christi Procession and the *Biblia Pauperum.*" *JEGP* 35 (1936): 1–16.

———. "Processional Drama and Dramatic Procession in Germany in the Late Middle Ages." *JEGP* 32 (1933): 141–71.

Brown, Arthur. "A Tradition of the Chester Plays." *London Medieval Studies 2* (1951): 68–72.

———. "York and Its Plays in the Middle Ages." In *Chaucer und seine Zeit: Symposion für Walter F. Schirmer,* ed. Arno Esch, pp. 407–18. Tübingen: M. Niemeyer, 1968.

Butt, John. Rev. of *The Trial and Flagellation, with Other Studies in the Chester Cycle,* ed. W. W. Greg and F. M. Salter. *Review of English Studies 15* (1939): 91–92.

A Calendar of Dramatic Records in the Books of the Livery Companies of London, 1485–1640. Ed. Jean Robertson and D. J. Gordon. Malone Society Collections 3. Oxford, 1964.

Cameron, Kenneth, and Kahrl, Stanley J. "The N-Town Plays at Lincoln." *Theatre Notebook* 20 (1965/6): 61–69.

———. "Staging the N-Town Cycle." *Theatre Notebook* 21 (1967): 122–38, 152–65.

The Catholic Encyclopedia. Ed. Charles G. Habermann et al. New York: Appleton Press, 1911.

Chambers, E. K. *English Literature at the Close of the Middle Ages.* Oxford History of English Literature. New York: Oxford U. P., 1945, rpt. 1961.

———. *The Mediaeval Stage.* 2 vols. London: Oxford U. P. , 1903, rpt. 1963.

Chaucer, Geoffrey. *The Works of Geoffrey Chaucer.* Ed. F. N. Robinson. 2d ed. Boston: Houghton Mifflin, 1957.

Chaucer Life-Records. Ed. Martin M. Crow and Clair C. Olson. Oxford: Clarendon Press, 1966.

Chester Plays. Ed. H. Deimling and G. W. Matthews. EETS, e.s. 62, 115. London, 1893, 1916.

A Chronicle of London, from 1089 to 1493. Ed. E. Tyrrell and N. H. Nicolas. London: Camden Society, 1827.

Chronicle of the Grey Friars of London. Ed. John G. Nichols. Camden Society, o.s. 53. London, 1852.

Clark, William Smith. *The Early Irish Stage: The Beginnings to 1720.* Oxford: Clarendon Press, 1955.

Cooper, J. Meadows. "Accounts of St. Dunstan's Church, Canterbury." *Archaeologia Cantiana: Being Transactions of the Kent Archaeological Society* 17. London, 1887.

————. *The Accounts of the Churchwardens of St. Dunstan's, Canterbury, A.D. 1484-1580.* London, 1885.

The Cornish Ordinalia: A Medieval Dramatic Trilogy. Trans. Markham Harris. Washington, D.C.: Catholic University of America, 1969.

"Corpus Christi Pageants at Bungay, 1514." In *The Eastern Countries Collectanea: Being Notes and Queries on Subjects Relating to the Counties of Norfolk, Suffolk, Essex, and Cambridge.* Ed. John L'Estrange, p. 272. Norwich, 1872-73.

The Coventry Leet Book. Ed. Mary Dormer Harris. EETS, o.s. 134, 135, 138, 146. London, 1907-13.

Craig, Hardin. "The Corpus Christi Procession and the Corpus Christi Play." *JEGP* 13 (1914): 589-602.

————. *English Religious Drama of the Middle Ages.* Oxford: Clarendon Press, 1955, rpt. 1960.

————. "The Lincoln Cordwainers' Pageant." *PMLA* 32 (1917): 605-15.

————. "Mystery Plays at Lincoln—Further Research Needed." *Lincolnshire Historian* 2 (1964): 37-41.

Creizenach, Wilhelm. *Geschichte des neueren Dramas.* 5 vols. Halle a. S.: M. Niemeyer, 1909-23.

D'Ancona, Alessandro. *Origini del teatro italiano.* 2 vols. Turin: E. Loescher, 1891.

Davidson, Charles. "Concerning English Mystery Plays." *MLN* 7 (1892): 339-43.

————. *Studies in the English Mystery Plays.* New Haven: Yale U. P., 1892.

Davies, Robert. *Extracts from the Municipal Records of the City of York during the Reigns of Edward IV, Edward V, and Richard III.* London, 1843.

Dawson, Giles E. *Records of Plays and Players in Kent, 1450-1642.* Malone Society Collections 7. Oxford, 1965.

Devon, Frederick. *Issues of the Exchequer.* London, 1837.

The Digby Mysteries. Ed. F. J. Furnivall. EETS, e.s. 70. London, 1882.

Dodd, Kenneth M. "Another Elizabethan Theater in the Round." *Shakespeare Quarterly* 21 (1970): 125-56.

Dodsley, Robert. *A Select Collection of Old Plays.* 15 vols. London, 1744.

Dorrell, Margaret. "The Mayor of York and the Coronation Pageant." *Leeds Studies in English,* n.s. 5 (1971): 35-45.

Dorrell, Margaret, and Johnston, Alexandra F. "The Doomsday Pageant of the York Mercers, 1433." *Leeds Studies in English,* n.s. 5

(1971): 29–34.

Dörrer, Anton. *Tiroler Umgangsspiele.* Schlern-Schriften 160. Innsbruck, 1957.

Drake, Francis. *Eboracum; or The History and Antiquities of the City of York, from Its Original to the Present Times.* London, 1736.

Dudding, Reginald C. *The First Churchwardens' Book of Louth.* Oxford: Oxford U. P., 1941.

Dugdale, William. *Antiquities of Warwickshire.* London, 1656. 2d ed. rev. William Thomas. London, 1730.

Dunn, F. I. "The Norwich Grocers' Play and the Kirkpatrick Papers at Norwich." *Notes and Queries* 19 (1972): 202–3.

Dürrer, Albrecht. "Tagebuch der niederländischen Reise." In Albrecht Dürer, *Schriften, Tagebücher, Briefe,* ed. Max Steck, pp. 34–86. Stuttgart: W. Kohlhammer, 1961.

Eccles, Mark. "*Ludus Coventriae*: Lincoln or Norfolk?" *Medium Aevum* 40 (1971): 135–41.

Encyclopaedia Britannica. 11th ed. London, 1911.

Extracts from the Records of the Merchant Adventurers of Newcastle upon Tyne. Ed. J. R. Boyle and F. W. Dendy. Surtees Society 93, 101 (1–2). Durham, 1895.

Fairholt, F. W. *Lord Mayors' Pageants.* Percy Society 10. London, 1843.

Fitch, Robert. "Norwich Pageants, the Grocers' Play." *Norfolk Archaeology* 5 (1859): 8–31.

Foxe, John. *The Acts and Monuments of John Foxe.* Ed. Stephen R. Cattley. London, 1837–39.

Frampton, Mendal G. "The Date of the 'Wakefield Master': Bibliographical Evidence." *PMLA* 53 (1938): 86–117.

Froissart, John [i.e., Jean]. *Chronicles of England, France, Spain, and the Adjoining Countries.* Trans. Thomas Johnes. New York, 1857.

Gardiner, Harold C. *Mysteries' End.* Yale Studies in English 103. New Haven, 1946.

Gilbert, John T. *Calendar of Ancient Records of Dublin.* 17 vols. Dublin, 1889–1916.

Grace, Mary. *Records of the Gild of St. George in Norwich, 1389–1547.* Norfolk Record Society 9. Norwich, 1937.

Greg, W. W. *Bibliographical and Textual Problems of the English Miracle Cycles.* London: A. Morning, 1914.

"Gregory's Chronicle." In *Historical Collections of a Citizen of London,* ed. James Gardiner. Camden Society, n.s. 17. London, 1876.

Grupenhoff, Richard L. "The Lord Mayors' Shows: From Their Origins to 1640." *Theatre Studies* 18 (1971–72): 13–22.

Guenée, Bernard, and Lehoux, Françoise. *Les Entrées royales françaises de 1328 à 1515.* Sources d'histoire mediéval 5. Paris: Editions du Centre national de la recherche scientifique, 1968.

Halliwell-Phillips, J. O. *Outlines of the Life of Shakespeare.* 2 vols. London, 1887.

Harbage, Alfred. *Annals of English Drama, 975-1700.* 2d ed. rev. S. Schoenbaum. London: Methuen, 1964.

Hardison, O. B. *Christian Rite and Christian Drama in the Middle Ages.* Baltimore: Johns Hopkins Press, 1965.

————. Rev. of V. A. Kolve, *Play Called Corpus Christi. Modern Language Quarterly* 29 (1968): 94–98.

Harris, Mary Dormer. "The Ancient Records of Coventry." *Dugdale Society Occasional Papers* 1. Oxford, 1924.

Harrod, Henry. "A Few Particulars Concerning Early Norwich Pageants." *Norfolk Archaeology* 3 (1852): 3–18.

————. "Queen Elizabeth Woodville's Visit to Norwich in 1469." *Norfolk Archaeology* 5 (1859): 32–37.

Hassall, W. O. "Plays at Clerkenwell." *Modern Language Review* 33 (1938): 564–67.

Higden, Ranulph. *Polychronicon Ranulphi Higden Monachi Cestrensis.* Ed. Joseph Rawson Lumley. 9 vols. London, 1865–86.

Hill, James William Francis. *Medieval Lincoln.* Cambridge: Cambridge U. P., 1948.

————. "Three Lists of the Mayors, Bailiffs, and Sheriffs of the City of Lincoln." *Reports and Papers of the Associated Architectural and Archaeological Societies* 39 (1929): 217–56.

Historical Manuscripts Commission. *Reports.* [Alphabetical order by town.]

Report on the Manuscripts of the Corporation of Beverley. Ed. A. F. Leach. London, 1900.

"The Manuscripts of the Corporation of Bury St. Edmunds." Ed. William Dunn Macray. *Fourteenth Report,* Part 8, pp. 121–58. London, 1885.

"The Records of the City of Canterbury." Ed. J. Brigstocke Sheppard. *Ninth Report,* Part 1, pp. 129–77. London, 1883.

"The Manuscripts of the Corporation of Coventry." Ed. John Cordy Jeaffreson. *Fifteenth Report,* Part 10, pp. 101–58. London, 1899.

"Manuscripts of the Corporation of Hereford." Ed. William Dunn Macray. *Thirteenth Report,* pp. 283–353. London, 1892.

"The Manuscripts of the Corporation of Ipswich Co. Suffolk." Ed. John Cordy Jeaffreson. *Ninth Report,* Part 1, pp. 222–62. London, 1883.

"The Manuscripts Belonging to the Corporation of the Borough of King's Lynn Co. Norfolk." Ed. John Cordy Jeaffreson. *Eleventh Report,* Part 3, pp. 145–247. London, 1887.

"The Manuscripts of the Corporation of Lincoln." Ed. William Dunn Macray. *Fourteenth Report,* Part 8, pp. 1–120. London, 1895.

"Municipal Records of Shrewsbury." Ed. William Dunn Macray. *Fifteenth Report,* Part 10, pp. 1–65. London, 1899.

History of Yorkshire: The City of York. Ed. P. M. Tillott. The Victoria History of the Counties of England. London: Oxford U. P., 1961.

Hodges, C. Walter. *The Globe Restored: A Study of the Elizabethan Theatre.* London: E. Benn, 1953.

A Hundred Mery Talys. Ed. Hermann Oesterley. London, 1866. Reprinted with introduction by Leonard R. N. Ashley. Gainesville, Fl.: Scholars' Facsimiles and Reprints, 1970.

Hussey, Maurice. *The Chester Mystery Plays: Sixteen Pageant Plays from the Chester Craft Cycle.* London: W. Heinemann, 1957.

"Informal Minutes of Conference 53." *Research Opportunities in Renaissance Drama* 12 (1969): 85–92.

"Informal Notes of Seminar 17." *Research Opportunities in Renaissance Drama* 13–14 (1970/1): 203–20.

Jenkins, Hubert M. "Dr. Thomas's Edition of Sir William Dugdale's *Antiquities of Warwickshire." Dugdale Society Occasional Papers* 3. Oxford, 1931.

Johnson, Goddard. "Chronological Memoranda Touching the City of Norwich." *Norfolk Archaeology* 1 (1847): 140–66.

Johnson, Richard. *The Ancient Customs of the City of Hereford.* London, 1882.

Kahrl, Stanley J. "Medieval Drama in Louth." *Research Opportunities in Renaissance Drama* 10 (1967): 129–33.

Kavanagh, Peter. *The Irish Theatre: Being a History of the Drama in Ireland from the Earliest Period up to the Present Day.* Tralee: Kerryman, 1946.

Kendall, Paul Murray. *The Yorkist Age.* New York: W. W. Norton, 1962.

Kernodle, George R. *From Art to Theatre: Form and Convention in the Renaissance.* Chicago: University of Chicago Press, 1944.

———. "The Medieval Pageant Wagons of Louvain." *Theatre Annual* 2 (1943): 58–62.

Kolve, V. A. *The Play Called Corpus Christi.* Stanford: Stanford U. P., 1966.

Latham, R. E. *Revised Medieval Latin Word List.* London: Oxford U. P., 1965.

Leach, A. F. [No title.] *Proceedings of the Society of Antiquaries of London,* 2d ser. 15 (1893–95): 103–18.

———. "Some English Plays and Players." In *An English Miscellany Presented to Dr. Furnivall on the Occasion of His Seventy-Fifth Birthday,* pp. 205–34. Oxford: Clarendon Press, 1901.

Longsworth, Robert. *The Cornish Ordinalia: Religion and Dramaturgy.* Cambridge, Mass.: Harvard U. P., 1967.

Loomis, R. S. "Lincoln as a Dramatic Centre." In *Mélanges d'histoire du théâtre du moyen-âge et de la Renaissance, offerts à Gustave Cohen,* pp. 241–47. Paris: Librairie Nizet, 1950.

Ludus Coventriae, or The Plaie Called Corpus Christi. Ed. K. S. Block. EETS, e.s. 120. Oxford, 1922, rpt. 1960.

Lydgate, John. *Minor Poems, I.* Ed. H. N. MacCracken. EETS, e.s. 107. London, 1911, rpt. 1968.

Machyn, Henry. *The Diary of Henry Machyn.* Ed. John G. Nichols. Camden Society 42. London, 1848.

Mackerell, [Benjamin]. "Account of the Company of St. George in Norwich." *Norfolk Archaeology* 3 (1852): 315–74.

Michael, Wolfgang F. *Die geistlichen Prozessionsspiele in Deutschland.* Hesperia 22. Baltimore, 1947.

Mill, Anna J. *Medieval Plays in Scotland.* St. Andrews University Publications 24. Edinburgh, 1927.

———. "The Stations of the York Corpus Christi Play." *Yorkshire Archaeological Journal* 37 (1948–51): 497–502.

Mone, Franz Joseph. *Altteutsche Schauspiele.* Quedlinburg and Leipzig, 1841.

Morris, Rupert. *Chester in the Plantagenet and Tudor Reigns.* Chester, [1895].

Murray, J. T. *English Dramatic Companies, 1558–1642.* 2 vols. Boston and New York: Houghton Mifflin, 1910.

Naogeorgus [Kirchmayer], Thomas. *The Popish Kingdom, or Reign of Antichrist, written in Latine verse by Thomas Naogeorgus, and englyshed by Barnabe Googe.* London, 1570.

Nelson, Alan H. "On Recovering the Lost Norwich Corpus Christi Cycle." *Comparative Drama* 4 (1970/1): 241–52.

———. "Principles of Processional Staging: York Cycle." *Modern Philology* 67 (1970): 303–20.

———. Rev. of Woolf, *English Mystery Plays. Modern Philology* 71 (May 1974).

———. "Six-Wheeled Carts: An Underview." *Technology and Culture* 13 (1972): 391–416.

———. "Some Configurations of Staging in Medieval English Drama." In *Medieval English Drama: Essays Critical and Contextual,* ed. Jerome Taylor and Alan H. Nelson, pp. 116–47. Chicago: University of Chicago Press, 1972.

———. "The Wakefield Corpus Christi Play: Pageant Procession and Dramatic Cycle." *Research Opportunities in Renaissance Drama* 13–14 (1970/1): 221–33.

Nichols, John. *The History and Antiquities of the County of Leicester.* London, 1815.

Non-Cycle Plays and Fragments. Ed. Norman Davis. EETS, s.s. 1. London, 1970.

Ormerod, George. *The History of the County Palatine and City of Chester.* 2d ed. rev. Thomas Helsby. 3 vols. London, 1882.

The Oxford English Dictionary. Ed. James A. H. Murray et al. 13 vols. Oxford: Clarendon Press, 1933.

Paston Letters. Ed. Norman Davis. Oxford: Clarendon Press, 1958.

Petit de Julleville, Louis. *Histoire du théâtre en France: Les Mystères.* 2 vols. Paris, 1880.

Pevsner, Nikolaus. *The Buildings of England: North-East Norfolk and Norwich.* Hammondsworth, Middlesex: Penguin, 1962.

Pierson, Merle. "The Relation of the Corpus Christi Procession to the Corpus Christi Plays." *Transactions of the Wisconsin Academy of Sciences, Arts, and Letters* 18 (1915): 110–65.

Puyvelde, Leo van. *L'Ommegang de 1615 à Bruxelles.* Brussels, 1960.

Raine, Angelo. *Medieval York: A Topographical Survey Based on Original Sources.* London: J. Murray, 1955.

Records of the City of Norwich. Ed. William Hudson and John C. Tingey. 2 vols. Norwich, 1906, 1910.

Register of the Freemen of the City of York, I, 1272–1558. Surtees Society 96. Durham, 1897.

The Register of the Guild of Corpus Christi in the City of York. Surtees Society 57. Durham, 1872.

Rites of Durham, Being a Description or Brief Declaration of all the Ancient Monuments, Rites, & Customs Belonging or being within the Monastic Church of Durham before the Suppression. Written 1593. Ed. J. T. Fowler. Surtees Society 107. Durham, 1903.

Rose, Martial. *The Wakefield Mystery Plays.* London: Evans Bros., 1961.

Salter, Frederic Millet. "The Banns of the Chester Plays." *Review of English Studies* 15–16 (1939/40): 433–57, 1–17, 137–48.

————. *Medieval Drama in Chester.* Toronto: University of Toronto Press, 1955.

Sharp, Thomas. *Dissertation on the Pageants or Dramatic Mysteries Anciently Performed at Coventry.* Coventry, 1825.

————. *The Presentation in the Temple, a Pageant, as originally represented by the Corporation of Weavers in Coventry.* Edinburgh: Abbotsford Club, 1836.

Shull, Virginia. "Clerical Drama in Lincoln Cathedral, 1318–1561." *PMLA* 52 (1937): 946–66.

Simpson, Frank. "The City Gilds of Chester: The Smiths, Cutlers, and Plumbers' Company." *Journal of the Chester and North Wales Architectural, Archaeological, and Historic Society,* n.s. 20 (1914): 5–121.

Smith, L. Toulmin. "Ordinances of the Companies of Marshals and Smiths at York, A.D. 1409–1443." *Antiquary* 11 (1885): 105–9.

Smith, Toulmin. *English Gilds.* EETS, o.s. 40. London, 1870.

Southern, Richard. *The Medieval Theatre in the Round: A Study of the Staging of the Castle of Perseverance, and Related Matters.* London: Faber and Faber, 1957.

Spencer, Matthew Lyle. *Corpus Christi Pageants in England.* New York: Baker and Taylor, 1911.

Stemmler, Theo. *Liturgische Feiern und geistliche Spiele.* Buchreihe der Anglia Zeitschrift für englische Philologie 15. Tübingen, 1970.

———. "Zur Datierung der *Chester Plays.*" *Germanisch-Romanische Monatschrift* 49 [n.s. 18] (1968): 308–13.

Stevens, Martin. "The Missing Parts of the Towneley Cycle." *Speculum* 45 (1970): 261–64.

Stow, John. *A Survey of London.* Ed. C. L. Kingsford. 2 vols. Oxford: Clarendon Press, 1908.

Taylor, Jerome. "The Dramatic Structure of the Middle English Corpus Christi, or Cycle, Plays." In *Literature and Society,* ed. Bernice Slote, pp. 175–86. Lincoln, Neb.: University of Nebraska Press, 1964. Reprinted in *Medieval English Drama: Essays Critical and Contextual,* ed. Jerome Taylor and Alan H. Nelson, pp. 148–56. Chicago: University of Chicago Press, 1972.

Testamenta Eboracensia. Surtees Society 30. Durham, 1855.

The Towneley Plays. Ed. George England and Alfred W. Pollard. EETS, e.s. 71. London, 1897.

The Trial and Flagellation, with Other Studies in the Chester Cycle. Ed. W. W. Greg and F. M. Salter. London: Malone Society, 1935.

Two Coventry Corpus Christi Plays. Ed. Hardin Craig. EETS, e.s. 87. London, 1912, rpt. 1957.

V. S. D. [John Bowes Bunce, Vicar of St. Dunstan's]. Letter in *Gentleman's Magazine,* Dec. 1837, pp. 569–71.

Very, Francis George. *The Spanish Corpus Christi Procession: A Literary and Folkloric Study.* Valencia, 1962.

The Wakefield Pageants in the Towneley Cycle. Ed. A. C. Cawley. Manchester: Manchester U. P., 1958.

Walker, J. W. *Miscellanea II.* Yorkshire Archaeological Society. Record Series 74. Wakefield, 1929.

———. *Wakefield, its History and People.* 2 vols. Wakefield: [printed privately], 1939.

Warton, Thomas. *History of English Poetry.* Ed. W. Carew Hazlitt. 4 vols. London, 1871.

Weever, John. *Ancient Funerall Monuments.* London, 1631. 2d ed. rev. William Tooke. London, 1767.

Welsford, Enid. *The Court Masque.* Cambridge: Cambridge U. P., 1927.

Westlake, H. F. *The Parish Gilds of Medieval England.* London: Society for Promoting Christian Knowledge, 1919.

Wickham, Glynne. *Early English Stages, 1300–1660.* 2 vols in 3. London: Routledge and Kegan Paul; New York: Columbia U. P., 1959–72.

Williams, Sheila. "Les Ommegangs d'Anvers et les cortèges du Lord-Maire de Londres." In *Les Fêtes de la Renaissance,* ed. Jean Jacquot, 2: 349–57. Paris: Editions du Centre National de la Recherche Scientifique, 1956, 1960.

Williams, Sheila, and Jacquot, Jean. "Ommegangs Anversois du temps de Bruegel et de van Heemskerk." In *Les Fêtes de la Renaissance,* ed. Jean Jacquot, 2: 359–88. Paris: Editions du Centre National de la Recherche Scientifique, 1956, 1960.

Wills in the York Registry, 1389–1514, 1514–1553, 1568–1585, 1585–1594. Yorkshire Archaeological Association, Record Series 6, 11, 19, 22. Wakefield, 1887, 1891, 1895, 1897.

Withington, Robert. *English Pageantry: An Historical Outline.* 2 vols. Cambridge, Mass.: Harvard U. P., 1918–20.

Woolf, Rosemary. *The English Mystery Plays.* Berkeley and Los Angeles: University of California Press, 1972.

Wordsworth, Christopher. *Notes on Mediaeval Services in England.* London, 1898.

Wyclif, John. *The English Works of Wyclif.* Ed. F. D. Matthew. EETS, o.s. 74. London, 1880.

Wylie, James H. *History of England under Henry the Fourth.* 4 vols. London, 1884–98.

York Civic Records. Ed. Angelo Raine. Yorkshire Archaeological Society 98, 103, 106, 108, 110, 112, 115, 119 (1–8). Wakefield, 1939–53.

York Memorandum Book. Ed. Maud Sellers. Surtees Society 120, 125 (1–2). Durham, 1912, 1915.

The York Mercers and Merchant Adventurers. Surtees Society 129. Durham, 1918.

York Plays. Ed. L. Toulmin Smith. Oxford: Clarendon Press, 1885.

Young, Karl. *Drama of the Medieval Church.* 2 vols. Oxford: Clarendon Press, 1933.

———. "Records of the York Play of the *Pater Noster.*" *Speculum* 7 (1932): 540–46.

Zesmer, David M. *Guide to English Literature from Beowulf through Chaucer and Medieval Drama.* New York: Barnes and Noble, 1961.

INDEX